Gender and Leadership in Education

Gender and Leadership in Education

Women Achieving Against the Odds

Kay Fuller and
Judith Harford (eds)

PETER LANG

Oxford • Bern • Berlin • Bruxelles • Frankfurt am Main • New York • Wien

Bibliographic information published by Die Deutsche Nationalbibliothek.
Die Deutsche Nationalbibliothek lists this publication in the Deutsche National-
bibliografie; detailed bibliographic data is available on the Internet at
http://dnb.d-nb.de.

A catalogue record for this book is available from the British Library.

Library of Congress Control Number: 2015952227

Cover image © pimchawee/shutterstock.com

ISBN 978-3-0343-1923-2 (print)
ISBN 978-3-0353-0783-2 (eBook)

© Peter Lang AG, International Academic Publishers, Bern 2016
Hochfeldstrasse 32, CH-3012 Bern, Switzerland
info@peterlang.com, www.peterlang.com, www.peterlang.net

This publication has been peer reviewed.

Printed in Germany

Contents

TONY BUSH

Foreword

I have known Marianne Coleman for more than thirty years. We met when she was a teacher, and head of department of economics and business studies, at what was then Bushey Meads School in Hertfordshire. We worked together for two years and became good friends. A few years later, we met by chance at a teacher professional development day in Hertfordshire. Over lunch, she said: 'Do you know what I would really like to do? I would like to do research.' A few months later, I was looking for a research assistant for a Leverhulme Trust-funded project on grant-maintained schools. I contacted her and, following much thought and discussion with her husband John, she gave up a permanent position with Hertfordshire Local Authority to accept a short-term post with the University of Leicester. Her distinguished research career started in this modest way.

It will surprise nobody reading this book to learn that Marianne was outstandingly successful in this role. Despite little formal research knowledge or experience, she was excellent in her fieldwork and in writing research reports and chapters for the book that we wrote with our colleague Derek Glover. When the contract ended, after a short gap she was appointed as a lecturer in Leicester's Educational Management Development Unit (EMDU), where she worked alongside several other colleagues who have become leading researchers and writers in educational leadership and management. These include David Middlewood, Ann Briggs, John West-Burnham, John O'Neill, Les Bell, Mark Brundrett and Jacky Lumby, a contributor to this volume.

While at Leicester, Marianne registered for a PhD and decided to focus on women principals in secondary schools. This was the start of her engagement with leadership and gender. I was fortunate to be Marianne's supervisor, the easiest such role in more than twenty years of doctoral supervision. Her research involved a survey of all women secondary school heads and follow-up interviews with some of them. Her external examiner was Valerie Hall, who sadly died a few years later at the very early age of just fifty-nine.

Valerie was almost certainly the leading UK writer on gendered leadership before her untimely demise and, in a sense, the baton passed to Marianne.

Marianne's contribution to research on women leaders is immense. Her questionnaire with UK heads was adapted for use by other academics, including Kay Fuller, as the introduction to this volume attests. She also conducted research on gender in several other countries, including China, Hong Kong and South Africa. She was also an obvious choice when Megan Crawford and I co-edited the fortieth-anniversary issue of *Educational Management, Administration and Leadership* (*EMAL*) and wanted to include a paper on leadership and diversity.

Her distinctive contribution to the field in the UK was in building a solid evidence base to underpin her conclusions and theorising. Much of the writing on gender and management in the twentieth century was normative, based on indignation about the unfair under-representation of women. Marianne's work helped to build a body of research data to explore and to explain the reasons for the gendered nature of leadership. Her cool analysis moved the debate forward in important ways although she never lost the values which led her to embark on this research in the first place. The only time I can recall her losing her measured approach was in China when we were interviewing a male principal. He explained his commitment to equal opportunities but was challenged by Marianne to explain why there were no women on his school management team. His reply, that women were good at nurturing children but could not see the 'big picture' and hence were unsuited to management, angered Marianne but she was still able to maintain a professional approach.

It is my pleasure and privilege to contribute the foreword to this important volume. Kay Fuller and Judith Harford have assembled an impressive cast of authors, including several world-leading researchers on gender and leadership. That such a distinguished group of writers have agreed to contribute to this book demonstrates the high regard for Marianne's research and writing in this field, and for her excellent personal qualities. I anticipate that this volume will become 'required reading' for students and academics in many parts of the world. It is a fitting tribute to a distinguished academic and a wonderful human being.

Tony Bush
Professor of Educational Leadership
University of Nottingham

KAY FULLER AND JUDITH HARFORD

A Festschrift for Marianne Coleman

The under-representation of women in leadership positions in educational settings is a widely acknowledged, complex phenomenon. This persists, despite the fact that teaching as a profession is dominated by women. Over recent decades, scholars have interrogated this phenomenon with a view to identifying the factors that have contributed to the under-representation of women in leadership positions in education, with a particular focus on the personal, organisational and social/cultural levels. Leadership, Coleman (2011: 37) contends, 'is a very gendered concept. In a wide variety of cultural contexts, leadership continues to be identified with the male. Even though women occupy positions of leadership and responsibility, there is a tendency to assume that the rightful leader is male.' Reay and Ball (2000: 145) suggest that 'management is commonly conceptualized as 'masculine', concerned with 'male qualities of rationality and instrumentality.' They go on to note that in such contexts, women are 'more like men than men themselves' (ibid.). Blackmore (2002) also notes the deeply rooted belief that leadership is a male construct. This accepted norm, she argues, discourages women from pursuing a career in educational leadership as 'it takes an extraordinary woman to do what an ordinary man does' (ibid.: 56).

The idea for this book first emerged following the launch of the British Educational Leadership Management and Administration Society (BELMAS) Gender and Leadership Research Interest Group at the Institute of Education in London in April 2013. Marianne Coleman presented on 'Women in Leadership: Challenges, Choice and Change – An Individual Research Journey'. She looked back at the origins of her interest in gender and leadership, reflected on the major outcomes of surveys conducted in the 1990s and in 2004, as well as more recent research in the period 2010–11. Marianne concluded change was slow but there was improvement in many sectors, largely because of advances in technology and more family-friendly cultures. However, the difficulties of combining leadership at work with a family life recurred and the presence of mentoring and networking were important support factors. Marianne identified key areas for future research as women's reluctance to align themselves with feminism; the need to research the intersections of gender with 'race'/ ethnicity, social class and sexuality; the experience of younger women leaders; and leadership in non-Western contexts. The RIG has used these ideas to move forward with their activities by holding their first one-day conference focused on intersectionality.

In the discussion which followed the launch event, it became quickly evident that all present had been deeply influenced by Marianne's work and indeed many had chosen to pursue research on gender and leadership because of the trail blazed by Marianne many decades previously and because of her inspiration and nurturing. Soon after the event, we approached scholars who had been influenced by Marianne's work and asked them if they wished to contribute to an essay collection in recognition of her work. The response was overwhelming. The result is a collection of essays from a range of disciplines which collectively interrogate the complexity of the under-representation of women in leadership positions in educational settings internationally. Amongst the key questions the book asks are the following. Why does society continue to accept male leaders as the norm? What barriers do women who seek leadership positions face? What supports do women require in order to encourage them to pursue leadership positions? How do women working in leadership positions conceive of their role as leaders? How might women's leadership be best supported at an institutional level? At the same time it is vital that we acknowledge women do not comprise a homogenous group. Where women do succeed, they are predominantly white women. There is a need to problematise what has tended to be an essentialist discourse to consider Black and Global Majority women, and men from potentially marginalised groups. We need to ask how far the gender and educational leadership field has embraced multiple gender theories in recent decades to consider how women and men do leadership as well as which women and men do it. The chapters in this book chart the evolving landscape of women in educational leadership, provide a critique of the interplay between gender, leadership and education, drawing on a range of theoretical perspectives.

The book opened with a foreword from Tony Bush, who recounted his initial meeting with Marianne when she was a secondary school teacher in the UK. Tony reflected on Marianne's keen interest in research and in gender and leadership in particular, along with her humility and kindness, characteristics, all whom have met her recall. Tony became Marianne's PhD supervisor and her journey into academia thus began. The opening chapter by Izhar Oplatka, 'The Research on Gender in the Field of Educational Management: A Journals-Based Historical Overview of an Area of Study' appropriately provides a historical overview of the emergence of gender and education as a field of study. The paper is intended to enable scholars to grasp the unique development of 'gender' in the field of Educational Management (EM) and make sense of its theoretical and applied knowledge both cumulatively and systematically. Jacky Lumby's chapter 'Culture and Otherness in Gender Studies: Building on Marianne Coleman's Work' focuses on the importance of how those engaging in research on gender inequality position themselves. They are, Lumby notes, typically women, but also of a particular race, culture and history. Positioning raises a range of challenges in relation to the degree of self-awareness and the nature of 'otherness' perceived in those studied. This chapter focuses on this fundamental issue, using Marianne's work as a backdrop and discussing the relationship between the cultural embeddedness of research and the imperative for action to increase gender equality. Jacky provides Marianne's survey instrument which she notes has been used in many contexts, including by Kay (Fuller 2009). Following on from Lumby, Victoria Showunmi's chapter 'Diversity and Education in England' notes that population structures of schools and school communities in urban Europe in particular have been changing over the last few decades in the context of globalisation, eco-political developments and increased mobility. In the United Kingdom, the increasing diversity of the population is generally perceived as affecting schools' overall performance through the low achievement of children from many Black and Minority Ethnic (BME) groups and communities. Yet, this chapter goes on to demonstrate how research has produced varied and even conflicting evidence with regard to a direct link between achievement and factors such as ethnicity, socio-economic background, population mix, gender and the use of English as a second language.

This chapter is followed by Joan Smith's exposition on the impact of motherhood on women teachers' and headteachers' life and career choices, 'Motherhood and Women Teachers' Career Decisions: A Constant Battle'. Drawing on life history interviews with female teachers and headteachers working in secondary schools in the UK, this chapter considers how this cohort of women perceive motherhood to have impacted their career decisions. The chapter closes by considering how shifts in thinking are needed at national, institutional and domestic levels if gender equity in public, private and workplace domains is to be achieved. Staying with the theme of headteachers and career trajectories, Kay Fuller's chapter 'Headteacher Preparation: An Account of One Woman Headteacher's Supportive Practices' explores the findings from a case study of headteacher preparation practices of a single woman headteacher. It locates twelve practices, constructed by the headteacher and eight former and current members of the senior leadership team (SLT) at a school in the UK in the situated learning literature concerned with communities of practice. Empirical research is used to outline twelve practices as a process of successful headteacher preparation. Finally, a critical analysis reveals that within the SLT position, disposition, capital and power relations impact greatly on an individual's leadership aspirations and achievement of them. Again on the same theme, and inspired by Marianne's ground-breaking scholarship on headteachers and career trajectories, in 'Gender Matters: Women's Experience of the Route to Principalship in Ireland' Mary Cunneen and Judith Harford report a study undertaken from a life story perspective in the life history tradition, of the perceived enabling and constraining influences which a cohort of twelve women principals articulate as informing their career pathway to principalship in Ireland. Ireland constitutes a good site for engaging in such research as while it represents international trends, it also has an idiosyncratic dimension; up until the demise of nuns in Catholic girls' schools, nuns (females) dominated the principalship in girls' religious-order run schools. Key findings indicate that the perceived challenges women principals in the Republic of Ireland have encountered include the cultural expectations around who should occupy leadership roles, especially in Catholic-run schools, organisational cultures which do not support childcare-friendly practices and a neoliberal policy agenda which is considered to be at odds with a social justice agenda. Perceived enablers include supportive partners and/or family members as well as the significance of mentors and role models.

In 'Roads Less Travelled: Female Elementary School Principals Aspiring to the School District Superintendency', Jill Sperandio and Jennifer Polinchock contend that knowledge of patterns of gender discrimination allows women to position themselves to take on the roles for which they are well-qualified and to which they bring fresh perspectives and leadership styles. This chapter presents research which indicates one group of women – elementary school principals in the USA – are doing just this, by forging non-traditional paths to the top leadership position in US school districts, that of the district superintendent. In 'Venturing into the Habitat of the Powerful: Women Leaders in Higher Education', Tanya Fitzgerald draws on Marianne's work to complicate 'leadership' and tease out the ambiguities, silences and contradictions of women's lived leadership experiences. In particular, she focuses on women leaders in higher education contributing to the debates highlighted in Marianne's 2011 work *Women at the Top*, interrogating leadership in higher education as the 'habitat of the powerful'. Margaret Grogan and Klara Wahlster build on Marianne's work in 'In Books, on the Screen, and in Games: Leadership and Gender Stereotypes Shape Images of Young Women Leaders'. The purpose of this exploration is to consider whether contemporary young women are being offered less traditional ways of being in the world through fiction than their mothers and older sisters were. Some questions that guide this exploration include: Are the gender stereotypes identified by Coleman still alive and well in these works? How and where might gender and leadership stereotypes intersect? Are these images likely to influence the next generation of women positively or negatively as they consider leadership options? In 'Patriarchal Bargain for African Women in Leadership: Deal or No Deal?', Pontso Moorosi draws on findings from a research project which examines constructions of masculinities by corporate leaders in South Africa, focusing on African women's experiences sharing their successes in navigating their way to the top while attempting to strike a balance between family and work. The chapter draws comparisons between these women's experiences and those examined in Coleman's work, to demonstrate that in negotiating a balance between work and life, women end up striking a 'patriarchal bargain' that is both empowering and disempowering. Central to this argument is the extent to which the patriarchal bargain and the corporate policies that are supposed to enable change and benefit women, perpetuate the stereotypes about the role of men and women at work and in the home. Finally, in a fitting epilogue to the collection, Helen Sobehart, using the metaphor of a tapestry, traces the threads of Marianne's research charting how her research represents a tapestry of complex, probing and inter-connected threads. These are represented by the warp – the cords of Marianne's work, the weft – the crossweaves of many artists and the tapestry of legacy. We are delighted to present this collection in celebration of Marianne Coleman's academic career.

References

Blackmore, J. (2002). 'Troubling Women: The Upsides and Downsides of Leadership and the New Managerialism'. In C. Reynolds (ed.), *Women and School Leadership: International Perspectives*, 49–74. Albany: State University of New York Press.

Coleman, M. (2011). *Women at the Top*. Basingstoke: Palgrave Macmillan.

Fuller, K. (2009). 'Women Secondary Head Teachers: Alive and Well in Birmingham at the Beginning of the Twenty-First Century'. *Management in Education* 23 (1), 19–31.

Reay, D., and Ball, S. J. (2000). 'Essentials of Female Management: Women's Ways of Working in the Education Market Place'. *Education Management and Administration* 28 (2), 145–59.

IZHAR OPLATKA

The Research on Gender in the Field of Educational Management: A Journals-Based Historical Overview of an Area of Study

Since the 1970s, gender has become both an important topic of academic study and a major category to be used in analysis within the social sciences (Bradley 2007), including management and education. Spurred by the women's studies movement of the 1970s, researchers in many fields either focused directly on gender differences or used gender as a variable in their analysis

These streams of research have also penetrated the field of educational management (EM) which focuses on the leadership and organisation of educational institutions (Oplatka 2010). A great deal of research worldwide has addressed the differentiation between the attitudes and behaviours of men and women in educational leadership and administration during the last four decades thereby enriching our knowledge about the role of gender in schools and the unique characteristics of women in leadership.

The purpose of the current chapter is to trace the place of 'gender' in the field's discourse since the early 1960s, the decade in which the first academic journals in the field emerged. More specifically, this chapter aims to present the emergence of 'gender' as an area of study in the field's journals from a historical perspective and analyse the major topics related to this area of study and its types of publication.

Historical analysis offers a new approach to understand an area of study by charting according to date the main research contributions over a precisely defined period (Gray 2001). Likewise, it allows some meta-epistemological reflection of a relatively new area of study and, as Humes and Bryce (2001) note, tries to make the field more cumulative in character. Thus, this chapter is intended to enable scholars to grasp the unique development of 'gender' in the field of EM and make sense of its theoretical and applied knowledge cumulatively and systematically. After all, a field of knowledge is essentially open-ended as there is a never-ending proliferation of new disciplinary and sub-disciplinary fields (Hoskin 1993; Rodgers and Rodgers 2000), and the field of EM is no exception.

The remainder of this chapter is organised as follows: the first section displays the literatures on gender in social sciences and management that explore organisational phenomena usually in non-educational settings. The second section goes on to discuss the methodology used to analyse the journal articles. The third section, the major part of the chapter, provides an historical analysis of 'gender' in the field's journals in each of the last five decades.

Research on Gender in Life and Work

Gender is 'a busy term' (Glover and Kaplan 2000: ix), meaning that it is very widely used in many contexts and its usages are numerous and evolving. Holmes (2007) claimed that gender differences should be understood as a central feature of patriarchy, a social system in which men have come to be dominant in relation to women.

A distinction made by sociologists since the 1970s between sex (biological differences between males and females) and gender (socially produced differences between being feminine and being masculine) (Holmes 2007) is commonly used. Hawkesworth (1997) has developed a lexicon which summarises a number of important terminological and conceptual distinctions. Thus, while sex is construed in biological terms, gender identity is constructed as a psychological sense of oneself (as a man or a woman), and gender role is defined as a set of prescriptive culture-specific expectations about what is appropriate for men and women.

In contrast, a host of postmodern feminists (e.g., Butler 1993) have argued that the distinction between sex and gender is no longer sustainable and should be collapsed. For them, both concepts are inextricably linked and created in tandem through daily acts of 'playing out' male or female identity. In this sense, 'gender is cultural and socially constructed as natural and biological' (Bradley 2007: 15), i.e., it is something different from either biological sex or sexuality.

Regardless of this semantic controversy, sociologists have tried to explore gender differences not as 'natural' but as socially constructed. For example, Rubin (1975: 159) identified the sex/gender system as a 'set of arrangements by which a society transforms biological sexuality into products of human activity'. In this sense, gender, as the attribution of aspects of human personality, relationships, behaviours, privileges and prohibitions to the domain of either masculine or feminine, is a social effect rather than the result of human biology (Jordan-Young 2010). Put differently, gender differences are not a simple outcome of having a female or male body. Yet, the idea that physical differences between the sexes are significant is used to justify many injustices to women (Holmes 2007). This leads us to study the relationship between gender differences and issues of inequality and equity in human interactions (Mitchell 1971).

In recent years, the research has focused more and more on 'doing gender', i.e., on the ways by which individual women and men are actively engaged in creating and recreating their identity. Gender is considered to be something we do, although within social constraints. If people do gender they have to engage with ideas about how it 'should' be done, even if they find ways to do it differently (Holmes 2007). For example, it is interesting to explore the ways in which female school principals display their femininity in their post. Likewise, 'doing gender' cannot be avoided in organisations; we do gender and sometimes we undo gender, i.e., employees may conform to or break away from sex stereotypes within their workplace.

The research on gender by organisation scholars during the last several decades has revolved around gender distinctions between male and female employees in a wide variety of personal and organisational aspects, gender differences among male and female managers. Of the many streams of research related to gender in the organisation literature, two appear to be most relevant to managers – barriers to women's advancement and the particular career experiences of women managers.

To begin with the former, the research on women in organisations elucidated much reference to personal and structural barriers which impede women's progress within work organisations (Kremer 1998). These barriers include stereotypes towards working women, a shortage of family-friendly policies, inadequate childcare services for working women, sexual harassment in the workplace, and latent forms of gender discrimination.

Much attention has been given to the masculine stereotype of leadership as a major obstacle to women's advancement. In a meta-analysis conducted by Koenig et al. (2011), the authors found that the masculinity of the cultural stereotype of leadership is a large effect that is robust across variation in many aspects of leaders' social contexts. In other words, the masculine stereotype of leadership poses a problem for women aspiring to management roles because female stereotypes do not match expectations for leaders. Even women who possess outstanding qualifications for leadership may have the burden of overcoming preconceptions that they are not well equipped to lead like their male counterparts.

Amazingly, despite the many historical, political and social differences across countries, this stereotype is a cross-cultural and global phenomenon, especially among males in a wide variety of countries, such as China, Japan, the United Kingdom, Germany and the United States (Schein 2001). Thus, the construction of glass ceilings is related most strongly to the patriarchal nature of many organisations, where male managers may dwell comfortably in a men-only world (Kremer 1998) and resist any entrance of women into their 'club'.

Yet, as local work cultures influence how we are constructed and which values, norms and ideas are prevalent (Due Biling 2011), women managers who have succeeded in breaking the 'glass ceiling' in their own careers report coping with stereotypes and the old boys' network by anticipating negative attitudes and detaching from given stereotypes (Baumgartner and Schneider 2010). In other words, they have avoided taking stereotypes personally (detachment) and have not been afraid to invite themselves into male networks.

Another stream of research, although more limited in scope, has focused on the particular experiences of women in management. Earlier research had suggested that in order to succeed, women managers were

obliged to cloak their femininity (Kremer 1998) because thei
were incompatible with the traditional female stereotype bas
and nurturing. The model of the effective manager was thus conceptualised
in masculine terms.

Over time, however, the model of the ideal manager has evolved and
organisations have come to recognise that qualities traditionally associated with femininity should be encouraged among managers. They have
crossed traditional gender lines and challenged traditional ideas about what
is suitable work behaviour for women. Having worked in older organisations, which might have been more resistant to change, it may have been
important for them to act according to the prevalent rules of the game.

Feminist scholars in educational administration, like their counterparts in other disciplines and fields of study, have fought for a long time to
place women on the intellectual terrain of this field of study, and therefore
should be given due credit for the advances which they have made. Their
story is narrated in this chapter.

The Reviewing Method

The primary methodology employed to trace the place of 'social justice' in
the field's journals was qualitative content analysis (QCA) because a journal paper is seen as a document susceptible to textual analysis (Altheide
1996). QCA combines both quantitative and qualitative content analysis.
It involves collecting numerical and narrative data, i.e., the emphasis is on
simultaneously obtaining categorical and unique data for every text studied.

Thus, QCA provides a way of obtaining data to measure the frequency
and extent of messages following a serial progression of category construction, sampling, data collection and coding. It is the reflexive and highly
interactive nature of the investigator, concepts, data collection and analysis
that is unique in this method. Besides providing numerical information, it
is important to expose the reader to descriptive, interpretive information,
thereby illustrating the usefulness of constant comparison for discovering

emergent patterns, emphases and themes in an analysis of documents and texts. Likewise, QCA enables researchers to refer not only to categories and variables that initially guide the study but also to others which emerge throughout the study, including the use of constant comparison of relevant textual parts, images, meanings and nuances (Glaser and Strauss 1967).

Sample

For this chapter, the abstract of papers about gender in educational management/leadership published between 1962 and 2013 in seven dominant refereed journals in the area of EM were reviewed: *Educational Management, Administration and Leadership* (*EMAL*), *School Leadership and Management* (*SLM*), *Educational Administration Quarterly* (*EAQ*), *Leadership and Policy in School* (*LPS*), *Journal of Educational Administration* (*JEA*), *International Journal of Leadership in Education* (*IJLE*) and *International Journal of Educational Management* (*IJEM*). While the first two journals are more oriented to the UK, and the next two are American focused, the last three are more internationally focused, which, in turn, allows ample comparison across countries.

   Only papers focusing on gender were chosen for this review. Their identification was based on two criteria: (1) the terms 'female/women principals/heads', 'gender', 'sex', 'female teachers', 'feminism', 'post-feminism', 'feminine/masculine' or their adjectives (e.g., feminist) appear in their abstract; (2) the abstract contains some reference to issues of gender and/ or feminism explicitly and implicitly.

The Method of Analysis

The analysis was organised around two central issues: the topics addressed in every paper and the type of work (i.e., empirical, scholarly). Each paper was coded on four variables: topic, type of paper (empirical, comment, conceptual, etc.), subjects and methodology (if available) and the number of occurrences of the emergent categories. A similar procedure has been commonly used in the field's reviews (e.g., Murphy et al. 2007; Oplatka 2010).

Note, this analysis was not conducted by someone from an Anglo-American nation. (The author lives and works in Israel and English is his second language.) This position made him 'remote' in some sense from the contextual and cultural determinants that influenced the authors of many of the reviewed papers, on one hand, and allowed him to connect many of the insights/findings to an international audience, on the other hand.

The 1960s and the 1970s: Gender – What Is It?

A wide variety of social movements erupted during the 1960s in Europe and North America questioning traditional practices about how people had been treated on varied issues (e.g., civil rights, gender inequality, gay rights and the environment). Each, to a varying degree, has contributed to policy changes and to the growth of new ways of thinking in many countries even today, many decades later.

The questioning of social and political arrangements inspired people to establish organisations and movements to fight against injustice and inequality in their society. The women's movement was no exception. In light of second wave feminism, its pioneers took direct action (e.g., public marches, rallies, picketing, petitions) to raise gender inequality as an issue and call for policy changes towards women's rights. They contributed their time and energy in order to make our world a better and more just place for both sexes to live.

The pioneers' activities led in the 1970s to the establishment of women's organisations in many countries (National Organisation of Women, Coalition of Labour Union Women that also founded journals edited by women (e.g., *Ladies' Home Journal*), and to the emergence of gender/feminist studies in universities and colleges. The purposes of these new studies were to bring women and their experiences more fully into knowledge fields and to encourage scholars from different disciplines to promote research on women in their institutions. Indeed, this is the time when early books about women and feminism appeared and the research on gender began in social sciences.

Yet, the 1960s signal the beginning of the EM field's academic journals with the appearance of *JEA* (Australia) and *EAQ* (US) in the early 1960s and of *EMAL* (UK) in the early 1970s. Unsurprisingly, the waves of feminism had not yet spread among EM scholars and researchers were occupied at this time with issues of methodology due to their need to justify their research and increase the academic legitimacy of their field. Only thirteen works published in these three journals had dealt with issues of gender, sex, and women's work in education. None contained the phrases 'feminism', 'feminine' or 'masculine', that would become very popular in the field's knowledge base in the decades to come. None of them had been published in the British journal of the field although one should bear in mind that this review is based only on journal articles. It is likely, though, that some reports about gender/women in education were published elsewhere in England at that time.

Of the thirteen works, four papers focused on women in headship or on women's career advancement in education, all of them published in the second half of the 1970s. Ross Telfer, for example, examined in 1978 the effect of the administrator's sex on decision-making. He did not justify affirmation of the hypothesis that schools with only male administrators would have higher agreement in perception of decision points than would schools with both male and female administrators.

From a different perspective, other authors explored public prejudice against women school administrators in the US and the differences between women teachers who did or did not aspire to promotion. The second paper, described below, tells us a lot about the many changes we have witnessed in the last number of decades:

> This research study compares women elementary school teachers who have and have not applied for promotion. The variables considered include degree of family responsibilities, and extent of commitment to the roles played both inside and outside the home. A picture of the woman applicant for promotion emerges. While she is as likely as other women teachers to follow the traditional marriage with children pattern, she does take a markedly different approach to her home life and responsibilities there. (McIntosh 1974: 28)

More interestingly, two works concerned with the entry of female employees into many workplaces – a new phenomenon for that time – examined the attitudes of male graduate students of departments of EM and of administrators towards professional women. Paul (1975), for example, analysed the roles and attitudes of men and women in the same environment in order to explore the ways in which male administrators manage female employees.

Most of the authors who mentioned the issue of gender in that period used 'sex' as another independent or dependent variable in their research design. Put differently, gender was not the focus of their study but rather was used as one aspect in the examination of another phenomenon. Thus, the factor of sex (among other factors such as age, education, teaching experience) was examined in studies which examined teacher satisfaction, perceived need deficiencies of teachers and administrators, and bureaucratic orientations among teachers. To illustrate, Trusty and Sergiovanni (1966) discovered that factors such as age, sex and professional role are significantly related to the perception of need deficiencies.

Remarkably, two studies investigated the relationship of intelligence, sex and selected 'home background' variables to student perceptions of the high school environment and their vocational aspirations, admittedly not the kind of papers published in the field of EM today. Similarly, the sex factor was examined also in relation to male and female professors' careers in varied aspects (e.g., participation in decision-making, work satisfaction and tension).

Before closing our discussion of the 1960s and the 1970s, a very illuminating paper for its time titled 'Educational Administration: A Feminine Profession' reviewed the feminisation of educational administration in the US and elucidated some reference to reports and papers published in professional magazines, reports, or journals about gender/women (that had been founded during the 1970s) about males and females in management (Frasher and Frasher 1979). Among the cited works are Gross and Trask's 'Men and Women as Elementary School Principal' (final report from 1964), Fisher and Pottker's 'Performance of Women Principals', and Bach's 'Of Women, School Administration, and Discipline'. Their conclusion merits highlighting as it is so relevant even thirty-five years later:

We are concerned about the likelihood that future female administrators will behave more like their male than their female predecessors. If women who wish to be educational leaders feel that they must adopt an authoritarian style, short-cut their experience as teaching professionals, and focus on techniques employed and advocated by male models, there is little reason to believe that they will have a significant, positive impact on the American education system. If young women with administrative aspirations sacrifice teaching experience in favour of seeking early administrative appointments, as men have, they too may feel inadequate in instructional supervision and deemphasize a critical aspect of their responsibility. (Frasher and Frasher 1979: 10)

Their warning was further explored in many studies over the decades to come as we will see in the next few pages.

The 1980s: A Mix of Gender-Related Topics

The new decade opened with far-reaching changes in the political leadership of major western countries. Ronald Reagan, a determined foe of abortion and reproduction rights, affirmative action, government regulation and many liberal social services programmes, assumed the presidency in the US in 1980. A year before, another conservative leader – Margaret Thatcher came to power in the UK. Both would challenge many institutional, economic and social arrangements.

As these countries as a whole became more conservative in many areas of political life, the women's movement entered a new phase, characterised by both advancement and backlash. Many feminists became discouraged with the continuation of sexist attitudes and behaviours, the inferior status of women of colour and female immigrants, poverty, sexual harassment, and huge gender salary gaps. In addition, a growing number of female breadwinners found themselves doing two jobs – working at full-time jobs during the day and a second job at home as they continued to assume responsibility for most of the childcare and family duties. A sense of disillusionment grew – despite the victories of the women's movement in previous decades, many realised that the full liberation of women and the hopes for gender equality and egalitarian society were less and less plausible under the new political regime.

Feminist politicians focused at that time on issues of affirmative action, race relations, and women's employment and struggled, for instance, for the right to taxpayer-funded abortion-on-demand and publicly financed day-care. Similarly, feminist scholars began to engage with the question of gender itself, comparing gender distinctions across societies and cultures, tracing the origins of masculinity and femininity, exploring power relations and gender and extending the feminist debate into issues of social class, race, ethnicity and other differences.

The field of EM at this time extended to more countries and new journals devoted to its purposes and scholarly contents were issued. Indeed, thirty papers related to our historical review were published during this decade, ranging from statistical descriptions of gender gaps or women's representation, through works that centred on gender distinctions in a wide variety of areas, to works that used 'sex', like before, as one variable among many others in the research design.

Influenced by feminist attempts to better understand the particular women's world, a growing number of field authors focused directly on gender difference among administrators, teachers and other educators. They compared the career paths of male and female secondary school heads, explored male and female teachers' aspirations to administrative positions and investigated characteristics of access for men and women superintendents. The last topic is illustrated in the following abstract:

> Access to the superintendency was examined for 10 men and 10 women who are or have been school superintendents in metropolitan area school districts with pupil enrolments of 1,000 to 7,000. The qualitative investigation addressed the subjects' background characteristics and early socialization, and the elements in organizational structures related to their access to management positions. The purpose of the inquiry was to determine some predictors of access to the school superintendency for men and women, with particular emphasis on predictors of access for women [...]. (Grow-Maienza 1986: 245)

Others examined sex bias in the evaluation of superintendents indicating that females in this role were rated as less fair and less flexible than males

(Frasher and Frasher 1980) or investigated the typical explanations for general male/female salary differentials or questioned their relevance for educational administrators (Pounder 1988).

Yet, the works about female leadership were extremely limited, published only in the British journals of the field (*EMAL*, *SLM*). The responsibilities of women in managerial roles and their image in the eyes of schoolteachers were explored through qualitative methodologies, uncommon procedures in those years. Along the same lines, a very influential work in the study of women in management was published in 1987 by Gray who explored the relationship between gender concepts and styles of management. He further explained:

> It is suggested that primary schools are generally 'feminine' in culture and therefore require appropriate 'feminine' styles of management behaviour from heads. This presents a problem for male heads who try to follow 'masculine' paradigms of management behaviour. Secondary schools are seen as being predominantly 'masculine' or even 'patriarchal' in culture and the question is raised as to whether such a culture is appropriate to an organization that could be expected to be nurturing and characterized by needs that would be better attended to by a characteristically 'feminine' style of management. It is pointed out that individual heads whose personal style does not suit the conventional expectations of how a head should behave, based upon sexist perspectives will have a sense of personal incongruence as a school manager and leader and may experience considerable personal stress as a consequence. (297)

The barriers to women's advancement in education examined in the preceding decades continued to gain the attention of EM researchers during the 1980s. Authors illuminated the difficulties of women from minorities in educational administration or the sexism in teacher education, and suggested ways to increase the number of women in leadership positions in schools (e.g., through special courses in principal training programmes or career education in which sex-stereotypes were combated and challenged).

Two works merit highlighting in this respect. The first, written by McBurney and Hough from England in 1989, found that fewer women were being confined to stereotypical roles within senior management teams in comparison with a decade before, an optimistic finding for the future. The second, written by a very famous scholar in the forthcoming years, Charol Shakeshaft, criticised the androcentric bias in *EAQ* in the 1970s

(Shakeshaft and Hanson 1986). She found that the most common bias was in the methods employed; all male samples generalised to both genders and interpretations of results ignored females' ways of viewing the world. A similar paper was published in *EMAL* by Hough (1988) who investigated gender bias in articles from this journal over five years and found that its authors tended to pay insufficient attention to gender as a variable of interest.

To a lesser extent than before, though, and in sharp contrast to Hough's conclusion, the field's journals (except *EMAL*) continued to publish works that used 'sex' as one of other independent or dependent variables in their research design. Thus, researchers examined factors, including sex, associated with teacher participation in decision-making, supervisory behaviour, and teacher satisfaction, providing us, nevertheless, with inconclusive evidence about the relation between sex/gender and teacher participation in school management.

Finally, although the 1980s have been characterised by more scholarly and empirical attention given to the research on gender and women in educational administration, the inchoate nature of this research can be seen by a lack of clear direction (e.g., should researchers focus on gender differences, on the career of women in management, on bias in other streams of research?) and the appearance of gender-related works that are weakly connected to each other or to any scientific core in terms of conceptual framework, type of institution or content. For example, Over (1983) presented underrepresentation of women in university appointments in Australia, Pounder (1989) explored the problem of a male/female salary differential for professors and its determinants, and Cross (1985) published a paper that suggested a feminist assessment of current assumptions in the co-education/single-sex schools debate in England, a topic that is out of the scholarly boundaries of EM. Other topics revolved around sex bias in school curriculum, determinants of educational plans of indeterminate male and female high school graduates and gender distinctions in perceptions of sexual harassment in schools.

No doubt, many topics and areas of study of weak relevance to EM have been published in the field's journals, and gender-related issues were no exception. This might be accounted for by the initial stages of the field's development and its, yet premature, attempts to define its unique scholarly identity.

The 1990s: More Attention to Women Leaders

The transition to the 1990s signals the beginning of third-wave feminism. Whereas the focus of second wave feminism was on total gender equality, the current wave criticised the previous one for failing to incorporate the voices of many young women, lesbian women and women of colour. Indeed, the voices of women from marginalised groups have been heard in public since the early 1990s; lesbian, bisexual, African-American, Hispanic, under-privileged women were 'allowed' now to express their identity and life style.

Likewise, those who defined themselves as third-wave feminists were more likely to engage with global and multicultural feminisms, and have handled issues of anti-racism, womanism and transgender politics. They have fought to enhance the number of women in politics and media and struggled to empower women who live in developing countries and tra-ditional societies.

Many feminist scholars have translated these ideas into undergraduate and graduate programmes in gender studies. More and more universities worldwide have established programmes aimed at studying women and gender, feminist thought and gender in society and culture. Other schol-ars have encouraged inter-disciplinary research on such topics as gender, women, masculinity, equality, equity. Some of them, as we will see in the subsequent pages, found the journals of EM a proper outlet to deliver their ideas.

Fifty-five gender-related papers have been published in the EM field's journals during the 1990s, paying more attention to understanding the lives and careers of women leaders in education than ever before. Likewise, as part of the proliferation of the research on gender and educational administration, there was a decrease in the works that used 'sex' as another factor in their research design and, in contrast, an increase in the works that focused directly on exploring/examining gender distinctions as their main purpose.

Interestingly, this is the first decade that articles grounded in feminist views are evident in the field's journals. Thus, authors, who published their articles mainly in American journals (only one has been published in *SLM*), suggested taking on, sometimes among other new theoretical paradigms, a feminist view to analyse issues in EM, such as equity, race and class issues; teacher participation in urban schools or the concept of strategy and school development planning. Usually, these authors suggested an alternative view for a certain concept or issue deriving from a feminist literature. Two works, though, centred directly on feminist analysis of approaches in E.M. Glazer's (1991) study exemplifies this analysis:

> Feminist theory, methodology, and research applications are discussed in this article. Emphasis is placed on the relationship of feminism and professionalism and the role of feminist perspectives in transforming teaching and educational administration. (321)

Several years later, Capper (1998) further analysed the potential contribution of critical, feminist, and postmodern perspectives to EM by asking three questions:

> The purpose of this article is three-fold: (a) to locate and describe several aspects of what the author terms critically oriented theories, which in addition to critical theory and feminist theory include critical race theory and queer theory; (b) to describe more fully poststructural perspectives including critical pragmatism and feminist poststructuralism; and (c) to identify key questions from each perspective that can help persons in the field of educational administration think about and respond to research and specific leadership situations in ways that push beyond traditional approaches ... The author offers teaching suggestions to stimulate further conversation about making critical and postmodern ideas more accessible to educational leaders. In so doing, these ideas can lend support to leaders who wish to co-create inclusive school communities. (355)

No doubt, these and other voices have urged more feminist scholars to challenge the field's knowledge base more than before and (this time) from alternative theoretical lenses. In some sense, these voices corroborated those who called to study the unique world of the female educational leader.

Much more empirical attention has been given now to women leaders per se – their leadership style, career experiences and barriers to advancement. Thus, qualitative inquiries from England, Australia, the USA, Hong Kong and New Zealand focusing on women principals' and superintendents' leadership styles have been published in this decade. Coleman's (1996) study of the management style of female headteachers in England illustrates this kind of research:

> Women are highly under-represented amongst senior managers in education in the UK. The stereotype of the leader as male perpetuates this situation. This study sought to build upon the links which are now being made between 'feminine' styles and effective management. Five female headteachers of mixed secondary schools in one shirecounty in the UK were interviewed and asked to identify their characteristics as leaders and managers. The picture that emerged was of an 'androgynous' leader, able to draw upon a range of qualities. The success of the female headteacher was seen by those who were the subjects of this research to some extent to be due to the possession of qualities similar to the traditional male leader but they were also able to identify ways in which being a woman was helpful. (163)

Similarly, researchers were concerned about the impact of School-Based Management upon women administrators' ways of leading and career, re-conceptualisation of effective leadership through the stories of African-American female principals, the effect of context and gender on leading schools, experiences of women principals with power in the course of daily leadership and perceptions of women principals' leadership and teachers' work attitudes. The authors emphasised issues of 'power with', 'power through', the centrality of the student, and emotions (e.g., Fennell 1999; Strachan 1999) as major elements of female leadership, to name just a few. Findings about gender-related leadership styles were summed up by Eagly and her colleagues (1992) in a review paper they published:

> This article uses meta-analytic methods to review 50 studies that compared the leader-ship styles of principals of public schools and finds some evidence for differences between the sexes. In general, female principals scored somewhat higher than male principals on measures of task-oriented style, but there was less evidence for a sex difference on measures of interpersonally oriented style. A third aspect of

leadership style, the tendency to lead democratically or autocratically, produced the largest sex difference, with female principals adopting a more democratic or participative style and a less autocratic or directive style than male principals [...]. (76)

Whereas the research on females' leadership styles was in vogue during the 1990s, far fewer authors centred on issues of careers among women leaders in education. Authors investigated the professional identity of women headteachers in the nineteenth century, the ways to retain women superintendents in their jobs, the ways women administrators think and speak about their worlds and the strategies used by successful superintendents during their career. Interviews and historical case studies have been used as main methodologies aimed at unearthing the career stories of women educational leaders. For example, Kyle (1993) used theoretical viewpoints emerging from a biographical and historical analysis in order to provide a detailed account of the social, historical and political dimensions of particular Australian women leaders' lives.

Surprisingly, in spite of the extensive research on women leaders during that decade, very few works were written about barriers to women's advancement in education as if there was no longer gender inequality and discrimination. The few authors who acknowledged women's underrepresentation in educational administration explored women's lack of access to mentoring programmes that were more suitable for women actively seeking leadership positions within schools, or older women teachers' early retirement due to discriminatory practices in access to higher level positions. Notably, they not only explored barriers to career advancement among women but also suggested solutions in the form of better organisational interventions or mentoring programmes. One paper, written by Brown (1996), is worth mentioning because it symbolises the initial internationalisation of the research on women. Brown reviewed the internal and external barriers faced by African women, particularly women from Uganda, who sought access to managerial positions in schools, providing a number of strategies which could help these women to overcome these barriers. In some sense, it was a voice crying in the wilderness that predicted the extension of studies about women in education to many developing countries in the forthcoming decades.

As in the previous decades, but to a greater extent, authors continued to publish papers intentionally about gender distinctions in varied areas and work aspects, using quantitative research methods or governmental/ public databases. However, they neither centred on a certain group of employees in education, nor used any common conceptual framework to guide their comparative analysis. Thus, there are studies about the attitudes of men and women primary school teachers to promotion and educational administration, compensation differentials for female and male educational administrators, gender and race differentiations among applicants in educational leadership programmes, and gender differences in mentoring. Authors even attempted to explain the differences in examination outcomes between boys and girls, an area of study of little association with the EM knowledge base. Unsurprisingly, their results indicated that women administrators were paid less than comparable male counterparts and showed significant differences in the scores of black and Hispanic female applicants in educational leadership programmes on standardised tests, i.e., emphasised the dominance of gender distinctions in EM.

Similarly, EM researchers kept including, even more than before, the sex variable in their research design, i.e., the sex factor was one among other factors under investigation in their study. On the higher education level, researchers examined the concept of service values in business education and found that male students were more inclined to focus on social value during service consumption and that females were more critical of the price/quality relationship as it related to value (LeBlanc and Nguyen 1999). Others examined the influence of gender (and other antecedents) on job stress, psychological health, perceived role of trustees in higher education institutions, etc.

At school level, the sex factor was examined in studies about teachers and principals in a wide variety of issues and role aspects such as job satisfaction, teachers' receptivity to a proposed system-wide educational change, deputies' familiarity with the headteacher role and their views on its attractions and disadvantages, teacher absenteeism and psychological stress in secondary teaching. As before, sex-related distinctions were found in some studies; for example, absenteeism among teachers was significantly related to distance to work, gender, job involvement and overall job satisfaction (Scott and Wimbush 1991). Similarly, gender interacted significantly with stress factors in teaching and principalship. By contrast, teacher characteristics, including sex, had no significant impact on student evaluation of teaching in Singapore (Koh and Tan 1997).

Increasingly, authors reviewed the gender differences in papers published in *EAQ* and traced the levels of androcentric bias in this journal as Shakeshaft had done a decade earlier. In England, Valerie Hall (1997) reviewed the topic of gender in *EMAL*, the English journal of the field:

> This paper focuses on gender and educational management in the context of a critical review of the treatment of this issue in *Educational Management and Administration* since 1972. Gender emerged as a discrete topic in the journal only after 1980 and the first major call for a serious treatment of this issue did not take place until 1988. The paper argues that making gender figure rather than ground in studies of school leadership contributes to a more comprehensive picture of current practice. It raises questions about the relationship between home and work, family and career, early socialization and later performance [...]. (309)

These works set the stage for many new works on gender, women, feminism and even masculinity (only one paper mentioned the other side on the spectrum of gender) in the decades to come.

The 2000s: Massive Extension and Internationalisation

While there were some voices questioning the relevance of feminism since the beginning of the twenty-first century, at least in part because many Anglo-American and European women achieved many political firsts in that time, EM authors extended their interest in issues of gender, feminism and even masculinity and enriched their research designs and methodologies. In parallel, many international EM members started to explore gender-related issues in their geographical and national educational arenas (e.g., Romania, Nigeria, Greece, China, Iran, Turkey, Israel), thereby extending our knowledge base about women in educational administration from a social-cultural perspective. More books than ever were published about women superintendents, women in educational administration, gender and educational reforms and so forth from the 2000s.

Let's start our historical discussion of the 2000s onwards with several conceptual and review papers written by scholars such as Jill Blackmore, Marianne Coleman, Tanya Fitzgerald and others that symbolise the considerable scholarly progress of gender and female leadership in the field of EM. Some works have criticised western ethnocentric and masculine notions of leadership from feminist, post-feminist and post-modern perspectives and suggested an adequate reconceptualisation of leadership, while others use feminist concepts to analyse discourses of racism, diversity, marginality, inclusivity and social justice. Blackmore (2010), for example, confronts normative whiteness in educational administration from the perspective of feminist and critical race theory, considering how foregrounding whiteness in leadership is a necessary condition of inclusive education and leadership. The voices of marginalised women such as indigenous women from New Zealand have been also been highlighted. For instance, Fitzgerald (2010) strives to authenticate and legitimate Indigenous women's voices through theorising their leadership realities and by situating such knowledge in the cultural spaces that they occupy. Grogan's (2000) paper is an example of these works:

> This article reviews the literature on the superintendency over the past 50 years to understand what has been written about the position. By juxtaposing the traditional with ideas from feminist and postmodern literature, a possible re-conception of the superintendency is offered. This is grounded in acknowledging postmodern paradoxes that emerge using this approach. Recognizing such paradoxes allows the questioning of the current superintendency. This leads to suggested leadership strategies that differ from the traditional in hopes of a more socially committed superintendency in the future. (117)

Interestingly, although the field of EM has become more focused on the school organisation during the last two decades, there were several innovative papers about women leaders in higher education institutions from feminist and post-structuralist views, such as women deans in American universities, the childhood of women university presidents and women academics in university administration. Other works continued to examine the potential effects of gender on student performance (e.g., presentation evaluations) and on transformational learning and resistance in educational leadership programmes. For example, Blackmore and Sachs (2000) focused specifically on the experiences of women in universities in leadership positions in the Australian higher education system and identified five paradoxes that were shaping the work of women in these positions. They found that women were still largely excluded from much of the power structures in the local higher education system.

A considerable increase is evident also in the number of works that focused directly on gender differences in education. This comparative analysis included male and female teachers, middle-managers, primary headteachers, secondary principals, superintendents and other groups of educational leaders. A sample of these comparative works includes the effect of gender on educators' perceptions of the personal well-being (Sackney et al. 2000), the values underpinning the work of female and male educational leaders in Iceland (Lárusdóttir 2007), the impact of gender dynamics on middle managers' career aspirations and development (Choi 2013) and gender differences in transformational leadership (Zeinabady 2013).

As in previous decades, some gender differences were found; female school leaders have more diversified behaviour to other women than male leaders show in regard to men (Addi-Raccach 2006), many men administrators had worked in line-role positions and moved vertically up to the superintendency while women generally travelled to the superintendency through staff roles and their career mobility patterns were more often horizontal (Kim and Brunner 2009), and many other differences, as appeared in Coleman's (2007) paper:

> This paper presents a comparison of the views of men and women headteachers (principals) of secondary schools in England in the 1990s and in 2004. The same survey instrument was used on both occasions. The perceptions of the headteachers show change in some areas and no change in others. Overall, women are more likely to become headteachers and are now less likely to be categorised into pastoral roles, but in some cases women still meet prejudice from governors and others in the wider community. Women headteachers are more likely to have partners and children than in the 1990s, sharing equally or carrying most of the domestic responsibilities, whereas

male colleagues are most likely to have partners who take the majority of responsibility in the home ... Women headteachers are likely to see some benefits in being a woman in a role stereotypically associated with men. However, there has been an increase in the proportion of women who feel that they have to prove their worth as a leader, and this may be linked with increased levels of accountability in schools. (384)

As compared to previous decades, the topics for comparison became more diverse, ranging from 'old' concepts such as work satisfaction, career paths and development, to complex issues of principal-teachers relations, moral dilemmas, gender identities and gender-related variability in the selection of educators and school leaders. In fact, field members interested in gender issues extended their comparative research topics and areas of study. Note, in addition, that the number of works that used 'sex' or 'gender' as one of several variables in their research design also increased dramatically, but its nature, topics and type were similar to these in previous years (e.g., authors kept examining the correlation between several variables, including sex, and teachers' or principals' job satisfaction, occupational stress and work commitment). Very few examined 'sex' in relation to new organisational phenomena such as 'organisational citizenship behaviour' or 'principal-teachers' relationships.

Similarly, the number of works centring directly on women leaders increased dramatically, using new theoretical and methodological perspectives and extending to new geographical areas and societies. Likewise, it was no longer the white woman leader who received major attention in the literature; more and more works explored the lives and careers of women from minorities (e.g., African-American superintendents, Arab women leaders) in a host of leadership positions.

As before, the barriers to women's advancement were explored but this time with much more attention being given to particular barriers faced by women in traditional societies and in minorities. In this sense, EM researchers continued to deepen understanding of the complexities associated with American and English women's advancement to superintedency, the effect and effectiveness of leadership development programmes for aspiring women (e.g., McLay and Brown 2001), the gendered nature of the UK further education sector, etc. One paper examined the 'glass ceilings' and 'glass walls' faced by women from different parts of the world (Cubillo and Brown 2003) emphasising, therefore, the initial internationalisation of the research on women leaders.

From these studies we learned more about a wide variety of constraints on the decisions and choices of women seeking to advance to leadership positions. Some of these constraints derived, at least in part, from sex discrimination (Coleman 2001). These constraints were not only external but also internal as Oplatka and Tamir (2009) showed:

> The current study aimed at tracing the career stories of 25 Israeli female deputy heads who explicitly do not aspire to headship. These deputies hold a stance that is in sharp contrast with widespread beliefs on career aspiration and advancement, albeit that they are considered to be competent candidates for headship. The female deputies' stories revealed that they construct a clear and sharp distinction between the deputy's role and that of the school head. Whereas the former is perceived to be challenging and less complicated, leaving them sufficient space to establish informal, warm relationships with staff and students, the latter is portrayed as stressful, formal and essentially administrative-oriented. This distinction corroborates the dichotomy of masculine versus feminine leadership [...]. (216)

In the last decade, though, more attention has been paid than ever before to women's personal decisions to become school leaders, i.e., researchers sought to shed more light on issues of career aspiration, choice and perception. An interesting paper in this area focused on the managerial aspirations of women teachers from Uganda (Sperandio and Kagoda 2010) and revealed that the majority of them aspired to school leadership but few had positioned themselves to do well in the competitive applications process. Similarly, some works have extended our knowledge about the career development of female school leaders, such as the key role of the mentors in the success of new women school leaders and the process of self-renewal among women principals in mid-career.

Several EM authors probed into the lives and careers of women in educational leadership positions. They traced the career experiences of women superintendents from their own viewpoints, attempted to characterise the world of African-American women administrators, 'unearthed' the factors affecting women leaders' retention in their job, and so forth.

Some papers merit illuminating for their new and challenging research questions as depicted below:

- To illuminate differences and commonalities in how women administrators from different generations and racial/ethnic identities negotiate work-family conflicts (Loder 2005);
- To tell the stories of six female supervisors who have successfully managed to access this high-level position in the Bedouin educational system (Abu-Rabia Quader and Oplatka 2008);
- To consider what all-women networks have, and might offer, in terms of support and development of women in educational leadership (Coleman 2010).

The wealth of new topics, research questions and theoretical views observed in the works about women leaders' experiences in post characterises also the study about females' leadership style. Notably, authors emphasised the complexity of masculine and feminine leadership style, moved to study androgynous models of leadership, explored women's ways of implementing and legitimising their initiatives and leadership, and examined the problems arising from feminine leadership styles. Their research design was qualitative using mostly in-depth, semi-structured interviews and case studies. An example of the transition of the research on women in leadership from relatively simple binaries of masculinity versus femininity to more complex understandings of multiple realities is Reay and Ball's (2000) paper:

> A growing number of feminist accounts assert that gender matters when we examine leadership styles in schools and other educational establishments. We argue that gendered identities are in context more fluid and shifting than often depicted in such texts. There are many different femininities and the form they take is powerfully shaped by the roles women undertake, the context within which they perform these roles and the amount of power they have access to. We draw on a small case study of female headteachers to exemplify a number of the problems involved in depicting female management as essentially different from 'male' ways of managing. (145)

Similarly, Perumal (2009) aimed to explore how women school principals in South Africa navigate the complexities of educational leadership in disadvantaged communities ravaged by HIV and child abuse while also negotiating their status within the education fraternity that has historically relegated them to second-class citizenship. From a different perspective, Cliffe (2011) connected emotional intelligence and female leadership indicating that women leaders could make intelligent use of their emotions, not without negative effect, however.

Before closing, some reference should be made to the global expansion of the research on women educational leaders in recent years. International researchers sought to identify Muslim teachers' constructions of 'masculinity' and 'femininity' of the school principal (e.g., Arar and Oplatka 2013), examined female principal leadership practices that are considered crucial in the effectiveness and improvement of schools in Ghana (Agezo 2010) and explored the reasons for the relatively small number of women principals in Turkish elementary schools (Celikten 2005). Reports on female leadership have been published also by authors from Asia, the Middle East and the Arab society of Israel.

Concluding Comments

From the historical analysis described in this chapter, a number of insights can be provided. Firstly, during the last fifty years, the research on women educational leaders and gender in educational administration has undergone major upheavals, beginning as a very limited stream of research in terms of topics, research questions, and geographical focus (e.g., American-oriented, 'sex' is used as one variable among others in the research design), moving to a much wider and varied research in the last decade. It is now more global, focused explicitly on gender and female educational leadership and draws on a host of theoretical perspectives.

Secondly, as compared to feminist writings and gender studies, the research on gender permeated the field of EM relatively slowly, disconnecting from the development of gender studies and the women's movement, and appearing in the field's journals unsystematically. In addition, this research lacked sufficient critical feminist thought; the publication of papers grounded in feminist or post-feminist theories was relatively limited, for example. Although this developed throughout the 2000s, it seems that authors concentrated on few topics without much in-depth diversity.

Thirdly, as the research on women principals seems to have reached a mature phase, reading between the lines unearths some developing areas of study in their incipient stage, such as gender analysis of the team and the whole-school levels, queer theory, male-based leadership (masculine conceptions of leadership in our era of androgynous time), masculine notions, androgynous leadership styles. These broad areas would appear to be the foci of study that will enrich and diversify the research on gender in EM in the coming years.

References

Abu-Rabia Quader, S., and Oplatka, I. (2008). 'The Power of Femininity: Exploring the Gender and Ethnic Experiences of Muslim Women Who Accessed Supervisory Roles in a Bedouin Society'. *Journal of Educational Administration* 46 (3), 396–415.

Addi-Raccach, A. (2006). 'Accessing Internal Leadership Positions at School: Testing the Similarity-Attraction Approach Regarding Gender in Three Educational Systems in Israel'. *Educational Administration Quarterly* 42 (3), 291–323.

Agezo, C.K. (2010). 'Female Leadership and School Effectiveness in Junior High Schools in Ghana'. *Journal of Educational Administration* 48 (6), 689–703.

Altheide, D.L. (1996). *Qualitative Media Analysis.* Thousand Oaks, CA: Sage Publications.

Arar, K.H., and Oplatka, I. (2013). 'The Gender Debate and Teachers' Constructions Of Masculinity Vs. Femininity of The School Principals: The Case of Muslim Teachers Israel'. *School Leadership and Management* 33 (1), 97–112.

Baumgartner, M.S., and Schneider, D.E. (2010). 'Perceptions of Women In Management: A Thematic Analysis of Razing The Glass Ceiling'. *Journal of Career Development* 37 (2), 559–76.

Blackmore, J. (2010). '"The Other Within': Race/Gender Disruptions to the Professional Learning of White Educational Leaders'. *International Journal of Leadership in Education* 13 (1), 45–61.

Blackmore, J., and Sachs, J. (2000). 'Paradoxes of Leadership and Management in Higher Education in Times of Change: Some Australian Reflections'. *International Journal of Leadership in Education* 3 (1), 1–16.

Bradley, H. (2007). *Gender*. Cambridge: Polity.

Brown, M. (1996). 'Barriers to Women Managers' Advancement in Education in Uganda'. *International Journal of Educational Management* 10 (6), 18–23.

Butler, J. (1993). *Bodies that Matter: On the Discursive Limits of Sex*. London: Routledge.

Capper, C.A. (1998). 'Critically Oriented and Postmodern Perspectives: Sorting Out the Differences and Applications for Practice'. *Educational Administration Quarterly* 34 (3), 354–79.

Celikten, M. (2005). 'A Perspective on Women Principals in Turkey'. *International Journal of Leadership in Education* 8 (3), 207–21.

Choi, P.L. (2013). 'Gender Identities and Career Aspiration of Middle Leaders: Cases in Hong Kong Secondary Schools'. *International Journal of Educational Management* 27 (1), 38–53.

Cliffe, J. (2011). 'Emotional Intelligence: A Study of Female Secondary School Headteachers'. *Educational Management, Administration and Leadership* 39 (2), 205–18.

Coleman, M. (2010). 'Women-Only (Homophilous) Networks Supporting Women Leaders in Education'. *Journal of Educational Administration* 48 (6), 769–81.

Coleman, M. (2007). 'Gender and Education Leadership in England: A Comparison of Secondary Headteachers' Views Over Time'. *School Leadership and Management* 27 (4), 383–99.

Coleman, M. (2001). 'Achievement Against the Odds: The Female Secondary Headteachers in England and Wales'. *School Leadership and Management* 21 (1), 23–45.

Coleman, M. (1996). 'The Management Style of Female Headteachers'. *Educational Management, Administration and Leadership* 24 (2), 163–74.

Cross, E. (1985). 'Swimming against the Tide of Male Mythology: A Feminist Assessment of Current Assumptions in the Co-education/Single-Sex Schools Debate'. *School Leadership and Management* 5 (1), 69–77.

Cubillo, L., and Brown, M. (2003). 'Women into Educational Leadership and Management: International Differences?' *Journal of Educational Administration* 41 (3), 278–91.

Due Biling, Y. (2011). 'Are Women in Management Victims of the Phantom of the Male Norm?' *Gender, Work and Organization* 18 (3), 298–317.

Eagly, A.H., Karau, S.J., and Johnson, B.T. (1992). 'Gender and Leadership Style Among School Principals: A Meta-analysis'. *Educational Administration Quarterly* 28 (1), 76–102.

Fennell, H.A. (1999). 'Power in the Principalship: Four Women's Experiences'. *Journal of Educational Administration* 37 (1), 23–50.

Fitzgerald, T. (2010). 'Spaces In-between: Indigenous Women Leaders Speak Back to Dominant Discourses and Practices in Educational Leadership'. *International Journal of Leadership in Education* 13 (1), 93–105.

Frasher, J.M., and Frasher, R.S. (1979). 'Educational Administration: A Feminine Profession'. *Educational Administration Quarterly* 15 (1), 1–13.

Frasher, J.M., and Frasher, R.S. (1980). 'Sex Bias in the Evaluation of Administrators'. *Journal of Educational Administration* 18 (2), 245–53.

Glaser, G. and Strauss, A. (1967). *The Discovery of Grounded Theory*. Chicago: Aldine.

Glazer, J.S. (1991). 'Feminism and Professionalism in Teaching and Educational Administration'. *Educational Administration Quarterly* 27 (3), 321–42.

Glover, D., and Kaplan, K. (2000). *Genders*. London: Routledge.

Gray, D.P. (2001). 'Historical Analysis: A New Approach Comparing Publications from Inside and Outside the Discipline over Time', *Medical Education* 35 (3), 404–8.

Gray, H.L. (1987). 'Gender Considerations in School Management: Masculine and Feminine Leadership Style'. *School Leadership and Management* 7 (3), 297–302.

Grogan, M. (2000). 'Laying the Groundwork for Reconception of the Superintendency from Feminist Postmodern Perspectives'. *Educational Administration Quarterly* 36 (1), 117–42.

Grow-Maienza, J. (1986). 'The Superintendency: Characteristics of Access for Men and Women'. *Educational Administration Quarterly* 22 (1), 59–79.

Hall, V. (1997). 'Dusting Off the Phoenix: Gender and Educational Leadership Revisited'. *Educational Management, Administration and Leadership* 25 (3), 309–24.

Hawkesworth, M. (1997). 'Confounding Gender'. *Signs: Journal of Women in Culture and Society* 22 (3), 649–84.

Holmes, M. (2007). *What is Gender? Sociological Approaches*. London: SAGE.

Hoskin, K.W. (1993). 'Education and the Genesis of Disciplinarity: The Unexpected Reversal'. In E. Messer-Davidow, D.R. Shumway and D.J. Sylvan (eds), *Knowledges: Historical and Critical Studies in Disciplinarity*, 271–304. Charlottesville: University Press of Virginia.

Hough, J. (1988). 'Gender Bias in Educational Management and Administration'. *Educational Management, Administration and Leadership* 16 (1), 69–74.

Humes, W., and Bryce, T. (2001). 'Scholarship, Research and the Evidential Basis of Policy Development in Education'. *British Journal of Educational Studies* 49 (3), 323–52.

Jordan-Young, R.M. (2010). *Brain Storm: The Flaws in the Science of Sex Differences*. Cambridge, MA: Harvard University Press.

Kim, Y.L., and Brunner, C.C. (2009). 'School Administrators' Career Mobility to the Superintendency: Gender Differences in Career Development'. *Journal of Educational Administration* 47 (1), 75–107.

Koenig, A.M., Eagly, A.H., Mitchell, A.A., and Ristikari, T. (2011). 'Are Leader Stereotypes Masculine? A Meta-analysis of Three Research Paradigms'. *Psychological Bulletin* 137 (4), 616–42.

Koh, H.C., and Tan, T.M. (1997). 'Empirical Investigation of the Factors Affecting SET Results'. *International Journal of Educational Management* 11 (4), 170–8.

Kremer, J. (1998). 'Work'. In K. Trew and J. Kremer (eds), *Gender and Psychology*, 141–52. London: Arnold.

Kyle, N.J. (1993). 'Cara David: A Leading Woman in Australian Education'. *Journal of Educational Administration* 31 (4), 80–99.

Lárusdóttir, S.H. (2007). 'The Fact that I'm a Woman May have been the Defining Factor: The Moral Dilemmas of an Icelandic Headteacher'. *Educational Management, Administration and Leadership* 35 (2), 261–76.

LeBlanc, G., and Nguyen, N. (1999). 'Listening to the Customer's Voice: Examining Perceived Service Value among Business College Students'. *International Journal of Educational Management* 13 (4), 187–98.

Loder, T. (2005). 'Women Administrators Negotiate Work-Family Conflicts in Changing Times: An Intergenerational Perspective'. *Educational Administration Quarterly* 41 (5), 741–76.

McBurney, E.G., and Hough, J. (1989). 'Role Perceptions of Female Deputy Heads'. *Educational Management Administration and Leadership* 17 (1), 115–18.

McIntosh, J. (1974). 'Differences Between Women Teachers Who Do and Who Do Not Seek Promotion'. *Journal of Educational Administration* 12 (2), 28–41.

McLay, M. and Brown, M. (2001). 'Preparation and Training for School Leadership: Case Studies of Nine Women Headteachers in Secondary Independent Sector'. *School Leadership and Management* 21 (1), 101–15.

Mitchell, J. (1971). *Women's Estate*. Harmondsworth: Penguin.

Murphy, J., Vriesenga, M., and Storey, V. (2007). 'Educational Administration Quarterly, 1979–2003: An Analysis of Types of Work, Methods of Investigation, and Influences'. *Educational Administration Quarterly* 43 (5), 612–28.

Omair, K. (2008). 'Women in Management in the Arab Context'. *Education, Business and Society: Contemporary Middle Eastern Issues* 1 (2), 107–23

Oplatka, I. (2010). *The Legacy of Educational Administration: A Historical Analysis of an Academic Field*. Hamburg: Peter Lang.

Oplatka, I., and Tamir, V. (2009). 'I Don't Want to be a School Head: Women Deputy Heads' Insightful Constructions of Career Advancement and Retention'. *Educational Management, Administration and Leadership* 37 (2), 216–38.

Over, R. (1983). 'Career Prospects for Academics in the Education Department of Australian Universities'. *Journal of Educational Administration* 21 (1), 69–78.

Paul, R.J. (1975). 'Some Correlates of Role Ambiguity: Men and Women in the Same Work Environment', *Educational Administration Quarterly* 11 (3), 85–98.

Perumal, J. (2009). 'Reading and Creating Critically Leaderful Schools that Make Difference: The Post-Apartheid South African Case'. *International Journal of Leadership in Education* 12 (1), 35–49.

Pounder, D. (1988). 'The Male/Female Salary Differential for School Administrators: Implications for Career Patterns and Placement of Women'. *Educational Administration Quarterly* 24 (1), 5–19.

Pounder, D.G. (1989). 'The Gender Gap in Salaries of Educational Administration Professors'. *Educational Administration Quarterly* 25 (2), 181–200.

Reay, D., and Ball, S. (2000). 'Essentials of Female Management: Women's Ways of Working in the Education Marketplace'. *Educational Management, Administration and Leadership* 28 (2), 145–59.

Rodgers, R., and Rodgers, N. (2000). 'Defining the Boundaries of Public Administration: Undisciplined Mongrels Versus Disciplined Purists'. *Public Administration Review* 60 (5), 435–45.

Rubin, G. (1975). 'The Traffic in Women: Notes on the Political Economy of sex'. In R.R. Reiter (ed.), *Towards an Anthropology of Women*. New York: Monthly Review Press.

Sackney, L., Noonan, B., and Miller, C.M. (2000). 'Leadership for Educator Wellness: An Exploratory Study'. *International Journal of Leadership in Education* 3 (1), 41–56.

Schein, V.E. (2001). 'A Global Look at Psychological Barriers to Women's Progress in Management'. *Journal of Social Issues* 57 (4), 675–88.

Scott, K.D., and Wimbush, J.C. (1991). 'Teacher Absenteeism in Secondary Education'. *Educational Administration Quarterly* 27 (4), 506–29.

Shakeshaft, C., and Hanson, M. (1986). 'Androcentric Bias in the Educational Administration Quarterly'. *Educational Administration Quarterly* 22 (1), 68–92.

Sperandio, J., and Kagoda, A.M. (2010). 'Women Teachers' Aspirations to School Leadership in Uganda'. *International Journal of Educational Management* 24 (1), 22–33.

Strachan, J. (1999). 'Feminist Educational Leadership in a New Zealand Neo-liberal Context'. *Journal of Educational Administration* 37 (2), 121–38.

Telfer, R. (1978). 'Decision Congruence and the Sex of School Administrators'. *Journal of Educational Administration* 16 (1), 39–45.

Trusty, F.M., and Sergiovanni, T.J. (1966). 'Perceived Need Deficiencies of Teachers and Administrators: A Proposal for Restructuring Teacher Roles'. *Educational Administration Quarterly* 2 (3), 168–80.

Zeinabadi, H.R. (2013). 'Social Exchange Outcomes of Transformational Leadership: Comparing Male and Female Principals of Public Primary Schools in Iran'. *International Journal of Educational Management* 27 (7), 730–43.

JACKY LUMBY

Culture and Otherness in Gender Studies: Building on Marianne Coleman's Work

Those studying gender inequality grapple with how to position themselves. They are typically women, but also of a particular race, culture and history, moreover are researchers reflecting the ontological and epistemological predilections of their academic training. Positioning raises a range of challenges in relation to the degree of self-awareness and the nature of 'otherness' perceived in those studied. There are home contexts where distance between researcher and those researched may not be considered an issue; in Pillay's (2011: 657) words, the focus is 'the not other', though such a distinction may be illusory. Though many accept that 'gender congruity is not enough to overcome ethnic incongruity' (Bhopal 2001: 280), cultural or geographic congruity may not offer the inroad to understanding another that is supposed. There are more evident issues of distance when researchers present findings and sometimes recommendations about women with characteristics and experience different to their own or who lead in distant locations, as in international and comparative work.

Such research is often pursued by those from the Anglophone world, in part because these researchers have access to sufficient resources to undertake international projects and in part because international funding and sponsoring agencies may, unjustifiably, give greater credence to researchers and knowledge with provenance in an Anglophone setting. Engaging with the nature of distance and the ethical, methodological and political issues raised is central to researching gender. Whether researching in one's own or a less familiar cultural context, questions about the degree of congruence and interplay between the values and culture of researcher and researched remain problematic.

In the context of gender research, Alcoff (1991/92: 6) suggests that a belief persists that 'speaking for others is vain, arrogant, unethical and politically illegitimate'. Yet, in a sense, researchers always speak for those who are the focus of research. The issue is the relationship between the degree of otherness between the two and how 'truth' and related action are conceived. This chapter of the volume will focus on considering this question in undertaking research, using Marianne Coleman's work as a springboard and discussing the relationship between the cultural embeddedness of research and the imperative for action to increase gender equality.

Marianne Coleman's Work

An example of these challenges in practice can be explored using the survey instrument designed by Marianne Coleman to gather information on the experience of headteachers (see Appendix 1 on pages 55–62). It was first used in the United Kingdom in the 1990s (Coleman 2009) and was subsequently used as the basis of research in China (Coleman et al. 1998). Since then it has proved a useful tool for many researchers and has been adapted and implemented in many parts of the world, not only as a survey by questionnaire but as a basis for interviews. Numerous master's and doctoral degree students have sought permission to use the instrument in their country, for instance in Singapore in the 1990s. It was adapted to this context in relation to questions about domestic responsibilities, for example, because middle-class women headteachers had servants for childcare and so had different domestic responsibilities from women in England and Wales. The resulting data were reported in an article in *Compare* (Morris et al. 1999). The instrument was trialled in Uganda, Germany and the United States by members of the *Women Leading Education* international network prior to being further adapted by a team based in South Africa for use in that nation (Lumby et al. 2010). More recently, it has been used in Scandinavian countries and the US, and has been adapted to provide the basis for research with male Muslim teachers (Shah, with Shaikh 2010). It proved useful in all these contexts because of the comprehensive nature of the questions and because both women and men are asked questions about aspects of professional and personal life that are gendered and usually seen as women's concerns.

Coleman's instrument was originally intended to be administered within England and Wales. Although the instrument has always been adapted somewhat for use elsewhere, for example to reflect the school structure in a specific context, the degree to which those using it in other parts of the world have engaged with the implications of the cultural context has varied, for example how gender and gender equality are conceived by the researcher as well as by those researched. How this may impact on the use of the instrument is explored in varying depth. This is but one example of the way work with its origins in the West has travelled, potentially carrying with it ways of seeing and thinking that have provenance in a particular location but which may be assumed by some to be universal. Some researchers have used the instrument within its original intended context – the UK. However, this does not result in a process that is necessarily free from cultural misunderstanding. The insider–outsider binary is a simplistic division that obliterates the many dimensions in which we remain other, irrespective of apparent correspondence between researcher and research (Santoro & Smyth 2010). Many women protest: 'I am not the Other, capital O. I am part of the same, with a difference' (Arnott 1998: 17, quoted in Pillay 2011: 667).

The use of an instrument that has generated data in many parts of the world speaks to the value of the instrument itself and, arguably, has resulted in comparative data to build a picture of the experience of women internationally over time. However, such valued use of Coleman's work can serve as a stimulus to raise issues about how far data collected by means of the instrument might be conceived as generic to women in whatever context and the positionality of those undertaking the analysis.

Researching the Elsewhere

The majority of research and writing on gender and educational leadership has its provenance in the Anglophone world. Both theory and research methods may therefore be imbued with the values and cultural assumptions of the West, though they may be implicit rather than fully acknowledged and discussed (Lumby 2013). Researchers in the UK or the US, for example, do not usually explicitly depict the impact on their research of UK or US values. These are often a given within articles and research reports and, as is commonly the case in relation to culture, both writer and reader may take these for granted and be unaware of their nature.

The potential issues involved are not unique to researching gender:

> The notion that research is an inherently subjective exercise and that research prac-
> tices are embedded in a researcher's experiences and life views is well established in
> qualitative research methodology literature [...]. Data collection is not an objective,
> unbiased task that provides the 'raw materials' through which 'the truth' will be
> revealed upon analysis. (Santoro & Smyth 2010: 494)

Researchers have responded to such challenges by devising a range of methods to counter the distance, and particularly the power distance, between themselves and the subject of research and to breach differences of cultural understanding between those asking and those answering questions. Feminist research aims to prioritise women's voices and experience and to adjust unequal power relations between the researcher and researched (Hesse-Biber 2013). The challenge is how self-awareness and power adjustment are to be achieved. Methods are often similar to those used in other forms of qualitative research: 'Practices such as member checking, prolonged researcher time in the field, and the use of intensive semi-structured interviews are integral to and well established within ethnographic research' (op cit.: 497). Research training in some nations includes little emphasis on qualitative and feminist methods. Additionally, sufficient resource to fund such prolonged contact and extensive research is generally available only in economically wealthier nations and rare, even there. The majority must choose between not researching at all or using methods that are less resource heavy. It is in this context that Coleman's questionnaire has proved very useful. Another major tool proposed by feminist researchers is reflexivity. The challenges raised by such self-searching sensitivity are at the heart of this chapter.

If the distance between researcher and researched is an acknowledged, generic, methodological, ethical and political challenge, gender research may involve particularly difficult cultural issues in that concepts that are fundamental – gender itself, marriage, family, mothering, work – are so universal and familiar that assumptions about their nature are deeply embedded. Women may identify with others, believing, as is stressed in much feminist literature, that there is a collective experience of sexism (Firestone 2003) and that the shared language necessary for valid research is available to them in the body of feminist literature (Santoro & Smyth 2010). However, this is played out in everyday settings where differing religions, cultures and legal systems may fundamentally alter how such phenomena are experienced. Not least are very different notions of what equality or fairness between men and women would look like, and how other power differentials, such as between colonisers and the previously colonised, are relevant. For example, Jewkesa et al. (2003) suggest that research in South Africa must engage with the complex social disturbances brought about by the apartheid era, where what it means to be a man or a woman, to be married and to care for children were all influenced by social disruption and oppression by the regime (Lumby 2015), and continue to be influenced by structural factors relating to the economy. This is but one context in a global picture where not only are there many understandings of what it is to be a woman, but masculinities are multiplying:

> Multiple patterns of masculinity have been identified in many studies, in a variety of countries, and in different institutional and cultural settings. It is also a widespread research finding that certain masculinities are more socially central, or more associated with authority and social power, than others. The concept of hegemonic masculinity presumes the subordination of nonhegemonic masculinities, and this is a process that has now been documented in many settings, internationally. (Connell & Messerschmidt 2005: 846)

If femininities and masculinities are mutually constructed in specific social settings, then how women leaders wish to and are able to function is dependent on a wide spectrum of context sensitive factors. As a consequence, answers to questions, for example in Coleman's instrument around work and family responsibilities, are all likely to reflect the deeply historic construction of social roles.

Unpacking an Example Using Coleman's Work

The South African context in which the instrument was used provides an opportunity to explore the issues that arise in international research on educational leadership. A focus on a selection of questions offers an opportunity to discuss the justification for asking them and to explore how the analysis of responses may be similar or differ from those in the country of provenance, the UK, and why this matters. The instrument contains many sections relating to a range of aspects of professional and personal life. Those selected for discussion are in the section on domestic life. Given the unique issues in South Africa, where all aspects of family life have been influenced by the legacy of apartheid, the choice of questions is intended to highlight issues around otherness, positionality and interpretation of data:

6. To what extent do you and your partner share domestic responsibilities, e.g. housework, shopping, cooking, washing, gardening, organising holidays and social life? Indicate an approximate overall percentage undertaken by each of you.
7. Have you ever changed your job to follow your partner?
8. Has your partner ever changed their job to follow you?
9. Have you ever operated two separate households as a result of job commitments?
10. Do you have responsibility for the care of other dependants, including elderly relatives?

Domestic Responsibilities

Coleman's results document a persistent pattern in the nature of women leaders' lives and its impact on their access to and enactment of a leadership role in England and Wales:

> In both the 1990s and in 2004, those women who agreed that they had experienced discrimination (half in 2004, two-thirds in 1996), were most likely to link it to their domestic and family responsibilities. (Coleman 2007: 387)

The responsibility for domestic tasks was clearly unevenly shared:

> In three-quarters of the households of the men head teachers, their wives or part-
> ners take the major responsibility for all domestic matters, whilst the partners of
> women heads take major responsibility in only just over 30 per cent of the homes.
> (Coleman 2007: 390)

The tale of unequal adoption of domestic roles appears ongoing (Graves 2014) and international (Moorosi 2010; Zikhali & Perumal 2015), and is universally taken to demonstrate the impact on the workplace role of a sub-ordinate role in the family, to the detriment of women as leaders of schools.

The use of Coleman's adapted instrument in South Africa (Lumby et al. 2010: 21) discovered that '63 per cent of those in the survey with part-ners reported that partners took less than half of the domestic responsibili-ties'. This result is very similar to Coleman's 2007 finding, given above. It would seem that only about a third of women school leaders have partners who take an equal or greater share of domestic responsibilities. One might interpret this finding as evidence of near-universal gendered assumptions about the appropriate division of domestic responsibilities and the resulting additional burden placed on women leaders compared to men. Moorosi (2007) suggests that this is the case in South Africa, but also argues for a more nuanced consideration of the impact of history and context.

Achieving a change in long-habituated practice; that is, achieving a more equal division of domestic responsibilities challenges concepts of what it is to be a man or a woman. The apartheid era in itself robbed black and Asian heritage women and men of power and dignity. It also depended economically on the disruption of family, as individual members were forced to work away from their home. Carter and May (2001; 1987) note the 'extraordinary levels of inequality and human insecurity' caused during the era and the effect of enfeebling men's self-confidence. Post-apartheid, the constitution established a vision of masculinity: 'The ideal South African man in this framework is one who is non-violent, a good father and husband, employed and able to provide for his family' (Walker 2005: 164). However, the new man had to act in a context where legislation for gender equality further challenged masculinities already undermined by an oppressive regime and where continuing economic insecurity pre-cluded acting as this ideal man. As a consequence, 'Traditional versions and expressions of masculinity and male sexuality have been disturbed and destabilised (Walker 2005: 161), resulting in a growing backlash and a blaming culture across South Africa that locates responsibility for at least some of the issues faced by men in the growing employment, seniority and economic power of women (Shefer 2014). White men, too, experienced the influence of the regime on their construction of masculinity during and since the apartheid era. As Orwell (1936) pointed out, the role of the coloniser or oppressor demands maintenance of aggression to subordinates, in this case women.

Such understanding of the disruptive context in which men continue to bear an unequal share of domestic responsibilities is not to act as apologist for such behaviour. Women operate in a society where traditional paternalistic assumptions translate not only into an unequal domestic burden but subject them to exclusion and violence. Nevertheless, it is necessary to consider more deeply what reporting the percentage of women school leaders who carry the greatest part of the domestic load might mean or achieve. Shefer (2014: 506) acknowledges the problem of women's disproportionate responsibility in the home internationally, but also calls on a report from Tronto (2013) to point out the entrenched web of factors leading to such division. There is a significant positive association between men's father's participation in domestic duties and their own; they learn their role in domestic responsibilities from their own family. Broadly, to further gender equality it is important that men take their share of family responsibilities. However, when many have not experienced their own father being engaged in this way, in a South African context often due to the economic necessity to work at a distance, Shefer suggests that merely repeatedly and negatively pointing out the failings of men is unhelpful:

> Such findings may point to the value of moving away from dwelling on boys' and men's continued engagement in normative and problematic practices, to strategically engage with and acknowledge existing participation of boys and men in alternative, equitable, and constructive practices, such as more active participation in caring practices. (507)

Above all, it may be that, in listening to the voice of women as a feminist methodology, the voice of men has been lost. Shefer's point is that we need to listen to both, to understand the interplay and also to identify and celebrate more equitable behaviour, as well as depicting those which are oppressive. The use of Coleman's questionnaire in South Africa generated relevant data about the more positive aspects of the relationship between women and their partner or husband, and its impact on their work as school leaders:

> Many reported their partners or spouses were a great support and help, giving encouragement, advice and accompanying them to school or related functions. Some principals even reported that their partners regularly help out around the school by running errands or assisting with issues surrounding security of school property. Principals who are married to a supportive partner view their marital status as an advantage to their career progress. (Lumby et al. 2010: 21)

Reporting data produced by using Coleman's instrument can build on previous work and move beyond narratives of trauma and injustice. Mere repetition of statistics on relative shares of domestic responsibilities, while argued to raise consciousness, may in fact be counter-productive, trapping women further in merely narrating tales of distress rather than empowering them to take action. A deeper understanding of the circumstances in which habitual practice has arisen and greater emphasis on the lessons from positive relations might hold more promise of change. Above all, understanding the contextual factors that have exacerbated the issue is axiomatic to begin to achieve change. A survey instrument is always open to charges of superficiality but, as illustrated briefly in this section, data generated by Coleman's instrument hold the potential to move beyond consciousness-raising and to stimulate culturally sensitive reflection on ways forward. In part, this is due to its insistence on considering the perspectives of both women and men.

Family Relocation

Several questions in the instrument enquire about the choice of living with a partner and the relationship of this to job moves. In the West, women leaving a job to follow a male partner who has taken on a new post has historically been a norm, signalling to many that the dominant male part-ner's career and economic support of the family takes precedence. Harvey (1998: 309) refers to the 'trailing partner' as a well-established pattern; indeed, early research suggested that family relocation was one of the rea-sons that women found it difficult to build a career as quickly and efficiently as their male partners (Bielby & Bielby 1992). Valcour and Tolbert (2003) compare Bielby and Bielby's findings with their own:

> Using 1977 data, Bielby and Bielby (1992) found that men's careers were typically given priority over their wives'. More than twenty years later, our data indicate that men's careers are still more frequently given priority, even within dual-career couples. (783)

They go on to suggest a disparity in career outcomes, in that women pay a higher price for career success dependent on moving jobs, with a higher rate of divorce and of remaining childless or with fewer children. Coleman (2002) found this to be true in her survey of secondary schools in England and Wales. However, in some countries domicile patterns amongst families are changing, with growth in 'living apart together' (LAT) arrangements. Levin (2004) anticipates an increase in flexibility that will benefit women:

> Formerly, the matter was framed as a way of showing one's love: 'If you love me enough, you will relocate.' The job and the partner are seen as being in competition, and one has to choose between them. In particular there would have been social expectations pressurizing the woman to relocate [...]. Today, there is acceptance of the idea that she can keep her job and her friends, as well as her relationship with children, parents and other relatives, and at the same time have a relationship with a man and maintain separate dwellings. (232)

Using Coleman's adapted instrument in the South African survey, a similar result was found to that of earlier surveys in England and Wales. Whilst the large majority, 69 per cent, of respondent principals were married, 15 per cent were divorced and 12 per cent were single. Some found marriage a hindrance to their career and others had chosen to remain single, the better to forward their career. Only 4 per cent of male partners had changed their job to follow their partner, as in the international pattern. However, only 6.5 per cent of women leaders had changed their job to follow their partner;

93 per cent had not, while 10.5 per cent of the women leaders operated two households for job reasons, a relatively small percentage.

Interpreting the answers to these questions might be understood in relation to the family social patterns in the West, both traditional and emerging, but this would miss the very specific conditions within South Africa. Bank (2001) suggests that the forms of partnership in South Africa reflect more than just the exigencies of economic necessity. Living together unmarried, or *ukuthlalisana*, is potentially a protest against previous traditional and patriarchal structures, an expression of positive choice by women and a negative reluctance by men to entertain obligations to support a family:

> As ideology, *ukuthlalisana* propagated a retreat from the structural obligations associated with the multigenerational, patriarchal household, in favour of more horizontal, dyadic and voluntaristic relationships. (Bank 2001: 139)

The complexity of the South African context demands that we interpret data on the single or married status of women leaders, the experience of moving job to accommodate a partner and running two households, in ways that engage with very different meanings to those that might be used in Anglophone settings. The data collected by means of Coleman's adapted instrument remain valuable; it is the use to which they are put that demands cultural sensitivity. Partnerships and marriage have always been terms that obscure myriad understandings of what is implied. The variability is increasing as domestic arrangements continue to change, for example with the acceptance in many countries of same-sex marriage. The value of the data remains; the context in which they must be interpreted becomes ever more challenging to comprehend.

Responsibility for the Care of Other Dependants

Care of children, particularly when sick, and other dependants such as elderly parents, raises issues about who takes the major responsibility. The South African survey used Coleman's questions on caring responsibilities, particularly for children. A discrepancy between men and women's caring responsibilities was evident in South Africa. The survey found a much lower percentage of male partners caring for sick children. Only 4 per cent of the women respondents indicated that their partner did so, sometimes with the help of others, while sole care fell to 36 per cent.

It would appear that the data confirm the unequal burden of dependants placed upon women. However, Folbre (2006) rehearses the complexities of understanding how the changes brought about by developing economic opportunities for women translate to changes in childcare and the gendered discourse around such issues. In the context of South Africa, Montgomery et al. (2006) studied care of children in Kwazulu-Natal and raised questions about the dominant discourse and, as a consequence, the reliance that can be placed upon data. The authors discovered that both women respondents and researchers themselves were likely to record data that confirmed, rather than challenged, the prevailing view of women taking responsibility for childcare, and men failing to do so:

> We find that men are positively involved with their families and households in a wide range of ways. They care for patients and children, financially support immediate and extended family members and are present at home, thereby enabling women to work or support other households. As the qualitative data demonstrates, however, such activities are often not acknowledged. The dominant perception of both female respondents and research assistants continues to be that men are not caring for their families because they are irresponsible and profligate. (Montgomery et al. 2006: 2)

The authors suggest that, in this study, men were stigmatised for their absence from the family home, yet women who were absent because of their job, leaving children to the care of grandparents or other relatives, suffered no equivalent stigma. Equally, they suggest that women who earned sufficient to pay for nannies or other forms of childcare were not subject to criticism. The authors do not dispute that 'a large proportion of female respondents had experienced situations of neglect and abandonment that reinforced their negative view of male behaviour' (19); their point is that both research and development of policy are compromised by a cultural filter, based on a hegemonic view of who cares for children and stereotypical gender roles within it.

In the Anglophone world, the narrative of women's unequal responsibility for caring for children is deeply embedded. In one narrative, women are both criticised for leaving their children in the care of others and, if they are stay-at-home mothers, awarded lower status and stigmatised for being 'just' a mother (Steiner 2007). However this narrative is being joined by more varied discourses. Some women have proposed turning childcare into a competitive career in its own right (Story 2005). A further narrative suggests that women should be applauded rather than criticised for placing the care of their children with others as soon as possible after birth:

> As noted earlier, women in traditional organizations are accepted at a managerial level if they hide their differences and work 'like men'. Taking maternity leave 'like a man' – doing 'macho maternity' – is an extreme but common example of this. (Smithson & Stokoe 2005: 160)

Arguably, the narratives concerning men and childcare are less varied, with the dominant discourse on their failings to take a full share. There is a much less extensive body of literature about the complex choices facing men than on those facing women (Henwood & Procter 2003). Feminist literature tends also to utilise a narrow range of gender theory rather than drawing more widely from a range of disciplines. For example, the notion that 'men's involvement in family life has varied historically with the mode of economic production' (Hook, 2006: 649) is developed further by the authors using economics theory to consider why, although men's contribution to childcare and domestic responsibilities increased from the 1970s level, it remains lower overall than women's in the twenty nations studied. Modes of production, forms of employment and national policies are all implicated in both shifting and unchanging patterns of domestic responsibility. Studies on women school leaders rarely engage with the wider economic context to consider the multiple and complex interplay of factors; rather, the failings of men in terms of domestic responsibility tend to be a given.

In South Africa specifically, the context for researching women and men's care of children is therefore suggested by Montgomery et al. (2006) to be biased by assumptions that essentialise men in negative ways. It may be further skewed by feminist literature that tends not to criticise women for leaving the majority of childcare to a male partner yet is likely to criticise men for leaving it to women. Suggesting that this may reflect some degree of prejudice would open it to accusations of attacking the victim and or acting as an apologist for men. Nevertheless, the cultural and gender bias that may be influencing responses and interpretation of data could be considered more seriously. Analysis of data about responsibility for care therefore needs to be cautious and perhaps less simplistic in conclusions about the interplay of factors.

Building on Coleman's Work

In the instrument designed by Coleman and in her other work we have a wonderful legacy that has developed over time. It has supported a growing understanding of the experience of women leaders in education and of what they contribute to schools and learners. We who share that legacy are obliged to build on the work in ever more effective ways, and to engage with the complexities of context and multiple intersected characteristics in the lives of women leaders.

This chapter has focused only on selected questions from the instrument in a single specific context to illustrate the potential for cultural distance to impact on interpretation. However, reflexive self-searching about the assumptions and bias present when researching women in educational leadership are relevant, whatever the context. Even in locations where the researcher may assume she or he is focusing on the 'not other', society moves on – understanding of concepts such as gender, family and work move on – demanding that we interrogate our culturally and historically constructed concepts and methods in self-aware ways. Above all, we need to move beyond reporting data as evidence of inequality to analysing it in ways that progress societal and organisational practice. It is not enough to collect data in order to lament. We need to use it to increase understanding in profound ways that lead not to blame, but to shifts in attitude and action. This would be a fitting rejoinder to the work of Marianne Coleman.

Acknowledgements

The South African data was collected in a project sponsored by the Commonwealth Council for Educational Administration. Thanks are also due for the financial support of the Commonwealth Foundation, the Matthew Goniwe School of Leadership and Governance in South Africa and the University of Southampton, UK. The contribution of Cristina Azaola, Anna-Magriet de Wet, Hyacinth Skervin, Arlene Walsh and Alison Williamson in collecting data is gratefully acknowledged.

References

Alcoff, L. (1991/92). 'The Problem of Speaking for Others'. *Cultural Critique* 20, 5–32.

Arnott, J.M. (1998). 'Who is the Other Woman? Representation, Alterity and Ethics in the Work of Gayatri Chakravorty Spivak'. PhD dissertation, University of Natal.

Bank, L. (2001). 'Living Together, Moving Apart: Homemade Agendas, Identity Politics and Urban-Rural Linkages in the Eastern Cape, South Africa'. *Journal of Contemporary African Studies* 19 (1), 129–47.

Bhopal, K. (2001). 'Researching South Asian Women: Issues of Sameness and Difference in the Research Process'. *Journal of Gender Studies* 10 (3), 279–86.

Bielby, W.T., and Bielby, D.D. (1992). 'I Will Follow Him: Family Ties, Gender-Role Beliefs, and Reluctance to Relocate for a Better Job'. *American Journal of Sociology* 97 (5), 1241–67.

Carter, M.R., and May, J. (2001). 'One Kind of Freedom: Poverty Dynamics in Post-Apartheid South Africa'. *World Development* 29 (12), 1987–2006.

Coleman, M. (2002). *Women as Head Teachers: Striking the Balance*. Stoke on Trent: Trentham Books.

Coleman, M. (2007). 'Gender and Educational Leadership in England: A Comparison of Secondary Head Teachers' Views over Time'. *School Leadership and Management* 27 (4), 383–99.

Coleman, M. (2009). 'Women in Educational Leadership in England'. In H. Sobehart (ed.), *Women Leading Education across the Continents: Sharing the Spirit, Fanning the Flame*, 13–20. Lanham, MD: Rowman and Littlefield.

Coleman, M., Qiang, H., and Li, Y. (1998). 'Women in Educational Management in China: Experience in Shaanxi Province'. *Compare* 28 (2), 141–54.

Connell, R.W., and Messerschmidt, J.W. (2005). 'Hegemonic Masculinity Rethinking the Concept'. *Gender & Society* 19 (6), 829–59.

Firestone, S. (2003). *The Dialectic of Sex: The Case for Feminist Revolution*. Basingstoke: Palgrave Macmillan.

Folbre, N. (2006). 'Measuring Care: Gender, Empowerment, and the Care Economy'. *Journal of Human Development* 7 (2), 183–99.

Graves, S. (2014). 'New Roles, Old Stereotypes: Developing a School Workforce in English Schools'. *School Leadership & Management: Formerly School Organisation* 34 (3), 255–68.

Harvey, M. (1998). 'Dual-Career Couples During International Relocation: The Trailing Spouse'. *International Journal of Human Resource Management* 9 (2), 309–31.

Henwood, K., and Procter, J. (2003). 'The "Good Father": Reading Men's Accounts of Paternal Involvement during the Transition to First-Time Fatherhood'. *British Journal of Social Psychology* 42 (3), 337–55.

Hesse-Biber, S.N. (2013). 'A Re-Invitation to Feminist Research'. In S.N. Hesse-Biber (ed.), *Feminist Research Practice: A Primer*, 1–13. Los Angeles: Sage.

Hook, J.L. (2006). 'Care in Context: Men's Unpaid Work in 20 Countries, 1965–2003'. *American Sociological Review* 71 (4), 639–60.

Jewkesa, R.K., Levin, J.B., and Penn-Kekana, L.A. (2003). 'Gender Inequalities, Intimate Partner Violence and HIV Preventive Practices: Findings of a South African Cross-Sectional Study'. *Social Science & Medicine* 56 (1), 125–34 <http://www.africomnet.org/events/practicum/2007/resources/resource1%20 (2).pdf> accessed 18 October 2013.

Levin, I. (2004). 'Living Apart Together: A New Family Form'. *Current Sociology* 52 (2), 223–40.

Lumby, J. (2013) 'Valuing Knowledge Over Action: The Example of Gender in Educational Leadership'. *Gender and Education* 25 (4), 432–43.

Lumby, J. (2015). 'Women Leading South African Schools in Communities of Multiple Deprivation'. *Educational Management Administration & Leadership* 43 (3), 400–17.

Lumby, J., Azaola, C., de Wet, A., Skervin, H., Walsh, A., and Williamson, A. (2010). *Women School Principals in South Africa: Leading the Way*. Southampton: University of Southampton.

Moorosi, P. (2007). 'Creating Linkages between Private and Public: Challenges Facing Woman Principals in South Africa'. *South African Journal of Education* 27 (3), 507–22.

Moorosi, P. (2010). 'South African Female Principals' Career Paths: Understanding the Gender Gap in Secondary School Management'. *Educational Management Administration & Leadership* 38 (5), 547–62.

Montgomery, C.M., Hosegood, V., Busza, J., and Timaeus, I.M. (2006). 'Men's Involvement in the South African Family: Engendering Change in the AIDS Era'. *Social Science Medicine* 62 (10), 2411–19 <http://researchonline.lshtm.ac.uk/11784/1/ssm-d-05-00225%20reviewed%20copy.pdf> accessed 18 October 2013.

Morris, S.B., Low, G.T., and Coleman, M. (1999). 'Leadership Stereotypes and Female Singaporean Principals'. *Compare* 29 (2), 191.

Orwell, G. (1936). *Shooting an Elephant* <http://www.orwell.ru/library/articles/elephant/english/e_eleph> accessed 12 July 2015.

Pillay, V. (2011). 'White Women Speak, Black Women Write: The Politics of Locution And Location in the Other Researching the Not Other'. *International Journal of Qualitative Studies in Education* 24 (6), 657–72.

Santoro, N., and Smyth, G. (2010). 'Researching Ethnic "Others": Conducting Critical Ethnographic Research in Australia and Scotland'. *Intercultural Education* 21 (6), 493–503.

Shah, S., with Shaikh, J. (2010). 'Leadership Progression of Muslim Male Teachers: Interplay of ethnicity, faith and visibility'. Special issue of *School Leadership & Management* 30 (1), 19–33.

Shefer, T. (2014). 'Pathways to Gender Equitable Men: Reflections on Findings from the International Men and Gender Equality Survey in the Light of Twenty Years of Gender Change in South Africa'. *Men and Masculinities* 17 (5), 502–9.

Smithson, J., and Stokoe, E.H. (2005). 'Discourses of Work–Life Balance: Negotiating "Genderblind" Terms in Organizations'. *Gender, Work & Organization* 12 (2), 147–68.

Steiner, L.M. (2007). *Mommy Wars: Stay-At-Home and Career Moms Face Off on Their Choices, Their Lives, Their Families*. New York: Random House.

Story, L. (2005). 'Many Women at Elite Colleges Set Career Path to Motherhood'. *New York Times*, 20, A1.

Tronto, J. (2013). *Caring Democracy: Markets, Equality, and Justice*. New York: New York University Press.

Valcour, P.M., and Tolbert, P. (2003). 'Gender, Family and Career in the Era of Boundarylessness: Determinants and Effects of Intra- and Inter-Organizational Mobility'. *International Journal of Human Resource Management* 14 (5), 768–87.

Walker, L. (2005). 'Negotiating the Boundaries of Masculinity in Post-Apartheid South Africa. In Reid, G., and Walker, J. (eds), *Men Behaving Differently*, 161–82. Cape Town: Double Storey.

Zikhali, J., and Perumal, J. (2015). 'Leading in Disadvantaged Zimbabwean School Contexts: Female School Heads' Experiences of Emotional Labour'. *Educational Management Administration & Leadership*, online <http://ema.sagepub.com/content/early/2015/02/27/1741143214558572.abstract> accessed 12 July 2015.

Appendix 1: Questionnaire for Secondary School Principals in England and Wales

Name ....

Please indicate which qualifications you have

BA/BSc		B Ed	
MA/MSc/MEd		Certificate of Education	
PhD		Ed D	
Other (please name)			

Which of the following apply to you?

Male		Female	
Married or living with a partner		Single	
Separated		Divorced	
Widowed			

Age group

Under 30		30–35		36–39	
40–45		46–50		51–55	
56–60		61+			

Ethnic origin

Asian	Indian		Pakistani		Other Asian			
Black or Black British	Caribbean		African		Other Black or Black British			
Mixed	White & Asian		White & Black African		White and Black Caribbean		Other mixed	
White	British		Irish		Other White			
Chinese	Chinese							
Other								

Do you have a disability?

Yes		No	

If yes, please state the nature of your disability ....
School Name..
LEA.. County..

Please indicate which of the following apply to your school:

Primary	
Secondary	
Special	
Middle	

Co-ed	
Girls	
Boys	

Community	Foundation	Independent	Voluntary-aided	Voluntary – controlled
CTC	Specialist College	City Academy	PRU	

1. Year of appointment to present post
2. Is this your first headship?

Yes		No	

3. Before you became a principal, were you a deputy?

Yes		No	

If yes please indicate the number and duration (in years) of deputy headship (s)

deputy headship one		years
deputy headship two		years
deputy headship three		years

What were your main area (s) of responsibility as deputy head?

Curriculum	
Pastoral	
Personnel	
Finance	
Premises	
Other (please state)	

4. Which of the following posts have you held? Please tick the appropriate box

Acting Principal		Assistant Principal	
Other member of Senior Management Team		Head of Faculty/Department	
Advanced Skills Teacher		Head of Year	
Other (please specify)		Senior teacher	

5. Indicate your specialist subject area

English		Creative	
Maths		Technology	
Science		Early years	
Modern Languages		Social Sciences	
Humanities		Special needs	
Other (please specify			

6. At what stage of your life did you formulate a career plan that included principalship or deputy principalship?

at school		in higher education	
on becoming a teacher		on gaining a post of responsibility	
Never		other	

7. What or who has had a major influence on your career path? (indicate all those that apply)

your parents		partner	
friends		those who taught you	
domestic circumstances		previous principal (s)	
		other	

If you have children, please answer questions 8 and 9.

8. Number of children .... their present age (s) ....

9. If you have children, what were/are the main methods of child-care used?

Partner		Nursery	
Nanny		Childminder	
		Other relative (indicate which)	

Were/are you able to make childcare arrangements satisfactory to you and your family?

Yes		No	

Comment ....

Who looks/looked after your child/children when ill ....

Please answer questions 10–14 if applicable to you.

10. What is your partner's job? ....

11. To what extent do you and your partner share domestic responsibilities e.g. housework, shopping, cooking, washing, gardening, organising holidays and social life? Indicate an approximate overall percentage undertaken by each of you.

Me		Partner	

12. Have you ever changed your job to follow your partner?

Yes		No	

13. Has your partner ever changed their job to follow you?

Yes		No	

14. Have you ever operated two separate households as a result of career commitments?

Yes		No	

15. Apart from children, do you have responsibility for the care of other dependents including elderly relatives?

Yes		No	

If yes, please indicate nature of responsibilities ....

16. Have you had a career break?

Yes		No	

(Please indicate length of break in weeks, e.g. 52 weeks rather than one year)

Longer term child care		Maternity/paternity leave	
Secondment to obtain qualifications		Secondment to industry	
Travel		Other	

17. If you took maternity/paternity leave, please comment on its adequacy and impact ....

....

18. If you had a career break were you able to resume your career at the same level as before the break?

Yes		No	

19. Have you ever been aware of sexist attitudes toward you in connection with job applications or promotion?

Yes		No	

If yes, please indicate the circumstances ....

....

....

20. Have you been aware of sexist attitudes toward you from your peers or from those you work with?

Yes		No	

If yes please indicate the circumstances ....
....
....

21. Were you encouraged at any time to apply for promotion?

Yes		No	

If so, by whom?   (mark all those that apply)

Partner/family		Colleagues at work	
Senior managers at work		Principal	
Other			

22. Have you had a mentor, or role model who encouraged or inspired you?

Yes		No	

If yes, please indicate their role ....
If you had a mentor, please indicate if they were male or female

Male		Female	

22. Of the interview panel that selected you as principal, approximately how many were men and how many were women?

Men		Women	

23. Was there a point in your career when you thought you would not achieve headship?

Yes		No	

If so when and why? ....
....

24. Do you feel that as a woman or as a man you ever had to "prove your worth" in a management position?

Yes		No	

If yes, please give an example? ....
....

25. Give three key words to describe your style of management ....
....

26. What are the key values that you are trying to promote in your school?
....
....

27. What opportunities are there for staff to talk to you?

Any time as long as you are not in a meeting		Any time within specified limits	
By appointment			

28. While you are in school, what proportion of your time do you spend out of your office?

under 10%		between 10–25%	
between 25–50%		between 50–75%	

29. How do you encourage all the teachers in your school to develop their careers?

Mentoring		Special one to one meetings	
Courses		Appraisal/Performance Management	
Other (please specify below)		Short term projects or responsibilities	

....

30. How do you encourage female teachers in your school to develop their careers?

No special ways		Courses for women only	
Mentoring		Other (please specify below)	
Short term projects or responsibilities			

....

31. Why do you think that you were so successful in such a competitive field?

Through hard work		Support from others	
Knowing what you wanted from life		Academic achievement	
Other (please specify below)			

....

32. As a principal, have you ever found your gender an advantage?

Yes		No	

Please give an example ....
....

33. Would you be prepared to be interviewed as a follow up to this questionnaire?

Yes		No	

Finally, please would you tick in the list below, those qualities that you feel apply to you:

Caring		Creative	
Intuitive		Aware of individual differences	
Non-competitive		Tolerant	
Subjective		Informal	
Highly regulated		Conformist	
Normative		Competitive	
Evaluative		Disciplined	
Objective		Formal	

Thank you very much for taking the time to complete this questionnaire.

VICTORIA SHOWUNMI

Diversity and Education in England

Introduction

Population structures of schools and school communities, particularly in urban Europe, have been changing over the last few decades in the context of globalisation, eco-political developments and increased mobility. In the United Kingdom, the increasing diversity of the population is generally perceived as affecting schools' overall performance through the low achievement of children from many Black and Minority Ethnic (BME) groups and communities. This association between under-achievement and ethnicity, race, social class, gender or other variables is often highlighted by statistics, and emphasised in the literature, conveniently relieving the educational structures and professionals of the burden of responsibility (Tomlinson 1991; Abbas 2006). However, research has produced varied and even conflicting evidence with regard to a direct link between achievement and factors such as ethnicity, socio-economic background, population mix, gender and the use of English as a second language (Kincheloe and Steinberg 2007; Office for National Statistics 2004; OFSTED 2004), which has added to the complexity of the challenges faced by today's schools.

In my contribution to the collection of chapters in celebration of Marianne Coleman's work, I wanted to start with a short dialogue that gives the reader an insight into why I agreed to write this chapter. I remember a conversation I had with Marianne a few weeks after arriving at the Institute of Education (now UCL IOE) in 2008. At the time, I was located in the London Centre for Leadership and Learning (LCLL) as a Regional Lead for the Teacher Development Agency project. Marianne approached me after I had presented at a lunchtime research seminar which focused on my research.

'Hi, my name is Marianne.'
I looked up and said 'I'm Victoria.'
'Oh, I hear that you are working in LCLL.'
'Yes, you're right ...'
'I used to work in LCLL, and if there is anything that I can do to help do contact me.'

At the time, I was not sure why this person would think I might need any help. As time progressed and our relationship grew, my understanding of Marianne's true character emerged. Her sense of being was all about equality and social justice. This was evident through her work and everyday practice; for example, in her desire to take care of people whom she noticed as being new to the IOE. During our discussion for this paper I asked Marianne why she was so interested in someone like me. Her reply was that she knew how hard it was to be included when one's interests were on the 'margins', even when the area of interest was extremely important. The reference was to the work that I chose to study, namely that of gender and leadership, with a particular focus on 'race'. What was even more revealing of her personality was her apologetic sense of not wishing to come across as patronising in her offer of help.

As our relationship developed we were able to share and explore the many complexities surrounding the use of the term 'Black and Minority Ethnic' (BME) in the context of leadership, even discussing what we mean by 'Black' when we consider our different experiences and perspectives as we move deeper into the unknown. Our conversation continued with a shared desire to include an intersectional approach when discussing the recruitment, development and advancement of educational leaders. It is important for us to acknowledge that the majority of leaders are 'white and male', and while women are making a mark, they are predominantly white.

Diverse Population in Schools and BME Under-Achievement

The most recent census data in Britain (ONS 2011) indicates the non-white British population has grown from 6.6 million in 2001 to 9.1 million in 2011. The white British population has stayed the same since 2001. The non-white British population has grown by 4.1 per cent a year, or a total of 2.5 million over the whole period. The increase has taken non-White ethnic minorities to 16.65 per cent of the total population of Britain (Office for National Statistics 2014).

Within the school population, students who are classified as belonging to ethnic minorities accounted for 24.5 per cent of all primary and 20.6 per cent state-funded secondary school students in 2009. This represents increases of 1.2 per cent and 1.1 per cent, respectively, over the figures for 2008 (Department for Children, Schools and Families, 2009). It is interesting that the Department for Children, Schools and Families (DCSF) included all ethnic groups not classified as White British under the heading of 'ethnic minority', whereas the Office for National Statistics (ONS) states the: 'non-White ethnic group includes all minority ethnic groups but not White Irish or Other White groups' (Office for National Statistics 2004: 1). Academics such as Archer and Francis (2007) argue that this approach of lumping ethnic groups together into broad categories such as 'White' or 'Asian' proves to be rather problematic, as constituent groups may differ so significantly as to lead to a misrepresentation of the characteristics of the overall category and thus its constituent groups. When considering these statistics it is important to recognise that they differ greatly between urban areas, particularly London, and rural areas, where much of the data is presented in single figures.

Consequences of Misinterpreting BME Under-Achievement

> The Black/White achievement gap in England has the hallmarks of locked-in inequality. That is, an inequality so great and so deep seated that it cannot be closed through the 'normal' workings of the system. (Gillborn 2008: 240)

Much of the current critical research in the area of BME under-achievement points to systematic and structural failings in education and is understood as part of the wider discourse on race, ethnicity and inequality. A good example is the disproportionate number of exclusions of Black Caribbean students from British schools, which are said to occur 'irrespective of the socioeconomic context of the school, its performance, or its educational effectiveness' (Office for National Statistics 2004: 1).

Not all BME students are negatively stereotyped as underachievers; two groups in particular are positively labelled as 'success stories' and 'model' minorities: Chinese and Indian students. In 2009, Chinese students achieved the highest grades of any group, with 72 per cent gaining five good GCSEs, followed in second place by Indian students with 67.2 per cent (Department for Children, Schools and Families 2009b); these trends are also reflected throughout all key stages (Bhattacharya 2002). This, however, needs to be put into the wider context of mainstream discourses on race and inequality. According to Archer and Francis (2005: 167), such positive stereotyping of Chinese and Indian students forms part of a 'racialized narrative which seeks to compartmentalize these groups as diligent, conformist and docile, constructing them as the ideal immigrants'.

During the previous Labour Government the publication of a report commissioned by the then Department for Children, Schools and Families 2009 (now DfE) on Black children and exclusion (i.e. temporary or permanent removal from school) was forced when it was passed on to Diane Abbott MP and then leaked to the press. It is a matter of grave concern that the Department had hoped that the report and its findings would not be published. Priority Review into the disproportionate levels of Black exclusion had come to the firm conclusion that this level of exclusion was due to institutional racism. According to Abbott (2010) this was an incendiary conclusion because the British educational establishment and teachers' unions in particular had always refused to contemplate the possibility that institutional racism was present in Britain's schools. More importantly, it potentially put Britain's schools in breach of the Race Relations Amendment Act (2000). A key message stemming from the report stated that the disproportionate levels of Black pupils being excluded from school could not be attributed solely to factors such as culture, class background or home life. Rather, the report said that what happened in school was the key to the levels of exclusion.

In particular, it pointed to teachers' (sometimes subconscious) attitudes towards Black children. The report itself had clear recommendations. It wanted the Department to set targets for bringing down Black exclusions and in particular to focus on the 100 schools with the worst record for excluding Black children. Several meetings took place between Diane Abbott MP and the then Schools Minister Lord Adonis to seek clarification regarding the implementation of the recommendations. Despite the intervention from Diane Abbott, designing a research project that would work with the 100 worst schools was ruled out. Instead a pilot project was launched which resulted in more questions than answers, mainly to do with the research design, and which targeted a group of schools that 'volunteered' after being selected by the local authority to participate in the pilot.

A real concern about the pilot project was that most of the schools which took part had cohorts of White pupils only. However, the purpose of the pilot project was to focus on understanding why BME pupils had the highest exclusion rates. What is even more disturbing is that the funding was allocated to participating schools with no targets or monitoring (Weekes-Bernard 2010). What was the purpose of the funding? Was the pilot just a way of appearing to take action whilst allowing schools to carry on with business as usual? What happened to the original recommendation that the schools with the worst records for Black exclusions should be targeted?

The concern is that things are still as bad as they were fifty years ago. When a Black child is excluded from school, the 'family feel as though history is repeating itself' (Lorenzi 2013). Recent figures (DFE 2010b) indicate that Black Caribbean pupils are three times more likely to be permanently excluded than the school population as a whole. In light of the data, is the UK, particularly England, willing or able to start to accept the need to fully embrace the meaning of a diverse community?

The White Paper on Schools

In 2010, a White Paper, *The Importance of Teaching* (DfE 2010a), indicated critical deteriorations in achievement and performance in the case of English schools. The White Paper emphasised the role of leadership and the quality of teaching and teachers in improving students' level of achievement, stressing the need for continuous training and professional development. The paper presented an agenda for change described as 'radical reform of our schools' (DfE 2010a: 4). In the UK, a government White Paper was published formally to set out planned legislation and arguments in support. Some argue (e.g. Lumby 2013) that the purpose of this particular White Paper was to educate and to invite response.

This White Paper has important implications for issues of gender, race, language and cultural equality and identity in and around UK schools. It invites discussion of the 'training and professional development' of education professionals in managing and responding to diversity against the backdrop of achievement/under-achievement of BME students in schools. Careful engagement in the debate is required in order to identify the elements missing from the '*quality* of teaching and teachers' when revising the existing 'training and professional development' provisions; otherwise, this could be another futile exercise in policy-making, which would have no effective impact on improving practice or the performance of low-achieving students.

The White Paper 'sets out a radical reform programme for the schools system, with schools freed from the constraints of central Government direction and teachers placed firmly at the heart of school improvement' (DfE 2010b: 40). Indeed, the report reads like an 'exemplary neo-liberal recipe for DIY self-hood' (Harris 2004: 23), via de-centralisation, devolution, and the championing of individual educational leaders and schools as the units of educational enterprise in the brave new schooling world of the 'Big Society'.

It follows that key aspects of the report include a focus on 'improving discipline by trialling a new approach to exclusions' (David et al. 2010). The Secretary of State for Education states that the current process for appeals against an exclusion, where cases are referred to independent appeals panels, is problematic in several ways. The appeals process can become 'unduly adversarial' (David et al. 2010), rather than encouraging schools and parents to work together in the interests of the child. Therefore, the possible reinstatement of an excluded pupil rarely happens (Harris et. al. 2000, Communities Empowerment Network 2015). The new approach intends to legislate to reform independent appeals panels so that there is still an independent review of decision-making, although the review will not be able to compel reinstatement. If the review panel judges that there were flaws in the exclusion process they can request that governors reconsider their decision, and schools may be required to contribute towards the cost of additional support for the excluded pupil. Schools, however, will not be forced to re-admit children who have been excluded.

One of the important implications of the report is a return to 'core subjects' for every student to 'master', so the National Curriculum can operate as a 'rigorous benchmark' (David et al 2010). It is not at all clear where this leaves the 'softer' cross-curricular, non-assessed work in areas such as Personal Social Health Education (PSHE), and citizenship, which had offered spaces for engagement with inequality issues in schools. While the need to tackle 'prejudice-based' and 'homophobic bullying' (David et al 2010) is mentioned in the paper, awareness of rising rates of gender and sexualised violence and bullying in schools is conspicuously absent. A contradiction and ambiguity in the report lies in the relationship between the local authorities and the prioritising of 'school autonomy', since the report waxes lyrical about the need to allow every school to 'frame its own ethos, develop its own specialisms, free of either central or local bureaucratic constraint' (DfE 2010a: 58). Serious questions arise over how any form of distributive justice can be ensured and duties such as gender and race equality can be fulfilled, in the type of laissez-faire, free-for-all scenario of school autonomy called for in the report.

The report also suggests that there will be greater transparency in how the money on schools is being spent – in other words, greater accountability in school funding. The Government will also 'reform performance tables so that they set out our high expectations – every pupil should have a broad education (the English Baccalaureate) [and] a firm grip of the basics and be making progress' (DfE 2010a: 56). This will provide 'a new measure of how well deprived pupils do and introduce a measure of how young people do when they leave school' (DfE 2010a: 56). This tracking mechanism will be in the form of a 'Pupil Premium' to target more resources towards the most deprived pupils.

However, this type of extremely close focus on the performance of schools and pupils encourages a competitive ethos that may well serve to

put even greater emphasis on those individual pupils and schools who fail
to 'master' the 'broad' 'English' basics that education is being reduced to.
This has serious implications for the most marginalised, who may well be
more easily and systematically excluded from the platforms of 'choice, freedom and responsibility' underpinning the White Paper (David et al. 2010).

Equal Opportunities and the Development of Student Teachers

If one takes a close look at a sample of prospectuses taken from teacher
education departments at universities, many of them provide a statement
that shows their commitment to equal opportunity across the courses they
provide. The following extract is taken from the prospectus of an Initial
Teacher Training programme in a university in the South-East of England:

> The faculty of education is committed to providing Equality of Opportunity in all
> our provision.
>   The statement is based on the principle that the key purpose of education is to
> empower an increasingly diverse range of people through their learning, thereby
> contributing to the achievement of social justice. Many universities aspire to a com-
> mitment to widening access and addressing inequalities in education.

However, according to hooks (1994), when we critically examine the role of
the university in the sharing of knowledge and information, it is painfully
clear that biases that uphold and maintain white supremacy, imperialism,
sexism, and racism have distorted education so that it is no longer about
the practice of freedom. This knowledge shows us the necessity for developing teachers and educational leaders to have an understanding of diversity.
    The challenge of under-representation is evident in the statistics com-
piled by the DfE in 2013 (18) on Black and Minority Ethnic full-time teachers in November 2010. In these figures, 6 per cent of the BME teaching
population are headteachers. Over 95 per cent of headteachers are White
British, while deputy headteachers and assistant headteachers account

for 7 per cent of the teaching workforce and have an ethnic makeup again dominated by the 'White British' category, at 93 per cent (DfE, 2014: 10). This is without taking into account the 'White Irish' and 'Any Other White' background categories. There has been much more progress on 'increasing the workforce to reflect diversity' in the USA, which has been at the forefront in recognising the need for a diverse workforce. In 1987, the *Workforce 2000* report (Johnston and Packer 1987) informed North Americans that:

> by the year 2000 the majority of its workers would be African-Americans, Hispanics, Native Americans, women and other 'minority' groups. [...] The relegation of white males to 'minority' group status caused organisations in the USA to consider who their future managers might be. (Lorbiecki and Jack 2000: 20)

However, despite changes in the student demographic, the social makeup of senior management and the academic workforce in the USA and the UK is still mainly white, non-disabled, middle class and male (Bebbington 2009). Research has investigated issues of equality in education in the areas of race and gender, and, to some extent, sexual orientation and disability. Less attention has been paid to issues of religion and age. Concerning the relationship between scholarship and equality, Lumby with Coleman (2007) have noted that research that challenges power structures may be marginalised so that favoured themes and methodologies are reproduced. Traditional research paradigms are, however, being challenged by innovations from such fields as disability studies. Researchers have also examined the nature of leadership, although these studies have tended to overlook issues of social identity.

Teacher Recruitment and Training for Diversity

For many years there has been concern about the ability, preparedness and willingness of teachers to educate Black children. Many teachers, when asked, thought that a completely different method needed to be invented

to teach Black children so that they could meet the general academic standard (Maylor 2014).

Maylor (2014: 114) makes the following comment:

> I certainly do not believe that addressing the education of Black children requires
> 'strange' teaching methods but instead a willingness to develop greater awareness of
> how to meet their educational needs.

There have been numerous arguments concerning ways to tackle the challenge of recruiting and training teachers to enhance, develop and foster
diversity. Is the task being over-complicated? Why not (1) increase the
number of BME teachers, and (2) provide training to all teachers, new
and established, to assist them in dealing with diversity and increasing
BME achievement?

Recruitment of BME Teachers

The growing concerns about the experiences and achievements of Black
pupils (especially Black males) underlie the call for more Black people to
serve as teachers and lay mentors or role models in schools. Maylor (2014)
indicates the change in priorities for teacher recruitment in England to
increase the recruitment of BME teachers, against the continued debate
on the need for teachers to represent the minorities to which pupils in
English schools belong.

However, despite the various initiatives that have been available to
encourage BME teachers, there has been a decline in the numbers of people
from BME communities choosing teaching as a possible career (Maylor
2014). Furthermore, the people from BME communities who decide on
teaching as a career may face racism during their school placement. Many
student teachers find themselves isolated and can deal with their feelings
by adopting certain patterns of behaviour. They may feel compelled to
act out a stereotype, in an attempt to fit into what is expected of them. In

doing so, they internalise any racist vibes that surround them, and even deny their existence (Showunmi and Constantine-Simms 1995). It is not enough, however, merely to attract students onto courses. Establishments involved with the recruitment and development of teachers need to review their practices to ensure that Black students are given fair treatment and equal rights to develop their skills and talents and to progress within the profession.

In recent years, minority ethnic teacher recruitment in England has been prioritised, with targets set to encourage initial teacher training institutions to increase the recruitment of such teachers (see Carrington and Skelton 2003 for an overview of teacher recruitment initiatives). There has been a strong body of thought that the numbers of minority ethnic teachers should be increased to reflect the growing representation of minority ethnic pupils in English schools (e.g. Swann 1985; Cantle 2001; Maylor et al. 2007). Increased recruitment of minority ethnic teachers is also relevant to providing majority and minority ethnic pupils with a more representative view of society and the experience of teachers from diverse groups. It is welcome to see in black and white that the government is able to praise the way in which teachers have been educated within the UK (Maylor et al. 2007). There is presently a wide range of ways to learn to teach, which include initiatives such as employment-based routes, Teach First, university-based PGCE courses and Teaching Schools. The different routes that were previously available into teaching opened up access for people who were already highly qualified for a career in teaching, and for others who were able to gain teaching status through experience. The recent figures (DfE 2014) suggest that the diversity gap is widening.

However, the White Paper does not address the need for diversity within the routes into teacher training. Instead, the focus relies purely on 'offering financial incentives to attract the very best graduates in shortage subjects into teaching' (DfE 2010a; 105) and the expansion of Teach First. Again, there is no argument about the need for quality graduates to have the opportunity to teach; however, there is no concern expressed that teaching must have a diverse workforce. There is much evidence (Equality Challenge Unit 2009; Gillborn 2008; Richardson et al. 2005) to suggest that in order to raise the achievements of Black children (particularly African Caribbean children) we must ensure that there is a significant number of teachers from Black and minority ethnic groups within the classroom. As Teach First expands to attract Oxbridge students to develop as teachers, there is a failure to recognise the lack of diversity within the programme. If our focus is on attracting the best students from Oxbridge, it is important to consider that there was just one African Caribbean student who gained entrance to Oxford University during the 2009 intake (Operation Black Vote 2010). Therefore, if Teach First continues to concentrate on just the Russell Group universities, which have smaller numbers of Black students, the programme will not reflect the diversity within the community.

Diversity and Teacher Education

> We are all from different backgrounds and national cultures and we acquire 'baggage' as we progress through our lives. We learn stereotypical views that lead us to categorise individuals which then governs how we relate to individuals and the groups that we meet. These views may be held unconsciously, and it seems to me that it would be helpful for us all, especially our leaders, to examine our views and implicit values. (Coleman 2011: 13)

Educational leaders need to be aware of diversity issues and ways of encouraging ethnic minority achievement. It is no longer acceptable to rely on simply increasing the number of ethnic minority teachers, who – like any other teachers – may be good or bad role models. Some BME teachers may refuse to acknowledge their own identity and prefer to be assimilated into the dominant culture as the way to achieve success within the establishment (Showunmi and Constantine-Simms 1995). Before we start to understand the need to develop educationalists to manage and engage in diversity, it is essential that we ask what previous training and development they have had which has focused on equality issues. Some would say that things have now moved on and that the educational arena is now a much better environment in terms of equality. Nevertheless, the issue of BME under-achievement still exists, which would suggest that the current type of development is not working and needs to be addressed. Very little attention is given to issues of diversity and equality in the development of educational leaders (Coleman 2011: 11).

Teaching to Transgress (1994) by bell hooks provides a useful framework to discuss the development of teachers who are able to engage with and understand diversity. The book explains why it is crucial that educators are given the opportunity to be reflective so that they are able to understand the relationship between achievement/under-achievement and social justice. Even though the book was written in 1994 the challenges and discussion could easily be transferred into a 2015 classroom. In hooks' account, educating teachers to have an understanding of diversity involves encouraging students and their professors to become culturally literate through the exploration of diverse literature and to gain a deeper understanding of their own identity. iIt is argued by hooks (1994: 21) that:

> Empowerment cannot happen if we as educators refuse to be vulnerable while encouraging students to take risks. When teachers/trainers bring their own narratives of their experiences into classroom discussions it eliminates the possibility that we can function as all-knowing, silent interrogators. In diversity development it is often productive when the trainer/teacher takes the first risk, linking confessional narratives to academic discussions so as to show how experience can illuminate and enhance our understanding of academic material.

Maylor et al. (2007) provide an example of good practice. A case study of Woolmer University reported the development of an identity module that placed the emphasis on valuing individual identity (of teachers and pupils) and multiculturalism; raising student awareness of teaching in diverse contexts; and encouraging respect and equal treatment of diverse pupils. Creating a separate identity module allowed student teachers to reflect critically on their own cultural background and interrogate the biases of their own subject positions. The development of an identity module such as this would enable the students to be presented with a range of challenges, including comprehending the cultural backgrounds of minority ethnic communities, how they 'make meaning of the world' (Epstein and Kheimets 2000: 202), and the ways in which they articulate their experiences of racism and interact with difference. Such challenges are needed, especially if students have never worked with a Black teacher, or worked in a school where there is a high percentage of minority students and very few White students. Recent work by Beverly Daniel Tatum (2003) in the USA provides students with an understanding of the psychological causes and emotional reality of racism as it appears in everyday life. The course incorporates the use of lectures, readings, simulation exercises, group research projects and extensive class discussion to help students explore the psychological impact of racism on both the oppressor and the oppressed. The course (called Psychology of Racism) has been taught eighteen times at three different establishments, including a public university, a small state college and a private women's college. The feedback from students who attended the course was that they were amazed by the way in which the course changed their thinking on the subject of racism.

Training Leaders

In addition to the professional development of teachers, all educational leaders need to acquire sufficient understanding of the diversity issues facing UK schools and skills in handling these issues. Lumby with Coleman (2007: 142) states that there is increasing scrutiny of the part that leadership plays in relation to equality initiatives: 'Although leaders may not be alone in having power and access to resources within organisations, their power in terms of their formal role of authority and access to other sources of power mean that they have the capacity *and* possibility to unsettle power relations.' A number of arguments have been put forward for encompassing equality within leadership, including the idea that leaders may play a role in acknowledging and validating the experiences of disempowered groups or may provide support when staff experience a backlash against equality and diversity initiatives. Lumby also highlights the point that institutions are becoming increasingly diverse and that this makes the transformation of leadership all the more imperative.

In much of the literature, as Bebbington (2009: 10) notes, there is a tension between the need for leadership to advance the equality agenda and the reluctance of some leaders to engage with this area. In the context of the under-representation of BME staff in senior roles and the need for a larger number of BME applicants for headship, London has seen the development of an exceptional educational leadership programme, 'Investing in Diversity', provided through the London Centre for Leadership in Learning and funded by the National College for School Leadership (NCSL). Over 1000 BME leaders graduated from the year-long programme and many have progressed to senior roles in schools. The programme differs from other generic professional development courses as it explores the particular challenges faced by BME leaders under the direction of BME role models. The focus of the programme is to deepen the participants' knowledge of how to lead differently in diverse cultural, linguistic, religious and social contexts by refining the existing tools of school leadership to address issues of social justice and equality. A further element of the programme is that it offers the BME leaders the opportunity to network, do action research, work collaboratively and obtain peer support (Coleman and Campbell-Stephens 2010).

Conclusion

It is important to acknowledge that structures and procedures are necessary but not sufficient to bring about a culture which supports diversity and equality. There need to be systems that support ethical practice to ensure that people are not treated in a discriminatory manner. Procedures should be thought through and based on shared values. One way in which the ethos of an organisation might be changed is through having a focus on equality/diversity/social justice at the heart of on-going professional development. This paper has shown that the debates on diversity are complex and sensitive as it is an issue which poses particular challenges both for teachers and for leaders in education. The meaning of the word 'diversity' is not fixed and is somewhat contested. It is currently often understood as a synonym for ethnicity. In terms of leadership, the overall trend appears to be towards more equality, but change is slow and some problems appear fairly intractable. Those from ethnic minorities continue to be under-represented both as teachers and as educational leaders. There needs to be further research in the area of ethnicity, particularly in relation to religious affiliations, unpicking and examining the implications of this relationship in different contexts (Coleman 2012).

I recently met Marianne whilst attending a seminar showcasing work on educational leadership which was led by a colleague based at University College London Institute of Education (UCL IOE). As soon as I entered the room, our eyes made contact and she smiled. It was comforting to know that there was at least one other person who understood issues of diversity. During the break I approached Marianne and the first things she said were 'How are you, Victoria?' and 'How is the writing coming along?' Before I could even answer she showered me with further words: 'Oh, I hope that what I said to you was a help.' 'Marianne', I replied, 'it was more than helpful. Thank you for your time and support.' Perhaps you may be thinking: so why are you telling us this? I wanted to say that Marianne's critical reflectiveness on her whiteness and her understanding of diversity enable us to think through together how to keep the focus on inclusivity within education and leadership.

References

Abbas, T. (2006). *Muslims in Birmingham, UK*. Oxford: University of Oxford. Background paper for the Centre on Migration Policy and Society (COMPAS).

Abbott, D. (2010) 'Foreword', in O.D. Clennon, C. Earl, and K. Andrews, *Making Education a Priority*. Basingstoke: Palgrave Macmillan.

Archer, L., and Francis, B. (2005). '"They Don't Go Off the Rails Like Other Ethnic Groups": Teachers' Constructions of British Chinese Pupils' Gender Identities And Approaches To Learning'. *British Journal of Sociology of Education* 26 (2), 165–82.

Archer, L., and Francis, B. (2007). *Understanding Minority Ethnic Achievement: The Role of Race, Class, Gender and 'Success'.* London: Routledge.

Bebbington, D., (2009) *Diversity in Higher Education-Leadership Responsibilities and Challenges.* London: Leadership Foundation for Higher Education.

Bhattacharya, S. (2002). 'Introduction: An Approach to Education and Inequality'. In S. Bhattacharya (ed.), *Education and the Disprivileged*, 1–34. Hyderabad: Orient Longman.

Cantle, T. (2001). *Community Cohesion: A Report of the Independent Review Team.* London: Home Office.

Carrington, B., and Skelton, C. (2003). 'Re-Thinking "Role Models": Equal Opportunities in Teacher Recruitment in England and Wales'. *Journal of Education Policy* 18 (3), 253–65.

Coleman, M. (2007). 'Gender and Educational Leadership in England: A Comparison of Secondary Headteachers' Views Over Time'. *School Leadership and Management* 27 (4), 383–99.

Coleman, M. (2011). 'Educational Leadership for Diversity and Social justice: Implications for Ethical Practice'. Unpublished paper presented at ENIRDELM conference in Reykjavik, Iceland, 22–4 September 2011.

Coleman, M. (2012). 'Leadership and Diversity'. *Educational Management Administration and Leadership* 40 (5), 592–609.

Coleman, M., and Campbell-Stephens, R. (2010). 'Perceptions of Career Progress: The Experience of Black and Minority Ethnic School Leaders'. *School Leadership and Management* 30 (1), 35–49.

Communities Empowerment Network (2015) *The Detrimental Effect Exclusion Has On Children From Black and Minority Ethnic (BME) Backgrounds.* <http://www.schoolexclusionproject.com/the-detrimental-effect-exclusion-has-on-children-from-black-and-minority-ethnic-bme-backgrounds/> accessed 20 July 2015.

David, M., with Ringrose, J., and Showunmi, V. (2010). 'Browne Report + the White Paper = A Murky Outlook for Educational Equality', GEA Policy Report, October–December 2010. <http://www.genderandeducation.com/wp-content/uploads/2011/01/GEA_Policy_Report_October_December_20101.pdf> accessed 20 July 2015.

Department for Children Schools and Families. (2009). *The Independent Review Of The Primary Curriculum: Final Report.* Department for Children, Schools and Families.

Department for Children, Schools and Families (2009). *Deprivation and Education: The Evidence on Pupils in England, Foundation Stage to Key Stage 4* <http://dera.ioe.ac.uk/9431/1/DCSF-RTP-09-01.pdf> accessed 20 July 2015.

Department for Education (2010a). *The Importance of Teaching: The Schools' White Paper 2010*. Norwich: The Stationery Office.

Department for Education (2010b). *Statistical First Release: Schools, Pupils and Their Characteristics*. London.

Department for Education and Skills, (2004). *Aiming High: Understanding the Needs of Minority Ethnic Pupils in Mainly White Schools*. London: Department for Education and Skills.

Epstein, A., and Kheimets, N. (2000). 'Immigrant Intelligentsia and its Second Generation: Cultural Segregation as a Road to Social Integration?' *Journal of International Migration and Integration/Revue de L'integration et de la Migration Internationale* 1 (4), 461–76.

Equality Challenge Unit (2009). 'The Experience of Black and Minority Ethnic Staff Working in Higher Education'. London.

Gillborn, D. (2008). *Racism and Education: Coincidence or Conspiracy?* London: Routledge.

Harris, A. (2004). 'Distributed Leadership and School Improvement: Leading or Misleading?' *Educational Management Administration and Leadership* 32 (1), 11–24.

Harris, N.S., and Eden, K., with Blair, A. (2000). *Challenges to School Exclusion: Exclusion, Appeals, and the Law*. London: RoutledgeFalmer.

hooks, b. (1994). *Teaching to Transgress*. Abingdon: Routledge.

Johnston, W.B., and Packer, A.E. (1987). *Workforce 2000: Work and Workers for the Twenty-First Century*. London: DIANE Publishing.

Lorbiecki, A., and Jack, G. (2000). 'Critical Turns in the Evolution of Diversity Management'. *British Journal of Management* 11, S17–S31.

Lorenzi, M. (2013). *Fighting School Exclusions*. Institute of Race Relations. <http://www.irr.org.uk/news/fighting-school-exclusions/> accessed 20 July 2015.

Lumby, J. (2013). 'Distributed Leadership the Uses and Abuses of Power'. *Educational Management Administration and Leadership* 41 (5), 581–97.

Lumby, J., with Coleman, M. (2007). *Leadership and Diversity: Challenging Theory and Practice in Education*. London: Sage.

Maylor, U. (2014). *Teacher Training and the Education of Black Children: Bringing Color Into Difference*. London: Routledge.

Maylor, U., et al., (2007) *Diversity and Citizenship in the Curriculum: Research Review*. Research Report 819. Nottingham: DfES.

Office for National Statistics. (2004). *Living in Britain: Results from the 2002 General Household Survey*, Vol. 31 London: The Stationery Office.

Office For National Statistics (2011) *Origin-destination Statistics on Migration for Local Authorities in the United Kingdom and on Workplace for Output Areas and Workplace Zones, England and Wales* <http://www.ons.gov.uk/ons/rel/

census/2011-census/origin-destination-statistics-on-migration-and-students-for-local-authorities-in-the-united-kingdom/index.html> accessed 20 July 2015.

Office for National Statistics (2014). *Statistical First Release: School Workforce in England* <https://www.gov.uk/government/uploads/system/uploads/attachment_data/file/440577/Text_SFR21-2015.pdf> accessed 20 July 2015.

Race Relations (Amendment) Act 2000. HMSO. <http://www.legislation.gov.uk/ukpga/2000/34/pdfs/ukpga_20000034_en.pdf> accessed 20 July 2015.

Richardson, A.S., Bergen, H.A., Martin, G., Roeger, L., and Allison, S. (2005). 'Perceived Academic Performance as an Indicator of Risk of Attempted Suicide in Young Adolescents'. *Archives of Suicide Research* 9 (2), 163–76.

Showunmi, V., and Constantine-Simms, D. (eds) (1995). *Teachers for the Future*. Stoke on Trent: Trentham Books.

Swann, B.M.S. (1985). *Education for All: The Report of the Committee of Inquiry into the Education of Children from Ethnic Minority Groups* (Vol. 9453). London: HMSO.

Tatum, B.D. (2003). *'Why are all the Black kids sitting together in the cafeteria?' And Other Conversations About Race*. New York: Basic Books.

Tomlinson, S. (1991). 'Ethnicity and Educational Attainment in England: An Overview'. *Anthropology and Education Quarterly* 22 (2), 121–39.

Weekes-Bernard, D. (2010) *Did They Get It Right? A Re-Examination of School Exclusions and Race Equality*. London: The Runnymede Trust.

JOAN SMITH

Motherhood and Women Teachers' Career Decisions: A Constant Battle

Motherhood has been and continues to be identified as a major factor influencing women teachers' and headteachers' life and career choices (see for example, Coleman 2002; Bradbury and Gunter 2006; Smith 2011a and 2011b). It is particularly striking that, despite societal and legal changes, an enduring constant is the unquestioned and unspoken assumption that women will take primary responsibility for childcare.

Drawing on life history interviews with female teachers and headteachers (principals) working in UK secondary schools, this chapter considers how the women perceived that motherhood had framed their career decisions. Whilst many women had chosen teaching as a career because it was perceived to be compatible with family life, combining the two caused conflicts, practical difficulties and guilt for many. Support for women coping with the double load emerges as patchy, and where it exists, it can reinforce the notion that childcare is women's concern rather than men's. The chapter closes by considering how shifts in thinking are needed at national, institutional and domestic levels if we are to achieve gender equity in public, private and workplace domains.

Change and Constancy

During the twentieth century, women in the UK won the right to vote, the right to financial independence and, with the advent of freely available contraception, control over their own fertility. Discrimination at work was outlawed and women gained the right to the same pay as men. The legacy of this for twenty-first-century women is that, legally, in the public and professional spheres, women enjoy the same freedoms and choices as men.

If the playing field is now level, it is reasonable to expect that in the second decade of the twenty-first century we might see equal numbers of men and women in the most powerful positions in the workplace. Yet women continue, as Coleman (2011) notes, to be under-represented in the most senior posts, even in professions numerically dominated by women, like teaching.

In trying to account for the continued under-representation of women in senior leadership, it is tempting to think that many women are simply choosing not to pursue positions of power. Hakim (2000), for example, holds that, as a result of the changes that took place in the late twentieth century, twenty-first-century women have real options and opportunities, and are free to make genuine choices with regard to work and family: if women are under-represented in senior leadership, this is because they are acting in accordance with their preferences. Hakim (2000: 6) identifies three preference groups: 'home-centred', 'work-centred' and 'adaptive' women. 'Home-centred' women, she argues, 'choose lives centred on full-time homemaking, and hope never to be obliged to do paid work' (84). 'Work-centred' women 'effectively adopt the male lifestyle centred on competitive achievement in the public sphere' (ibid.), and many of them treat child-bearing as 'an optional extra, or hobby, certainly not the essence of adult life' (ibid.). 'Adaptive' women, the largest and most diverse group, account for up to about 80 per cent of all women. These are women who want to combine employment and family without prioritising either (ibid.). Hakim (ibid.: 277) predicts therefore that women will remain a minority in the most powerful positions in society 'because only a minority of women are work-centred in the way that most men are' (Hakim 2000: 277).

As has been argued elsewhere (Smith 2011b), the decision not to pursue a career in leadership can be a conscious and positive choice, rooted in a preference for classroom teaching and resistance to a contemporary educational leadership culture many women (and presumably some men) find abhorrent. However, Hakim's (2000: 1) claim that women have a 'genuine choice in affluent modern societies' between 'family work' or 'market work' assumes women are now free from all types of oppression, and takes no account of societal, familial and self-generated pressures on women to prioritise family responsibilities. In asserting that women are making free 'choices' in accordance with their 'preferences', Hakim (2000) fails to recognise the structural barriers to women's career progression (Coleman 2011), the constraints within which they make their life and career decisions, their differing capacities for overcoming constraints and the extent to which their roles are socially constructed (McCrae 2003).

Whilst there have been significant changes with regard to legal and policy reform, what has remained constant is the expectation that women will take responsibility for childrearing. Powerful social discourses of motherhood continue to find expression in the restrictive parameters within which many women make their life and career decisions. This is not to deny that women exert their agency (see Smith 2011b), but to recognise that they do so within a strikingly constant set of constraints. In attempting to account, therefore, for the continued under-representation of women in the most senior posts in education there is a need to take into consideration how women's private and domestic worlds intersect with their public and professional lives. In this chapter I draw on narrative research with women teachers and headteachers to explore the links between motherhood and women teachers' career decisions.

Motherhood and Career: A Life History Study

This chapter considers some of the findings emerging from a life history study investigating the main factors forty women teachers perceived to have influenced their career decisions. Motherhood emerged as particularly influential in framing and influencing the career decisions of women with children and those who planned to have children.

Open-ended life history interviews were conducted in order to allow the women to define for themselves, with minimal prompting from the researcher, what the important factors framing and influencing their career decisions had been (for an in-depth discussion of the methodology, see Smith 2012). The interwoven nature of women's personal and professional lives was very apparent in the narratives: participants frequently and voluntarily interspersed their narratives with details of personal relationships, family responsibilities and home life, and explained many of their career decisions in connection with these. The only question I asked about children was at the start of the interview, when I inquired as to whether the women had a partner or any children at present. Other than that, I did not return to the question of children. Any discussion about this therefore came from the narrators, and occurred spontaneously at various stages of the narratives, as seemed relevant to the interviewee.

The sample included:

- ten newly qualified teachers (NQTs), including one mother and others who were considering motherhood;
- twenty experienced teachers, including fourteen mothers, one foster mother and one woman who was pregnant for the first time at the time of the interview;
- ten headteachers, including five mothers.

This chapter draws on the narratives of the twenty mothers in the sample, plus a foster parent, a woman expecting her first baby at the time of the interview and five young women who were positively planning to have a family or thought it might be possible. As most of the mothers were in the 'experienced teachers' group, the data discussed here emanate mainly from these sixteen women, although I also refer to NQTs and headteachers where their accounts resonated with those of the experienced teachers. Findings peculiar to the NQTs and headteachers are summarised after the discussion on the experienced teachers.

All interviews were transcribed in full and manually colour-coded to identify emergent themes. The themes relevant to the discussion here included:

- relationship between personal and professional life;
- gender and career decisions;

- factors leading women to choose teaching as a career;
- ingredients for a happy working life;
- aspirations and perceptions of school leadership;
- self-perceptions as headteacher.

All participants worked in secondary schools in England. Pseudonyms are used throughout. Tables 1–3 provide mini-biographies of the women on whose narratives I draw in this discussion.

Table 1: Mini-biographies of Newly Qualified Teachers cited in this chapter

Name (Pseudonyms)	Age	Personal details	Teaching experience	Post at time of interview (full time unless otherwise indicated)
Cindy	39	married, 3 children	just finished PGCE (Post Graduate Certificate of Education)	secured MFL (Modern Foreign Languages) post as NQT (Newly Qualified Teacher)
Yvonne	23	living with partner, no children, did not think she wanted children but realised she might change her mind	in first year of teaching	Art teacher, NQT
Mandy	24	single at time of interview but thought motherhood was a possibility	in first year of teaching	MFL teacher, NQT
Mary	23	living alone but had been in a relationship for a few months. Intending to have children	in first year of teaching	MFL teacher, NQT
Daphne	28	living alone but had been in a relationship for one year. Intending to have children	in first year of teaching	English teacher, NQT
Pauline	33	living with partner and intending to have children	just finished PGCE	secured History teaching post as NQT

Table 2: Mini-biographies of Headteachers cited in this chapter

Name (Pseudonyms)	Age	Personal details	Teaching experience	Post at time of interview
Minnie	59	married, 4 children	30 years	Headteacher of selective girls' grammar school
Gladys	57	married, 1 daughter	30 years	Headteacher of selective girls' grammar school and executive head of local confederation of schools
Fiona	45	separated, 2 daughters	18 years	Headteacher of school for boys with educational and behavioural difficulties
Wilma	50	living with partner, 3 sons	27 years	Headteacher of mixed secondary school
Renee	52	married, 3 children	29 years	Headteacher of mixed secondary school

Table 3: Mini-biographies of Experienced Teachers cited in this chapter

Name (Pseudonyms)	Age	Personal details	Teaching experience	Post at time of interview (full-time unless otherwise indicated)
Gloria	50	separated, 1 daughter (20)	13 years	MFL teacher
Sarah	38	married, 2 young children	15 years	Head of Faculty (MFL) 0.8 FTE (Full-Time Equivalent)
Carol	40	married, pregnant	12 years	English teacher and Advanced Skills Teacher 0.8 FTE
Win	48	divorced, 1 daughter (19)	14 years	Special Educational Needs Coordinator & Head of Economics
Stella	43	married, 2 teenage sons	10 years	English teacher & Examinations Officer
Diana	34	divorced, living with partner, 2 young children	11 years	Head of Department (MFL)
Rhona	43	married, 2 teenage sons & 2 grown-up stepchildren	10 years	supply teacher

Name (Pseudonyms)	Age	Personal details	Teaching experience	Post at time of interview (full-time unless otherwise indicated)
Linda	54	divorced, 2 children (23 & 26), 2 grandchildren	13 years	Head of Department (MFL)
Coral	52	married, 2 daughters	27 years	supply teacher
Marjory	52	married, 4 children	30 years	MFL teacher
Olivia	53	married, 4 children	31 years	Head of MFL
Lisa	45	single, foster mother	23 years	Special school teacher
Olwen	60	married, 2 sons	32 years	just retired; was Head of Department (MFL)
Sandra	48	married, 3 children	28 years	just resigned from post as Deputy Director of post sixteen provision
Freda	51	married, 2 teenage children	29 years	just retired from post as teacher of Food and Life Skills
Christine	48	married, 2 children	25 years	Head of Science and Science College – Coordinator

Findings

The key findings are presented in this section under thematic headings relating to:

- the perception that classroom teaching is compatible with family responsibilities;
- the difficulties implicit in combining motherhood and teaching;
- the impact of the 'dual role' on career;
- the need for support.

Experienced Teachers

CLASSROOM TEACHING: 'A VERY GOOD CAREER FOR WOMEN WHO ARE GOING TO HAVE A FAMILY'

Motherhood had, to a greater or lesser extent, impacted upon the career paths of all of the mothers in the study. Many had chosen to enter the teaching profession in the first place at least in part because it was seen to be compatible with raising a family, or they had stayed in it for the same reasons. Some participants had worked in other careers previously, and entered teaching relatively late, perceiving it as a profession that offered greater potential for combining work and family responsibilities. Some had left teaching earlier but returned to it on marrying or starting a family. Olwen, for example, explained, 'I worked for the immigrants' advisory service [...] I was on call seven days a week and twenty-four hours a day, and my husband got very upset about that. So that's when I did actually go back to teaching [...] I went back [...] because it is a very good career, I think for women who are going to have a family'.

There were a number of reasons why teaching and family life were viewed as particularly compatible. A major advantage that was frequently cited was that teaching offered the flexibility to take care of the family during school holidays. Rhona's view was typical:

> One of the reasons I chose teaching was to fit in with the family, because of the school holidays [...] I know that's an old-fashioned idea now, but I think that's really important, to have your parents around [...] as a teacher I have always been there for [my own] children, with the exception of the odd meeting after school or the slight difference in finishing times. I'm there when they are and that was important for me, so that fitted in very well. (Rhona)

The financial security perceived to be offered by teaching, and the importance of this for supporting a family, were also alluded to by several mothers. Teaching salaries were seen to compare favourably with other jobs the women might have been able to consider, allowing them to provide a reasonable standard of living for their families.

Despite this prevalent view of teaching as compatible with raising a family, for many women, combining the two entailed significant practical and emotional difficulties that affected their career decisions, as I discuss below.

'MOTHERS CAN'T WIN': DIFFICULTIES IMPLICIT IN COMBINING FAMILY RESPONSIBILITIES AND TEACHING CAREER

Many of the women discussed how they had embarked upon their teaching careers expecting to be able to cope with motherhood and profession without feeling the need to sacrifice one for the other. However, all of the mothers in the study perceived that taking responsibility for childcare in the private domain had, to at least some degree, impacted upon their career decisions in the professional domain. Many perceived that having a family had limited the extent to which they had been able to focus on their career, and had impeded their career progression.

Most of the mothers' narratives were characterised by descriptions of home-work conflicts in their daily lives. These included practical and organisational considerations in the day-to-day running of the family and feelings of being pulled in two directions when professional commitments clashed with family needs. For example, a number of women talked about feeling unable to take time off work to care for sick children, and of the implicit difficulties in attending, for example, parents' evenings. Whilst, as seen below, they devised coping strategies to combine professional and family work, feelings of frustration and conflict remained. Freda, for example, recalled 'There used to be home-work conflicts when the children were little. If I had any work to do, I would never start doing it until they'd gone to bed, and so it was very hard. I look back and I think, how did I manage? I must've been Superwoman! I also used to do night classes as well, for extra money. I did a lot of things, but yes, there was a conflict'.

In many cases the sense of conflict was intensified as the women found themselves under pressure to prioritise motherhood over career. Freda's case provides a noteworthy example, as considerable pressure had been brought to bear on her by members of her wider family and social circle to give up her job in order to bring up her children. She explained, 'When

I went back into teaching after having children, my brother would hardly talk to me [...] my dad was of a generation when it was expected that you had to take time off, you stayed at home with your children [...] and I have friends who found it strange I went back to work'.

Whilst Freda resisted this pressure by returning to work full-time, the guilt she felt for doing so was clear in the emotive language she used, describing herself as 'a terrible parent'. This tendency for harsh self-judgment was not unusual in the narratives, and there were numerous manifestations of what McCrae (2003: 329) refers to as women's 'inner voices', providing evidence that women's expectations of themselves reflect those of the dominant discourses surrounding motherhood, leading women to believe their primary commitment should be to their family. Although Freda made the decision to return to work, it was not without a sense of guilt: her 'inner voices' (ibid.) reminded her that she ought to put her own children first.

There were further indications that women's own deeply–held assumptions about their mothering roles were at the root of dilemmas and inner conflicts regarding their double role. The sense of guilt to which Freda alluded was also apparent in women who had not experienced pressure of this sort from others in their social and family circles, and even where husbands or partners were fulfilling a caring role perfectly well. Olivia, for example, commented, 'I feel guilty that I don't spend enough time with the youngsters, helping them with their homework, my own children [...] But then they seem to prefer to go to their dad for help anyway. Now whether that's because I haven't been there to help them in the past I'm not sure'.

This indicates that the feelings of guilt can be self-generated: even if others are not consciously putting pressure on women to take on the main responsibility for childcare, the women themselves often feel they ought to be primarily responsible. It is interesting to note, for instance, that some women discussed how, although the feelings of guilt and inner conflict had been intense for them, their grown-up children in retrospect usually had no recollection of being in any way neglected. Olwen, for example, talked about this in the context of her earlier decision not to apply for deputy headship:

I didn't feel it was appropriate at that point, with the boys [...] I felt they needed me still [...] It created conflicts for me, not with the family, but within myself [...] I did work very hard, but I often used to get very guilt-ridden that I wasn't doing either job, at home or at school, as well as I could have done. The boys laugh at me when I say that now. They weren't aware of any lack [...] I think mothers can't win. If you don't go out to work and produce the extra money so that the kids can do things, you feel guilty, and if you do, you feel guilty because you're not giving them the time. So I think mothers are perpetual Catholics in search of absolution! (Olwen)

For single parents, the pressures and sense of guilt and conflict could be particularly intense at times. An example is that of Win, who described how on occasions she had been unable to arrange for babysitters and had had to take her young daughter to parents' evenings with her, or had had to take her into school with her when she was ill, commenting apologetically, 'That sounds really heartless doesn't it?' That Win seemed almost ashamed of what she had had to do as a result of the combined demands of her job and motherhood is indicative of the double bind in which women in her position inevitably find themselves. Whatever decision mothers make in such situations is likely to engender a sense of guilt and shame.

At the same time, as teachers and professionals, the women seemed typically to feel that they also ought to be dedicating themselves to their school and teaching role, which again gave rise to feelings of guilt for being unable to commit 100 per cent to either the teaching or the mothering role. Carol, who was pregnant for the first time at the time of the interview, was already experiencing acute pangs of guilt about the impact of her pregnancy on her professional work. Her experience of feeling guilty about being pregnant reflects the conflict for women in combining work and children, and it is difficult to imagine that any guilt-laden dilemma of comparable intensity might emerge from the career life history of a male colleague. Carol had started her current job only six months earlier. Her pregnancy had not been planned, and she felt very strongly that she was letting down her pupils and her school:

I'm already thinking [...] my year 11 group this year, I'm going to go off on maternity leave before they've finished. Now that could have a big effect on their results [...] I found it very, very difficult to tell [senior leaders] at school that I was pregnant [...] because [...] when I started [...] I mentioned that I'd just got married, and I said

that I wasn't planning to have kids [...]. We were really clear that we weren't going to
have children! [...] So now it's really difficult because there's another woman in the
department who's just taken maternity leave and may well take another one, because
she'd like a second baby and of course, it does make holes in provision [...]. I do really
feel guilty. So it was very, very difficult to tell them [...]. I did briefly consider a ter-
mination actually, initially [...]. Well, I do really [feel guilty [...] because it wasn't on
the agenda. And because I am always scrupulously honest with people, I would have
said, you know, 'Look, by the way, I probably am planning to have a family.' (Carol)

The strong sense of guilt Carol expressed reflected a personal commitment
and dedication to the job that appeared to be at least as important to her
as her private and home life. Her dilemma was thus almost intolerable
as she found herself forced to prioritise one over the other. The second
extract from her narrative, below, reflects some of the tensions for her when
pregnant, and also her expectation that it would be she who would need
to take steps to ensure she could accommodate her job and her childcare
responsibilities, despite the very strong, egalitarian relationship she enjoyed
with her husband:

[My husband is] just a fantastic support and we do very much share the housework.
In fact a lot of things [...] things I was responsible for before [we married], I now
share responsibility for, and that's great [...]. [We have] a good quality relationship
[...]. I can imagine with kids there are [home-work conflicts] [...]. I've got friends
who [...] have had their baby late and gone back to work and say it's an absolute
Godsend, and they really don't want to be at home all day with the baby, and I think
if you've had a really interesting, dynamic time working up until you're forty you're
not going to suddenly want to have five years at home going to the park every day!
So, no, that doesn't appeal to me really. But whether I'll want to reduce down the
hours to three days or [...]. I don't know. I do envisage going back to work and I do
envisage probably having a couple of years where it is a challenge to do both things.
And I think the assumption is that by doing both things you can't do either thing
well. I think maybe that if you've got the right sort of support and the right sort of
mind-set, you probably can do both things reasonably well. And there are women
who do that. So that's what I would like to do, and I suppose long term, I don't know
[...] I would possibly consider job-sharing a head of department role, possibly. (Carol)

As in the example above, in which Carol anticipates how she will need to
make adjustments to her 'mind-set' and her working arrangements in order

to ensure she can function in both roles, it appears from the narratives of the participants in this study that women are continuing to assume, or feel they ought to assume, primary responsibility for childcare, even if they are not intending to give up their paid work.

For a woman who is a mother, a professional career thus becomes an extra load, to be fitted in around and on top of the maternal role. As Coral commented, 'If I wanted my job I had to also make sure that I was available to sort out the other things as well. You end up by taking on a dual role'. In the section below, I present the evidence emerging from the women's narratives of how this 'dual role' is accommodated, and the impact this has on women teachers' career paths, decisions and aspirations.

'TAKING ON A DUAL ROLE': CAREER PATHS AND ACCOMMODATION OF FAMILY LIFE

There was considerable evidence that the women teachers in this study had fitted their career around their maternal and domestic responsibilities. Motherhood was cited as a career-influencing factor by all of the women with children of their own, although the extent and nature of its impact varied from one individual to another. All had taken their families' needs into account when making career decisions. Almost all explained that they were, or had been at some point, limited to one particular geographical area for reasons relating to home, family and relationships. All of the mothers spoke of shaping or modifying aspirations to a greater or lesser extent and/ or shedding professional responsibilities, and therefore pay and status, in order to meet the needs of their families. Marjory, a mother of four, for example, told me, 'the way my career's gone has been directly linked to having children ... I have not sought further development simply because I have not got the time to do it properly'.

It seemed the pressures on women teachers who were also mothers had impacted in significant and enduring ways on the women's career progression, which had been slowed down or halted as they navigated their way around the conflicting requirements of home and work. Moreover, what happened in career terms after having children was frequently at odds with what the women had originally intended. Sandra, for instance, recalled:

By the end of 1992, I had three children under three [...]. I had no intention of
returning to [school] for 92–3, because my husband was then working in [another
town] and we could not sustain both me going back to work and him travelling
long distances whilst having three children under three – that would have been
impossible. So I knew I wouldn't return, and I tagged along after my highly promoted husband to live further north with no status except that of mother, which I
wasn't ever too keen on. Certainly it was a million miles from my intentions when
I went there ten years prior as a twenty-seven-year-old woman who didn't want
children! I didn't completely capitulate – the U-turn wasn't sufficient to get me to
actually like small children or [my two] maternity leaves. Indeed, I threw my arms
into the air in celebration each time they were over and I could go back to work!
(Sandra)

In most cases, as in Sandra's, women who had adjusted their career aspirations after having children had done so because they were taking responsibility for childcare whilst their partners concentrated on their career.
Mid-career teacher Sarah, who was married to a vicar, had followed him
geographically according to his parish. Having had two children she still
aspired to deputy headship, but now expected this to take longer than if
she had remained childless. She saw deputy headship as the limit: headship,
with all its demands, she felt, would not be 'fair on the family'. Still ambitious, Sarah was also devoted to her family and had modified her career
goals to fit around the demands of home. Stella and Rhona had followed
their husbands for financial reasons and because of having children. Rhona
commented, 'I have followed [my husband] around the country with his
job. His earning power has always been a lot greater than mine [...]. He
now earns three times what I earn – why on earth would he follow me?
[...]. If it was a woman that earned more then you'd follow the woman, but
when does that actually happen in reality?'. Similarly Stella explained, 'My
career path was following his. He was earning more than me and he was
always going to be, because we intended to have children, he was always
going to be the one that we relied on for the income [...] everything, until
I got into the [job] that I'm doing now, has been geared around having
children and following my husband'.

   If career progression in education relies on geographical flexibility
and a willingness to move schools and areas, these restrictions may act
to limit women's potential career progression. In addition, the increased

likelihood of downscaled career aspirations when women become mothers also mean some women are less likely to progress to the upper echelons of school leadership.

More than half of the experienced teachers and NQTs were discouraged from applying for deputy headship and/or headship by the increased workload and pressure perceived to be associated with it, and what they saw to be the likely negative impact on their lives outside school. Headship in particular was seen as highly likely to be detrimental, leaving less time for family and home life. Taking on posts of increased responsibility was seen to involve extra work, and thus to be incompatible with family life. This was mentioned numerous times as a reason not to apply for leadership posts, for example:

> I think I am discouraged from applying for senior leadership by the balance [...]. I mean being a head of department now, I've realised that I've had less time to spend on the family [...]. People say you *can* do it, and our deputy head did it with young children, at our school [...] but I'm a bit of a perfectionist and I try to do everything well, and you have to let things go anyway if you're working and you have children. (Olivia)

The need to accommodate family and career led most of the mothers in the study to re-assess their priorities. Life-work balance, flexibility and having the time to function properly in both the teaching and mothering roles were major considerations for most women. Good health, a stable, happy home life and having the time to spend with and take good care of their families were cited by most of the experienced teachers as more important than promotion, power or status.

A small number of the older women had taken complete career breaks for child-rearing, rather than just statutory maternity leave. This had meant loss of status and an eventual return to the profession at a lower level in the career (and pay) hierarchy. Olwen, for example, like other 'returners', had given up a promoted post when she left the profession, re-entering initially as a supply teacher. In cases like Olwen's, taking a career break to raise a family acted as a disadvantage in career terms.

Most of the mothers in the experienced teacher group, like Cindy in the NQT group, had only entered the teaching profession after their own children were at least at school, thus the problem of leaving and re-entering the profession was not in their experience. On the other hand, as women who entered the teaching profession relatively late, several of the mothers in this study were also disadvantaged as they were likely to hit their ceiling in terms of promotion prospects more quickly. Awareness of the decreased likelihood of promotion as years went on had caused four of these women to lower their career expectations and aspirations. The four women ranged in age from forty-three to fifty-four – still some way from retirement age. It appears that mothers are less likely than other teachers to achieve promotion, and the leadership skills they might have brought to schools are being lost.

THE NEED FOR SUPPORT SYSTEMS

Support in various forms and from a range of sources was, unsurprisingly, discussed by many of the women as important in enabling them to fulfil their double role. Sources of support included relatives, senior leaders, teaching colleagues, their own children and in some cases, partners, although refer-ences to the latter were rather less prevalent amongst the older teachers, who, more typically, had relied on extended family members to take care of children. Coral, for instance, commented, 'If I hadn't had very helpful grandparents, I would have found it a lot more difficult when the children were young. I don't think I've had very much time off school at all actually, because of my own children, but I would've done had I not had grandpar-ents I could run them around to [...] they've been very helpful'. For women younger than Coral, who was fifty-two, this assistance from extended family seemed to be less readily available. There were very few indications how-ever that this support was being provided by husbands or partners instead.

A small number of women spoke positively of the support they had received in school. Headteachers who were understanding and tolerant were particularly appreciated by women who at times struggled to combine their professional and domestic roles. Diana, for example explained, 'The head [...] has been supportive of me [...] if I've not been able to make a parents' evening because I've not had a babysitter or something like that he's been really good about that sort of thing, so that's helpful'.

What becomes clear however is that institutional sources of support appear to be *ad hoc* and dependent on the goodwill of individuals, including some headteachers, rather than as part of any systematic, organised support for women teachers. The lack of support systems such as organised childcare at institutional, local or national levels, coupled with, for at least some women, a lack of informal support from family members, adds further conflict and pressure to women's dual roles and is likely to impact on career decisions.

I turn below to the experiences of NQTs and then headteachers, with regard to the links between career decisions and motherhood.

Newly Qualified Teachers (NQTs)

NQTs' thoughts about the future also indicated a tendency to see personal and professional lives as intertwined. Just one of the NQTs, Cindy, was already a mother of three. At thirty-nine, Cindy was older than the other NQTs. The interwoven nature of her family life and her career was clearly evident throughout her narrative. Her experiences overlapped with those of many of the experienced teachers who were also mothers.

With most of the other NQTs, discussion about the inter-relatedness of their personal and professional lives centred on their future plans rather than their current situation. Discussions about the future did, though, for more than half of the NQTs, incorporate thoughts about motherhood.

Six NQTs made reference to the likely impact of having children on their professional lives. Cindy, already a mother, was one. The other five included Yvonne, who did not think she wanted children but realised she might change her mind, Mandy, who mentioned it as a possibility, and Mary, Daphne and Pauline, who were very definite about their desire to have children, and to some extent aware of the impact that could have on their careers. Pauline commented: 'I'm going to have children, so that of course is going to impact strongly on the direction I go'. Thinking ahead to the prospect of having their own children, and the reality of combining this with a full-time teaching position, prompted the women to reflect on and articulate the dilemmas this would cause them. Daphne, for instance, reflected:

> You really do take a lot of the pressures and the stresses [...] home with you. [...] I want to have kids and I would obviously want my kids to be of primary importance [...]. Right now, my job takes over everything. [...] I would never want to put my students on the back burner, but I'd need to make sure that I did keep everything in perspective, that I wasn't ignoring what was going on at home [...] because right now I go home and I'm so tired, and there's so much to do. Talking to other people in the profession – one lady that works at another school, her kids were eleven and twelve – and she realised that she'd been too exhausted to raise them ... I'd never want that. [...] I would take time off, or put things on hold. [...] I'd definitely want to go to parents' evenings and be there when my children were little. [...] I would take a career break, which at the same time makes you think that maybe you don't want to progress and push forward in your career and get a lot of responsibility before that was to happen. [...] I guess your priorities really do change. [...] Ideally I would like to be a full-time mother for the initial years, but I wouldn't want to give up my career entirely because it is very important to me, and I have so much invested into developing it so far. [...] Everything is constantly changing in education. You miss a couple of days and it's hard to get back into [...] so I think it would be very detrimental to my career to take time off. (Daphne, NQT)

Daphne's comments were illustrative of the sort of concerns voiced by other NQTs in this regard. Comments in general related to the practicalities of combining both roles and the possible impact on career of taking time out for child-rearing. As with the experienced teachers, there was an implicit assumption that it would be the women's own responsibility to take charge of childcare. There was no mention of the possibility of fathers taking responsibility for children. There were no real indications that this younger generation of women was either conscious of, or intending to resist, pressures on them to prioritise childcare. It may be that the NQTs had not anticipated at this stage how motherhood might come to define their lives and careers, but it is noteworthy that even at this stage of their careers they were rejecting the possibility of careers in leadership out of consideration for as yet unborn children. It may also be that they understood implicitly that social pressures to put children first were so strong they could not contemplate doing otherwise.

Headteachers

Five of the headteachers were mothers. Interestingly, the five who were not mothers felt that being childfree had been an important factor in enabling them to progress through their careers and take on and function in the headship role. For the five headteachers who were mothers, there were some indications that career paths had been limited geographically as a result of home and family commitments of various sorts. This was not however so strong a theme as it was for the experienced teachers.

Their attitude to working full-time differentiated the headteacher mothers from the teacher mothers. Whereas typically teachers talked about the guilt and conflict as well as the practical difficulties they experienced in combining teaching and mothering, the headteachers were for the most part much clearer about the appropriateness of the decision they had made. Four of the five headteacher mothers talked about making a very positive choice to work rather than staying at home with children. Self-determination characterised their narratives: there was a very clear sense in which the women had engaged reflectively with social influences and taken action to shape their own lives and careers (see Smith 2011a and 2011b). Wilma, for instance, was aware of other women's dilemmas about combining profession and motherhood, but had been able to identify clearly for herself what she wanted rather than being over-influenced by socially determined expectations. She commented, 'I've never really felt torn between motherhood and the job, because I knew in my own mind when I had [my first child] [...] that I wanted to go back into work. [...] I never had the tugs that I see women experiencing here now. [...] I didn't have any difficulty making the choice, and having made the choice I never regretted it'.

It was also striking that relatively little time was spent during the head-teacher interviews discussing family issues. This was in contrast to the experienced teachers' interviews, when considerable attention was paid by narrators to explaining how their professional and family lives intertwined, and how this affected their career decisions. This was not to say that family did not matter to the headteachers, and indeed, two of the five mothers in this group strongly emphasised that whilst they were committed to their jobs they would prioritise family when and if it became necessary.

Gladys, for instance, remarked, 'It's family first. Whatever else happens, my family comes first. [...] They know that, even though sometimes the job comes first. [...] If my daughter 'phoned me and said, "I need you now", I would go. Nothing would stop me. [...] What matters to me is that I can prioritise home or school according to how I see the priorities, and I feel very free to do that'.

There were indications that the headteachers perceived that their position afforded them greater control over their lives, as reflected in Gladys' comments above. This contrasts with the experiences of the teacher mothers in the study, for whom struggling to balance responsibilities and emotional conflicts emerged as a much greater preoccupation, and who tended to view headship as a role that would control and restrict them (see Smith 2011b; Smith 2014).

Discussion

> Career decisions taken by women and men in partnership are generally influenced by expectations that women will take prime responsibility for the home and the raising of children while men prioritize work. (Coleman 2011: 97)

Consonant with the findings of Coleman (2002; 2011), the findings of this study suggest that perceived professional possibilities continue to be constrained by the still largely unquestioned assumption that women are primarily responsible for childcare. This expectation has remained stubbornly constant, despite the affordances and opportunities offered to women as a result of changes in law and policy. The inter-connectedness of women teachers' personal and professional lives is very apparent. For many, role conflict is alive and well. This forms the focus for the first part of the discussion in this section.

Moreover, it seems that the difficulties women face in combining profession and motherhood are exacerbated by the relative dearth of support systems at societal, institutional and family level. Even where formalised support systems exist, these can have the impact of reinforcing the view that women are ultimately responsible for childcare. This forms the focus for the second part of the discussion in this section.

Motherhood and Career Advancement: The 'Impossible Choice'

All of the women who were mothers, including the headteachers, perceived that having children had, to a greater or lesser extent, framed and influenced their career decisions. Many perceived that motherhood had placed major constraints on the career options that were realistically open to them, and found themselves faced with what Banyard (2010: 73) refers to as 'the impossible choice' of caring for their children or advancing their careers. The timing of childbearing also impacted on the participants' potential for career progression, and those taking career breaks were likely to find that they experienced 'a reduction in status that may never be fully repaired' (Coleman 2011: 99).

It was clearly apparent that the mothers in the study were assuming primary responsibility for child rearing. The unspoken expectation still seems to be that mothers will do this. This is consistent with findings of other researchers in the area (for example, Coleman 2002; Bradbury and Gunter 2006), and does not appear to be changing over time. No one participating in this study mentioned the possibility that husbands or partners could have taken on the main childcare responsibility – the assumption that mothers would do so was such a given that, seemingly, it did not need to be articulated. Indeed, there were relatively few references to husbands and partners in the narratives of the mothers, despite there being frequent discussions of children and home. NQT Cindy, for example, mentioned that she was married, but made no other reference to her husband, although her children featured throughout the narrative as career-shaping considerations.

There has been a significant shift in attitudes to marriage and divorce over the last few decades: single parents and step-parents are commonplace, civil partnerships and gay marriage are socially acceptable and adoption of children by same-sex partners is permitted. Given these changes, it is striking that socially constructed norms and expectations of mothers regarding what constitutes acceptable and appropriate behaviour have remained very stable: they are expected to stay with their children and take care of them for life (Jackson 1994). The expectation that mothers will take on the long-term, primary responsibility for child-care is endemic in contemporary western culture: its message continues to be so powerful that women who choose not to conform may risk ostracism, social exclusion and disapproval (ibid.).

Many of the women in this study had chosen teaching because they had perceived it to be a career that would fit well with family responsibilities. Despite the commonly-held perception that teaching was, in Olwen's terms, 'a very good career for women who are going to have a family', the reality for the majority was that combining teaching and motherhood resulted in feelings of guilt and frustration, as well as entailing practical difficulties and role conflict. This resonates with the experiences of the female headteachers in Coleman's (2002: 56) study about whom she reports, 'the natural expectation that it will be the woman who takes the lead role in family and childcare imposes a burden on the women heads with children. It was clear that many of the women headteachers were pre-occupied with the guilt engendered by their role conflict as mothers and career women'.

It is interesting to note that in Coleman's (2002) study, which included male and female headteachers, the sense of guilt and role conflict commonly reported by women was rarely mentioned by men. Rather, 'there was an assumption that the overall responsibility was not theirs' (Coleman 2002: 57). Whilst men do face issues in trying to balance home and work, 'there is generally less pressure on them in respect of home responsibilities' (Coleman 2002: 2).

It would seem that for most women who are parents, the pull of home and mothering commitments, practical and emotional, continues to be a strong factor leading to their unwillingness to take on the most senior positions. Banyard (2010: 83) argues that 'women still shoulder the bulk of caring and housework at home' and it is therefore 'very difficult for them to compete with others unencumbered by the responsibility to, for example, pick the kids up from school [...] make dinner [...] do the washing'. These combined pressures in many cases slow down or halt women teachers' career progression as they navigate the conflicting demands of work and home. As Coleman (2011: 2) observes, it is 'no coincidence that many women who are successful as managers and leaders are childfree'. Indeed, the five headteachers in this study who did not have children all said that this had been a factor enabling them to progress their careers.

On the other hand the five headteachers in this study who were mothers tended to view their senior position as a benefit in making decisions about work and home. It is perhaps worth noting that were female headteachers to be more proactive in communicating this advantage to potential women aspirants to leadership this might have an encouraging effect: as noted in Coleman's (2011) study, mentoring can be beneficial in enabling women to progress their careers.

However, the fact that the headteachers saw it as beneficial that their position offered them scope to make decisions about home suggests that, as in Coleman's (2002) study, they also saw themselves as primarily responsible for the domestic domain. Contrary to Hakim's (2000) thesis that women are making entirely 'free' and conscious choices with regard to work and family, it would seem that the career decisions women with children make are underpinned by family considerations, and strongly informed by powerful, unquestioned discourses relating to their primary role.

Looking forward with optimism, Coleman (2011: 15) argues that 'changes in society are impacting on how [women's] choices may be made, with men more likely to take some responsibility for their children'. However this is a slow revolution: a man's decision to devote more time to his family continues to be 'a personal choice' (McRobbie 2009: 81), whereas for a woman it is the norm or the socially expected decision. The narratives of the teacher mothers in this study suggest that the 'specific ideology of motherhood', which Jackson (1994: 17) identifies as having evolved over the last two centuries in the west, continues to predominate. Far more than a passive reflection of social reality, the 'iconography of good and bad mothers' (Jackson 1994: 18) continues to be 'an actively determining force, constantly renaming and reinforcing certain assumptions and definitions as to what properly constitutes maternity' (ibid.).

Images of motherhood and associated values are manufactured and reinforced in a range of ways, including through literature, the media, popular entertainment and culture, industries which, even though women can be found 'at the top' (Coleman 2011), work to reinforce traditional messages about women's roles. As McRobbie (2009: 34) comments, 'women's magazines, the fashion and beauty industries, as well as women's genres of film and television programmes, come to function as the primary disseminators of the new traditionalism'. By way of example, McRobbie (ibid.) highlights the 'fantasies of home and hearth peddled in UK cooking programmes', citing the example of 'domestic goddess' Nigella Lawson, and urging us to ask, 'Why this kind of fantasy? What are women viewers longing for or dreaming about, when they find themselves hooked into the soft focus images of happy families gathered round the table to enjoy a Sunday lunch cooked by a glamorous-looking and unstressed mother?'

The same discourses and assumptions underlying this romanticised view of motherhood also underpin mass media portrayal of working mothers, who are frequently blamed for 'damaging' children (see, for example, the *Daily Mail* headline on 1 August 2014, which reads, 'Working mothers risk damaging their child's prospects' (Doughty 2014)). The decision by writers of such reports to portray working mothers as the cause of a range of social ills, and to frame and headline them in this way is to show that, 'for large sections of the population, if there's a problem to do with caring then the buck stops with Mum, not Dad' (Banyard 2010: 80).

These implicit messages are internalised by women so that a woman's career choices are not only constrained by structural factors such as job availability and the cost and (non-) availability of childcare, but also by what McCrae (2003: 329) calls a woman's 'inner voices' and her beliefs, 'about being a mother, about being an employed mother, and about the implications of the latter [which] can curtail the choices that she considers are open to her' (ibid.). These beliefs are formulated through powerful social discourses that define women's role as mothers, and in relation to which their self-perceptions and self-expectations are formed.

These social and personal beliefs and expectations about women's proper roles are reinforced and maintained by policy. As Coleman (2002: 75) argues, 'the introduction of maternity leave may in some ways have made things worse for women [...] in reality, allowing women a number of weeks off for childbirth does not solve the childcare problems.

There continues to exist a significant gulf between what is viewed as normal in terms of parents' rights to maternity and paternity leave: 'Ordinary Paternity Leave' entitles a father to one to two weeks' paid leave (Gov.UK 2014) and even though there is an entitlement for fathers to take up to twenty-six weeks in the event of the mother returning to work, this is termed 'additional' leave and is infrequently accessed in the UK: just one in 172 fathers take up this option (TUC 2014). This suggests that there have been few shifts since Coleman's (2002: 75) study, in which men reported taking career breaks for secondment or to gain qualifications, but none reported a career break for childcare.

The Institute of Leadership and Management (2014) argue that cultural barriers prevent men from taking their full entitlement and so work to impede women's career progression. The assumption that women will not only bear children but will subsequently care for them seems to be a fundamental defining factor in the organisation of western industrial society, and changes to this model are, seemingly, not readily accepted in the workplace. The real question, as Banyard (2010: 75) asks, is 'why is it only women who have to choose between a family and maximizing their career potential?'

The Need for Support

Unsurprisingly, the need for support in order to function in the dual role of mother and teacher emerges from the study as very important. Coral, one of the older participants, talked about relying on helpful grandparents to assist when her children were ill, so that she did not need to take time off work, resonating with the experiences of some of the successful women in Coleman's (2011) study.

This support from extended family was not the norm however, particularly for younger mothers in the study, suggesting, as Jackson (1994: 86) argues, that 'massive social mobility and deracination in our society has killed many of the extended family structures that previously helped relieve pressures on one woman's parenting'. However, I am tentative in making sweeping statements based on this limited and unrepresentative sample of women, of whom all but one were white and European. It is possible that research into the lives and careers of a more diverse group of women would reap different results.

It might be argued that extended families are less prevalent in twenty-first-century society, meaning that the more communal forms of childcare are less readily available. At the same time there is an increased emphasis on the nuclear family model, intertwined with and strengthening discourses about women's mothering role. Those who take care of children within the nuclear family unit do so in relative isolation, largely unsupported, in ways that limit their freedoms in the public and professional domains.

Moreover, state and institutional support systems for childcare are inadequate. Support at the level of the school emerges from this study as patchy and inconsistent. There are indications from some of the women's narratives that at least some headteachers are understanding and tolerant, which, arguably is a positive change. However, the availability of support for women with children seems to be largely dependent on the goodwill and understanding of individual colleagues, rather than any organised systems of support.

It is interesting to contrast this view of twenty-first-century Britain with the picture that emerges from Nelson's (1992) study of the day-to-day working lives of women who taught in rural areas of Vermont during the first half of the twentieth century, a time when women teachers in England were not even allowed to marry. She found that many of the women 'spontaneously drew a comparison between family life and school life' (ibid.: 20) and that their lives were characterised by 'multiple intersections of home and work' (ibid.: 27): family responsibilities were seen as compatible with teaching, and support structures were in place that enabled women to combine the two. For the women of early twentieth century Vermont this intersection of the worlds of home and work offered practical solutions for the women in coping with what Nelson (ibid.: 26) terms the 'double burden' or the 'double day'. What was highly significant for the women of this period was that there was an overlap between their two worlds in terms of personnel and support systems:

> First [...] the community allowed these women to bring their small children to school with them, thus simply resolving the ongoing problem of what to do with children during working hours. Second, friends and relatives brought in during absences created through illness or maternity, assured those women that their jobs would still be available if and when they chose to return to work: a mother would give way to a daughter, a friend to a friend. Thus these intersections not only provided the solution for the immediate problem of 'who can be trusted to take over my school?' but for the longer-term problem of 'will my job still be there when I get back?' Third, the intersections at a temporal level provide us with ample evidence that women of the past could move in and out of their careers in response to domestic needs. (ibid.: 36)

What Nelson terms this 'intermingling of home and school' thus offered solutions to these rural schoolteachers, solutions which 'appear unavailable to women today' (ibid.). In the case of the women in Nelson's study, the support of husbands or partners who were prepared to share the domestic burden was also an important factor in enabling them to function professionally.

Seen in this light questions are raised about whether twenty-first-century women teachers are any more 'equal' to their male partners and colleagues than were their early twentieth-century counterparts, or whether the double demands that continue to be placed on them, and the relative dearth of support systems at societal, institutional and, for at least some, at domestic level as well, mean that their lives are in some ways more difficult than they would have been a hundred years ago in Vermont. Even with the right to maternity leave, the flexibility to 'move in and out of' (ibid.) careers as and when needed is not available to twenty-first-century women in Britain in the same way. Whilst there is a legal requirement for employers to offer some flexibility, this can result in reduced security of employment for women (for example, as part-time employees), and can mean that the choice to raise a family can also be a 'choice' to take a downward step professionally, or to slow down or halt career progression.

Even where state and institutional support systems exist, this is not unproblematic. Strategies that are ostensibly devised to 'support' working mothers, such as childcare provision or flexible working hours, can convey implicit messages that reinforce the expectation that mothers *should* find ways to manage the dual load, reifying rather than dismantling the notion that women with children and a career must take charge of both. Whilst, as McRobbie (2009: 80) argues, in twenty-first-century neo-liberal society women are not forced to remain in the home as mothers, there is instead pressure on them to 'do it all', to be active in the workforce as well as to take responsibility for child-rearing.

The resultant 'process of gender re-stabilisation' (McRobbie 2009: 79) sees 'young working mothers [...] draw back from entertaining any idea of debate on inequality in the household in favour of finding ways [...] to manage their dual responsibility' (ibid.). Thus domestic compromise works to limit the women's participation in the workplace: the onset of motherhood 'entails the scaling down of ambition in favour of a discourse of managing', as young women in this position are 'counseled to request flexibility of [their] employer[s]' (McRobbie 2009: 80). In this regard, it is interesting to note that flexible working is more common in the public sector, where larger numbers of women are employed (Hegewisch 2009).

Images in popular culture of 'the glamorous working mother, the so-called yummy mummy, the city high-flyer who is also a mother' (McRobbie 2009: 80) reinforce the notion that women can, and should, 'do it all', successful career, motherhood and of course, remaining beautiful at the same time. This message is reinforced through media representations of 'successful' women who *can* do everything, in many cases promoted by women who have 'made it' into powerful positions in those industries, including magazine editors and others. This is constructed as freedom of choice and an 'alternative to traditional economic dependence on a male breadwinner' (McRobbie 2009: 80), yet works to protect masculine hegemony, as the fundamental assumption that women care for children remains intact.

Concluding Comments

Family responsibilities are thus identified as one of the main reasons for women's subordinate positions in the labour force. The other remains the continued stereotyping of women as supportive and subordinate rather than being in charge. (Coleman 2011: 4)

If we are to move towards gender equitable social democracy, shifts in thinking are needed at national, institutional and domestic levels, reflected in policy reform, evolving workplace cultures and re-distribution of domestic responsibilities.

Whilst UK employment law potentially affords freedom of choice, there is scope for further reform. Coleman (2011: 110–11) mentions, for example, the 'current UK maternity leave which gives women the right to take up to one year off after the birth of a child but caps paternity leave at two weeks thus, further reinforcing the idea that childcare is the mother's responsibility'. It is informative to consider how the Scandinavian countries provide opportunities for both parents to engage in paid work and child rearing (see, for example, Eydal and Rostgaard 2014). Proactive campaigning for similarly targeted policies in the UK might pave the way for a more equitable distribution of parental, professional and leadership responsibilities, reflected in more equitable schools in which young people grow up understanding that they have real and meaningful freedom of choice.

There is also scope for change in terms of workplace expectations of women and men. Hegemonic discourses about women's 'natural' roles as carers and mothers extend into constructions of their work as teachers (see for example, Anfara and Brown 2000; Whitaker 2001; Abioro 2010), locking women into (and discouraging men out of) what are commonly perceived to be maternal, caring roles in the educational workplace. Within this culture, men who choose, for instance, to work with young children are placed under particular scrutiny and viewed with suspicion (see for example, Sargent 2002; King 2004; Hansen and Mulholland 2005), 'othered' in a society in which the care of small children is constructed as feminised work.

There is therefore a need to effect a shift in the way 'caring' is constructed in the context of educational institutions. It is useful to consider Noddings' (2001) observation that care, if viewed as a relational (rather than a feminised) attribute, allows both men and women to enact care in their roles as a part of their professionalism. At the same time, gender stereotypes which 'cast men as leaders [and] women as supporters and nurturers' (Coleman 2011: 13) effectively ensure many women remain for the most part 'outsiders' (ibid.) to leadership. This is exacerbated by workplace cultures that construct commitment as a willingness to work long hours. This has the dual impact of disadvantaging women who are caring for children or elderly relatives, and exerting pressure on men who are fathers to prioritise work over family.

There is a need to move towards discourses of androgyny in the construction of parenting, teaching and school leadership, if we are to maximise the involvement of men and women in raising and teaching our children and leading our schools. An emphasis on parenting rather than mothering, in tandem with a notion of professional care as a part of the teacher and leader ethic, rather than as typical of one sex or the other, may provide the foundation for more equal sharing of child-rearing, teaching and school leadership work and bring about real change to the strikingly constant set of constraints.

Acknowledgements

I am grateful to Marianne Coleman, Laura Guihen and Phil Wood for their helpful comments on previous drafts of this chapter. I would like to thank also the University of Leicester for granting me a period of study leave during which this work could be undertaken.

References

Abioro, E. (2010). 'Perceptions of Care: Self-Reflections of Women Teachers of African Descent Who Teach In Urban Settings'. EdD thesis, Loyola University Chicago.
Anfara, V.A., and Brown, K.M. (2000). 'An Unintended Consequence of a Middle School Reform: Advisories and the Feminization of Teaching'. *Middle School Journal* 31 (3), 26–31.
Banyard, K. (2010). *The Equality Illusion*. London: Faber and Faber.
Bradbury, L., and Gunter, H. (2006). 'Dialogic Identities: The Experiences of Women who are Headteachers and Mothers in English Primary Schools'. *School Leadership and Management* 26 (5), 489–504.

Coleman, M. (2002). *Women as Headteachers: Striking the Balance*. Stoke on Trent: Trentham Books.

Coleman, M. (2011). *Women at the Top: Challenges, Choices and Change*. Basingstoke: Palgrave Macmillan.

Doughty, S. (2014). 'Working Mothers Risk Damaging Their Child's Prospects'. *MailOnline* <http://www.dailymail.co.uk/news/article-30342/Working-mothers-risk-damaging-childs-prospects.html> accessed 1 July 2014.

Eydal, G.B., and Rostgaard, T. (2014). *Fatherhood in the Nordic Welfare States*. Bristol: Policy Press.

GOV.UK (2014). *Paternity Pay and Leave* <https://www.gov.uk/paternity-pay-leave/overview> accessed 16 October 2014.

Hakim, C. (2000). *Work-Lifestyle Choices in the Twenty-First Century: Preference Theory*. Oxford: Oxford University Press.

Hansen, P., and Mulholland J.A. (2005). 'Caring and Elementary Teaching: The Concerns of Male Beginning Teachers'. *Journal of Teacher Education* 56 (2), 119–31.

Hegewisch, A. (2009). *Flexible Working Policies: A Comparative Review*. Research report 16. Manchester: Equality and Human Rights Commission.

Institute of Leadership and Management (2014). *Poor Uptake of Paternity Leave Holding Back Female Career Progression* <https://www.i-l-m.com/~/media/ILM%20 Website/Documents/Information%20for%20media/Parental%20leave%20 press%20release_web%20pdf.ashx> accessed 16 October 2014.

Jackson, R. (1994). *Mothers Who Leave*. London: Pandora.

King, J.R. (2004). 'The (Im)Possibility of Gay Teachers for Young Children', *Theory into Practice* 43 (2), 122–7.

McCrae, S. (2003). 'Constraints and Choices in Mothers' Employment Careers: A Consideration of Hakim's Preference Theory'. *British Journal of Sociology* 54, 317–38.

McRobbie, A. (2009). *The Aftermath of Feminism*. London: Sage.

Nelson, M.K. (1992). 'The Intersection of Home and Work: Rural Vermont Schoolteachers 1915–1950'. In R.J. Altenbaugh (ed.), *The Teacher's Voice: A Social History of Teaching in Twentieth Century America*, 26–39. London: Falmer Press.

Noddings, N. (2001). 'Care and Coercion in School Reform'. *Journal of Educational Change* 2, 35–43.

Sargent, P. (2002). 'Under the Glass: Conversations with Men in Early Childhood Education'. *Young Children* 57 (6), 22–30.

Smith, J.M. (2011a). 'Agency and Female Teachers' Career Decisions: A Life History Study of Forty Women'. *Educational Management Administration and Leadership* 39 (1), 7–24.

Smith, J.M. (2011b). 'Aspirations to and Perceptions of Secondary Headship: Contrasting Women Teachers' and Headteachers' Perspectives'. *Educational Management Administration and Leadership* 39 (5), 516–35.

Smith, J.M. (2012). 'Reflections on Using Life History to Investigate Women Teachers' Aspirations and Career Decisions'. *Qualitative Research* 12 (4), 486–50.

Smith, J. (2014). 'Gendered Trends in Student Teachers' Professional Aspirations'. *Educational Management Administration and Leadership*, first published on 16 October as doi: 10.1177/1741143214543200.

TUC (2014). *Just One in 172 Fathers Taking Additional Paternity Leave* <http://www.tuc.org.uk/workplace-issues/just-one-172-fathers-taking-additional-paternity-leave> accessed 16 October 2014.

Whitaker, M.L. (2001). 'Doin' What Comes Naturally: When Mothers Become Teachers'. *Educational Foundations* 15 (3), 27–45.

KAY FULLER

Headteacher Preparation: An Account of One Woman Headteacher's Supportive Practices

Introduction

Marianne Coleman is well known for her research into women secondary school headteachers in England and Wales. She has investigated the barriers to, and facilitators of their careers; their becoming and being headteachers (see Coleman 2002). During research that followed her work (Fuller 2009), two women headteachers independently identified another woman who had supported each in their career. This coincidence sparked further investigation into the practice that was deemed supportive. The findings of that case study are further reported here (see also Fuller 2015). Despite sex and other equality legislation, there remains concern for the under-representation of women in secondary school headship in the twenty-first century (Fuller 2013). How headteachers support women into headship is likely to be of interest in the field of headteacher preparation as well as that of gender and leadership.

The women who achieved secondary school headship (Coleman 2001: 75), 'against the odds', identified being encouraged by others as an influential factor in that success. Encouragement of them came from headteacher, other senior colleagues and partners (Coleman 2002). Mentoring was by former headteachers (women and men), though it was not widely available (Coleman 2001). Networks for women set up in the 1990s have since been in decline (Coleman 2010). In Birmingham, England, where there was a high proportion of women secondary school headteachers, women (and men) were found to be much more influenced by their colleagues than nationally (Fuller 2009). Many more women had held a senior post prior to deputy headship than was found nationally (Fuller 2009). These women gained whole school leadership and management experience by working closely with the headteacher in senior leadership teams (SLT). This chapter explores the findings from a case study of headteacher preparation practices of a single woman headteacher. It locates twelve practices, constructed by her and eight former and current members of the SLT at Alan Road School, in the situated learning literature concerned with communities of practice (Lave and Wenger 1991; Wenger 1998) as it has been used by educational leadership theorists and in teachers' learning development literature (Hodkinson and Hodkinson 2003, 2004a, 2004b, 2005). The following sections explore the literature that refers to and critiques 'communities of practice' to conceptualise the SLT at Alan Road School as an expansive leadership learning environment. Empirical research is used to outline twelve practices as a process of successful headteacher preparation. Finally, a critical analysis reveals that within the SLT position, disposition, capital and power relations impact greatly on an individual's leadership aspirations and achievement of them.

From Communities of Practice to Expansive Learning Environments

A community of practice constitutes a group of 'apprentices, young masters [sic] with apprentices, and masters some of whose apprentices have themselves become masters' (Lave and Wenger 1991: 56). It is a space where workplace learning takes place, where participation changes as identities develop from 'newcomers' to 'old-timers'. Such an approach describes the 'traditional headteacher apprenticeship' (Daresh and Male 2000: 91) model seen fit only for passing on 'craft knowledge and technical skills' from one generation to another (13). An apprenticeship model neither serves the competence based educational leadership model (see DfES 2004); nor was it fit for purpose in a field that valued highly-qualified and experienced professional teachers who create knowledge about teaching and learning (Gunter 2006). Nevertheless, part of aspiring leaders learning how to lead takes place by working within senior leadership teams where valuable leadership experience is gained (Rhodes et al. 2009). Studies of educational leadership have drawn on, sometimes uncritically, this notion of 'communities of practice' (Lave and Wenger 1991; Wenger 1998). The literature about leadership and schools *as* communities of practice in which leadership preparation and development takes place has not been critical. Holden (2008) conceptualises the Leadership for Learning network as a community of practice. Waterhouse (2008) likens the development of Learning Catalysts to the cultivation of communities of practice as 'groups of people who share a concern, a set of problems, or a passion about a topic, and who deepen their knowledge and expertise in this area by interacting on an ongoing basis' (Wenger et al. 2002: 4). Møller (2009) locates the Leadership for Learning project (see Frost, 2006 for a discussion of the centrality of agency in the Carpe Vitam project) that applied a distributed perspective as a lens for thinking about the embeddedness of leadership and learning as 'closely linked' (254) to the socio-cultural perspective on learning articulated by Wenger (1998). Hammersley-Fletcher and Brundrett (2005) identify spaces where shared leadership might emerge in schools as communities of practice.

Leadership *of* communities of practice includes subject leadership by middle managers seeking to reduce role conflict (Wise 2003); the creation of spaces, beyond organisational units, where community members might develop and share knowledge (McGregor 2003); or where teaching practice might be enhanced by observation, discussion and reflection (Morley and Hosking 2003). Communities of practice are problematic for some. Morley and Hosking (2003: 47) argue 'the politics of relations within and between communities has been relatively neglected'; that 'communality, agreement and talk about 'what is' [should not be overestimated] at the expense of multiplicity, disagreement, and what might be' (48). Indeed differences in beliefs and values within groups and power relationships such as micro politics and the nature of 'headship' have been largely ignored (McGregor 2003). O'Neill (2003: 153) goes further in critiquing Wenger's (1998) analyses of learning as 'a veneer of ready applicability to complex social situations'. He advocates a critical policy scholarship approach to educational leadership research that requires a 'painstaking, reflexive approach to the understanding of educational practice' (154) as opposed to a labelling of experiences. Rhodes and Brundrett (2006) recognise communities of practice are not wholly benign. There is arbitrariness in aspirant headteachers' location in schools working with headteachers who do not necessarily create the conditions for headteacher preparation. Simkins (2009) suggests the distinction made by Hodkinson and Hodkinson (2004a) in the teacher learning literature between 'small, tight communities of practice such as a subject department and communities that arise in broader occupational and organisational contexts' might be applied to 'communities of practice among school leaders' (402). Hodkinson and Hodkinson's (2003, 2004a, 2004b, 2005) rethinking of communities of practice offers headteacher preparation and development research a useful analysis of the nature of the learning context and the individual's relationship with it.

As seen above, Hodkinson and Hodkinson (2004a) are not alone in their critical appraisal of communities of practice. Indeed, the concept has been much critiqued outside the educational leadership literature (see Barton and Tusting 2005; Hughes et al. 2007), including for the implicit alignment and merging of business and education (Gee 2000). Gender theorists have critiqued communities of practice for their assumption of benignancy (Paechter 2006), though that has been challenged (Fuller, 2007), and gender-blindness (Paechter 2003). Nevertheless, the concept has been used to consider how children learn to do masculinities and femininities (Paechter 2003) and the power relations exercised in policing boundaries within and between communities (Paechter 2003, 2006). The notion that 'full participants' police the boundaries and behaviours of 'legitimate peripheral participation' (Lave and Wenger 1991: 29) might be applied to the access afforded to leadership posts in the course of a career. The tendency by those with power to make senior appointments in their own image has been documented across a range of women's careers (see Coleman 2011). It leads to glass ceilings (impenetrable barriers), glass cliffs (women's appointments to difficult posts causing them to fall) and labyrinths (difficult routes to seniority). Thus the composition of senior leadership teams and the leadership discourses developed therein become even more important with regard to sex, social class and ethnicity.

Hodkinson and Hodkinson (2003, 2004b) draw on Bourdieu's social theory to explore the relationship between the individual and their learning context. They argue the teacher's habitus, or embodied dispositions influence how they approach learning opportunities, 'Different learners perceive the same opportunities differently, and react towards them differently, because of these differing dispositions, as well as their differing positions in relation to those opportunities' (Hodkinson and Hodkinson, 2003: 4–5). They show two teachers in similar learning contexts responding differently to opportunities that arise (Hodkinson and Hodkinson 2004b). One teacher appears to have 'greater and more valuable social capital' (178). The differences between the teachers occur 'through the interrelationships between position, disposition and capital, related to their career histories, the departmental communities of practice, and the wider field' (179). Variously tight-knit or loosely integrated subject teams impact on the nature and culture of different subject departments sometimes in the same school (Hodkinson and Hodkinson 2004a). The influence of the structures and practices of school teaching in the UK is also acknowledged. Finally, the concept of a continuum of expansive and restrictive learning environments (see Fuller and Unwin 2003) has been adapted for teachers (Hodkinson and Hodkinson 2005). This continuum has been adapted here for leadership learning (see Figure 1). I use it to think about the findings of a case study carried out to explore the supportive practices of a woman headteacher's preparation of members of the SLT for headship.

Stoll et al. (2006) describe the collective learning, including by leaders, taking place in Professional Learning Communities. A process of knowledge deconstruction as a result of reflection and analysis, reconstruction through action in context and the kind of co-construction of collaborative learning with peers in communities of practice takes place where 'participants gradually absorb and are absorbed in a "culture of practice"' (Stoll et al. 2006: 234). The apparent osmosis by which community members develop and are developed by a culture of practice involves a combination of learning construction and participation rather than knowledge acquisition (see Hodkinson and Hodkinson 2005).

EXPANSIVE	RESTRICTIVE
Close collaborative working within and beyond the Senior Leadership Team (SLT)	Isolated, individualist working
Colleagues mutually supportive in enhancing leadership learning	Colleagues obstruct or do not support each other's learning
An explicit focus on leadership learning, as a dimension of normal working practices including the opportunity for supported reflective practice in school	No explicit focus on leadership learning, except to meet crises or imposed initiatives
Supported opportunities for leadership development that goes beyond school or government priorities	Leadership learning mainly strategic compliance with government or school agendas
Out of school educational opportunities including time to stand back, reflect and think differently about leadership	Few out of school educational opportunities, only narrow, short training programmes
Opportunities to integrate off the job leadership learning into everyday practice	No opportunity to integrate off the job learning
Opportunities to lead and participate in more than one working group	Work restricted to single leadership focus within one school
Opportunity to extend professional identity through boundary crossing into other leadership roles, school activities, schools and beyond	Opportunities for boundary crossing only come with a job change
Support for local variation in ways of leading and learning for leaders and work groups	Standardised approaches to leadership learning are prescribed and imposed
Leaders use a wide range of leadership learning opportunities	Leaders use narrow range of learning approaches

Figure 1: Continuum of expansive and restrictive leadership learning environments adapted from Hodkinson and Hodkinson (2005)

The Case Study

This case study (see Yin 2009) explored how women and men headteachers successfully prepared, and continued to prepare for headship whilst working at a school led by one woman headteacher. It was undertaken amongst former and current members of the SLT at Alan Road School, a mixed comprehensive school for children aged eleven to sixteen. The school serves an area of multiple deprivations in the outer ring of a large urban local authority in the English Midlands. The school has consistently been graded as 'Outstanding' (the highest grade awarded) in successive school inspections carried out by the Office for Standards in Education, Children's Services and Skills (Ofsted). The study investigated the headteacher's preparation of members of the senior leadership team for headship. Members of a school SLT are leaders in their own right. They lead specific aspects of the organisation such as curriculum development or pastoral care, but they are learners with respect to learning about and preparing for headship in their daily work with the headteacher, their peers and members of the wider school population. Those preparing for headship as deputy and assistant headteachers are identified for the purpose of this research as *learning-leaders* and the headteacher (Rita) with whom they prepared as *teaching-leader*. This is a purposive sample. In the course of research reported elsewhere two women headteachers identified Rita and working at Alan Road School as influential in their career development and a source of ongoing support. Each had worked at the school as deputy headteacher but at different times. Rita collaborated by agreeing to be interviewed and enabled access to current and former members of the SLT including some who had not achieved headship. At the time of writing, five years after the collection of data, seven *learning-leaders* with whom Rita worked have become headteachers (women n = 5; men n = 2). Five agreed to participate in the project; their job roles at the time of interview are given in Table 1.

Nine semi-structured interviews were carried out with the *teaching-leader* and eight *learning-leaders* who worked with Rita. The sample of *learning-leaders* (Table 1) included two headteachers; four deputy headteachers (DHT); and two assistant headteachers (AHT) (women n = 7; men n = 2). In line with the current underrepresentation of Black and Global Majority women and men in secondary school leadership (DfE 2014) eight of the interviewees were white British and one woman was Asian British (she has achieved headship). Questions focused on Rita's mentoring and/or coaching practices. Interviewees widened the focus to include aspects of daily working practices and other influences in their responses. Thus semi-structured interviews or conversations with a purpose (Ribbins 2007) enabled the collection of rich qualitative data. Participants were aware the research focused on the preparation of women headteachers. The texts Rita and the *learning-leaders* produced were likely to have been influenced by that knowledge (see Møller 2009).

Table 1: Sample of senior leadership team interviewees by sex, job role at
Alan Road School, job role at the time of interview and job role
at the time of writing (adapted from Fuller 2015)

Senior leader	Sex	Job role in Alan Road School (School A)	Job role at time of interview	Job role at time of writing
Rita (teaching-leader)	F	Headteacher	Headteacher – School A[1]	Retired
Lucy	F	Deputy Headteacher	Headteacher – School B	Retired
Diana	F	Deputy Headteacher	Headteacher – School C	Regional educational leadership work
Michael	M	Deputy Headteacher	Deputy Headteacher – School A/Headteacher Designate School D	Headteacher – School E
Lawrence	M	Deputy Headteacher	Deputy Headteacher – School A	Deputy Headteacher – School A
Samantha	F	Deputy Headteacher	Deputy Headteacher – School A	Left (long-term illness[2])
Di	F	Assistant Headteacher	Assistant Headteacher – School A	Headteacher – School A
Jessica	F	Assistant Headteacher	Deputy Headteacher – School C	Headteacher – School C
Rebecca	F	Assistant Headteacher	Assistant Headteacher – School E	Assistant Headteacher – School E

1   Schools A, B, C and D were in the same local authority. School E was in a different neighbouring authority.
2   This illness was not work related. A debilitating physical condition was diagnosed after the interview took place.

Each of the interviewees was given a pseudonym. Interviews were digitally recorded and transcribed. They were stored and coded using Nvivo 8. Key codes were derived from the initial reading with respect to multiple feminist leadership discourses such as: the removal or reproduction of barriers to women accessing senior leadership posts; the notion of women's leadership; the feminist construction of leadership that uses power to work *with* to empower; and leadership heteroglossia as a conception of engagement with multiple gendered leadership discourses (see Fuller 2015, and Fuller 2014 for a discussion of gender heteroglossia). The transcripts have been re-coded with respect to ten features of expansive leadership learning environments identified in Figure 1.

A Headteacher Preparation Process within an Expansive Leadership Learning Environment

Accounts revealed Rita's work with the SLT at Alan Road School contributed greatly to headteacher preparation. Eight practices described elsewhere as dialogic encounters (see Fuller 2015) have been reframed here as twelve practices that constitute a process of leadership learning conducive to headteacher preparation. For clarification the original eight practices have been identified in brackets alongside the corresponding practice below.

Working with the whole school
1. *Modelling headship* (modelling headship)
2. *Standardising operating principles and practices* (implementing standardised operating practices)

Working with emerging leaders
3. *Identifying leadership talent* (initiating interest in leadership)

Working with the SLT
4. *Managing the leadership of others – support and challenge*
5. *Convening operational meetings (daily)* (SLT meetings)
6. *Convening strategy meetings (weekly)* (SLT meetings)
7. *Rehearsing leadership conversations (coaching)* (rehearsal of relational leadership)

8. Distributing leadership (project leadership)
9. Convening one-to-one reflective meetings (robust self-reflective conversations)

Expanding leadership repertoires
10. Supporting leadership learning opportunities outside school
11. Rotating roles and responsibilities

Working beyond the school
12. Mentoring formally and informally through networks (informal networking)
(adapted from Fuller 2015)

This should not be seen as a linear process though some practices clearly preceded others for some *learning-leaders*. Grouping the practices as *working with the whole school, working with emerging leaders, working with the SLT, expanding leadership repertoires* and *working beyond the school* demonstrates *learning-leaders* might gain and retain access to the process at different points. For example, *learning-leaders* who were promoted internally (Lawrence, Samantha, Di, Jessica, Rebecca) first worked with Rita as emerging leaders. *Learning-leaders* appointed from outside (Diana, Michael) and a *learning-leader* already in post (Lucy) first worked with Rita as members of the SLT. *Learning-leaders* who moved on to promoted posts elsewhere (Lucy, Diana, Jessica, Michael (as headteacher designate)) worked with Rita beyond the school. How the practices and process were constructed in terms of an expansive leadership learning environment are shown below (see Figure 1).

Working with the Whole School

MODELLING HEADSHIP

Being a good leader was 'being yourself but more so' (Rita). Rita sought consistency and coherence across the school. She modelled headship by greeting children and staff in the morning, leading assemblies, patrolling corridors, visiting classrooms and teaching lessons. She was highly visible and accessible. Lawrence described her modelling of meetings with parents:

> to have her ask you come to a meeting with her [to check] that she doesn't go overboard or she says the right thing; it almost empowers you to feel that you are there to keep tabs on Rita, when really you are there to learn from her whole handling of the meeting, and you are there to learn what she expects from kids, parents and staff. (Lawrence)

His presence had multiple purposes; one was to learn by observation. Samantha noted Rita's capacity for attention to detail was a model she could not emulate (see below).

STANDARDISING OPERATING PRINCIPLES AND PRACTICES

Rita attributed a close collaborative *teaching-leader* approach to team teaching with staff as a newly appointed headteacher, 'people were exposed to my [classroom] teaching very early on which made it easier for them to see [a collegiate role through which nurturing and growing took place]' (Rita). Operating principles and practices were established and standardised. Non-negotiable SLT working practices that benefited the whole school included *learning-leaders* maintaining an examination class teaching commitment. Rita taught Michael that

> you need to feel the pain. I think that is a very important credential in an aspiring leader, [that] a headteacher has to have. I think she is actually a great role model for getting her sleeves rolled up and getting her hands dirty and she actually empowers her leaders in the school, particularly senior leaders to do this. (Michael)

They shared the pressure on teachers to secure learning outcomes and supported them by managing pupil behaviour. Thus *learning-leaders* were accountable for examination results as teachers of examination classes; senior leaders line managing specific subjects; and in having whole school responsibility for a cohort's attainment. Leadership was focused on children's learning (MacBeath 2007; Grogan and Shakeshaft 2011).

Working with Emerging Leaders

IDENTIFYING LEADERSHIP TALENT

With an explicit focus on leadership learning at every level (Hodkinson and Hodkinson 2005; MacBeath 2007), Rita retained able teachers by engaging them in school-based research. She used intuition to identify leadership talent but confirmed it through a process of analysis, using triangulation to synthesise evidence. Her background in social science supported this work. Rita helped teachers 'imagine' what their careers might become. She 'stirr[ed] the nest' (Lawrence, adapted from Fuller 2015: 183) to prompt responses. Three approaches were made to Di:

> Rita does a lot of planting the seed and then leaving you to think about it. So she was never there saying I had to do it but it was a career opportunity [leading role in teaching and learning] and she would support me if I considered it. I think she might have mentioned it (with Rita it might never be off the cuff but it felt like off the cuff) three times over the course of a year and at the end of that I thought, 'Okay, I'll have a go' and I got it. (Di, adapted from Fuller 2015: 183)

Colleagues' responses depended on their different dispositions (Hodkinson and Hodkinson 2003), their

> ability to be open-minded and challenged and thoughtful [...]. If you are in a safe environment where you can take risks and be nurtured and challenged then you are going to grow. Some people will still grow faster than others. (Lawrence)

Leadership potential was identified early. Rita might see newly qualified teachers teach for 'five minutes, ten minutes of a lesson here, a lesson there' (Lawrence). She would be looking for reflective capacity (Hodkinson and Hodkinson 2005),

> subconsciously you recognise people [who have] the capacity, they're reflective. You don't have to do very much to get them on the right lines. So you can talk to them in a very sort of open way. About the typical coaching, *how* and all the rest of it and 'If something here was different, would you do that the same?', all that sort of stuff.' (Rita, adapted from Fuller 2015: 183)

Working with the SLT

MANAGING THE LEADERSHIP OF OTHERS: SUPPORT AND CHALLENGE

Rita's model was an assumption of teachers' ability and professionalism; her default position was to reprimand pupils for misbehaviour, remove them from classrooms and exclude them temporarily from school. The result was teachers' defence of pupils:

> frequently the staff will say, 'Well, I don't actually want them excluded because they're outside your office and I know it. They don't usually [behave like that].' So they don't have to push, they can give because I'm the one saying, 'No, I'm not having that. You're not going to be treated like that; nobody's going to speak to you like that.' (Rita)

Staff were generous to children because they were supported. Rita's approach diverged from headteachers elsewhere who identified values conflicts with staff around pupil behaviour management and inclusive education (Fuller 2013). The values underpinning her headship were associated with social justice (identified by Michael) and a passion for children (identified by Jessica) (see Grogan and Shakeshaft 2011). Her model was seen as enabling a culture of mutual support in line with an expansive learning environment where learning at every level might take place (Hodkinson and Hodkinson 2005; Stoll et al. 2006; MacBeath 2007).

Rita differentiated her management of senior leaders depending on their ability. One *learning-leader* might be left 'alone almost entirely'; another 'is hardly allowed to move a muscle without me being there' (Rita). Headteachers have worked with SLT members in different ways depending on levels of self-confidence or team roles (Fuller 2013). Rita supported Diana's curriculum leadership by 'protect[ing]' (Rita) her from the daily management of behaviour and pastoral issues that dominated school life. She supported Michael by not interfering with his management of the timetable. Rita also challenged poor leadership practice. Michael recalled the consequences of his poor handling of staff relations, '[Rita] will go in hard when she needs to but she will also reward incredibly' (Michael).

Rita recalled reprimanding Lucy for taking a hostile tone with staff at a whole school meeting:

> she just talked for ten minutes, telling everybody off about why this hadn't happened or why that hadn't happened, [...] I can't stand that. So afterwards we had that conversation, 'That isn't what we do. You go see those people. We're never going to have a meeting like that again, *ever*, where we tell people off. We tell people off individually; out there we do the big positive stuff.' Yeah, we can present the dilemmas and the challenges and all of that, but I can't stand blanket criticism. (Rita)

Such conversations were everyday working practices so the line blurred between what was line management and what constituted coaching and mentoring; they overlapped as in 'a Venn diagram' (Michael). Rita policed the boundaries of acceptable leadership practice for *learning-leaders*. However, that policing of practice was shared with SLT members and outside the team. Along with SLT members, a new middle leader observed the less respectful practice of a newcomer to the SLT (Fuller 2015). The micromanagement of the senior leadership team might be seen as a restrictive learning environment (Hodkinson and Hodkinson 2005). However, it was largely constructed by *learning-leaders* as modelling attention to detail and an opportunity to learn. Newly appointed women headteachers have managed male-dominated SLTs by directly challenging existing non-inclusive leadership practice (Fuller 2013).

CONVENING OPERATIONAL MEETINGS (DAILY)

Operational meetings enabled daily synchronisation of diaries to ensure colleagues provided mutual support for leadership work:

> Everybody knows [what each other is doing throughout the day] because [...] you can cross-reference your diaries but you are basically making sure that you need two senior members of staff always on duty, always here, available. (Michael)

Close collaborative work enabled openness about difficulty:

> there was Rita on the courtyard, on the playground, on the corridors [during] period five. I knew she was around certainly and other people did, probably because she knew I wasn't functioning as well as I should be [due to illness]. (Lawrence)

It was normal working practice to provide mutual support in leadership work (Hodkinson and Hodkinson 2005). A system and set of relationships were in place to identify and meet needs.

CONVENING STRATEGY MEETINGS (WEEKLY)

Strategic team meetings provided 'on-the-job training' (Lucy) in whole school leadership. Lucy, Lawrence and Rebecca constructed SLT meetings as an opportunity to gain an overview,

> we did share everything [...] we all discussed everything, so although you may have your specific duties and responsibilities in one area, you had that holistic view. You were constantly being encouraged to be in the helicopter so that you'd got the big picture and were encouraged to think strategically and consulted about strategic matters. (Lucy)

Temporary 'acting' responsibilities ensured members of staff outside the SLT gained this overview (see below). The practice resonated with accounts of additional members of staff being invited into the SLT to ensure staff voices were heard by senior leaders (Fuller 2013).

REHEARSING LEADERSHIP CONVERSATIONS (COACHING)

As seen above, Rita adopted a different approach with *learning-leaders* depending on their needs. They were expected to present analyses of information, make proposals for action and change at SLT strategy meetings. Proposals might be rehearsed in advance. Rita rehearsed a range of leadership conversations with Diana and Jessica. Each emulated the practice in their new school:

> you are just re-listening to stuff you have already heard once. But you are letting people tell the tale to a team. But the tale telling now has Rita's slant on it as well as your own, and so actually you are driving an agenda in your team and then therefore at the school's strategic movement level that's come through all of that coaching and support that you didn't realise you were being coached and supported in. (Diana)

Rita rehearsed staff management with Jessica:

sometimes she has to point it out to you that 'actually I want you to go and have a conversation with a member of staff'. And she would help you to role play. Role play is the wrong word but it was almost talk through how you would go through that conversation, what kind of things you might say, what the conclusions ought to be importantly; and whether any further action would be required [...]. So she was quite good at, I would almost say role play, coaching you through those conversations. (Jessica, adapted from Fuller 2015: 183)

Jessica had been coached in having conversations with parents:

she was always really clear when she was working with you on parents it was something you couldn't really get wrong. You couldn't afford to mess up when dealing with parents because you can spend a lot of time as a head dealing with it and sorting it out. (Jessica)

Relationships and dialogue with staff and parents were important. Although conversations were rehearsed with specific outcomes in mind, there was an emphasis on listening:

start with listening. Schools aren't full of staff who don't care and who don't care about the fact they missed their deadline. Schools are full of staff who want to meet the deadline and are personally disappointed at themselves if they have missed it. (Jessica)

Lawrence learned from those he managed and mentored, 'You have got to be open to other people's ideas' (Lawrence).

A dialogic and relational approach to leadership was promoted (Shields and Edwards, 2005; Grogan and Shakeshaft 2011). By encouraging *learning-leaders* to engage staff and parents in difficult conversations, Rita extended their professional identities by enabling them to cross boundaries (Hodkinson and Hodkinson 2005). In some schools, *learning-leaders* might not be trusted; headteachers might see their role as working with adults where others were working with children (Fuller 2013). Coaching events enabled reflection on leadership practice and leadership learning.

DISTRIBUTING LEADERSHIP

Learning-leaders were responsible for leading specific aspects of school life. Lucy led on community engagement then curriculum; Diana and Michael provided curriculum leadership; Lawrence and Rebecca led on pastoral matters; and Samantha on support services. Jessica and Di led on specific teaching and learning initiatives. Rita reluctantly referred to 'distributive leadership' (Rita) as sharing leadership opportunities in order to 'grow' (Rita) leaders inside and outside school (Bush 2011). Leadership emerged where colleagues had specific expertise (Woods et al. 2004).

Samantha acquired multiple support service leadership roles: 'health and safety arrived and I said 'that's me isn't it?' and she said 'yes, I think it [is] that has got to be you' (Samantha). Samantha challenged the school development planning process and took on its leadership. Her job description, salary grade and title changed. As deputy headteacher she gained immediate access to external facing leadership work she was barred from previously. *Learning-leaders* were enabled to lead in different ways with respect to subject and other whole school leadership matters (Hodkinson and Hodkinson 2005). Di led her subject differently to other heads of department; Jessica was allowed free rein with respect to a whole school issue. Such opportunities to exercise leadership enhanced it (MacBeath 2007).

Internal promotion to temporary or substantive senior leadership roles enabled middle leaders to develop their leadership. Di was temporarily appointed to the SLT:

> [Rita] works very well in terms of temporary appointments, so somebody like a head of year [name] is a temporary assistant head, [name] is a temporary assistant head, [Di] is a temporary and then she will get a full appointment. Really working at your key staff and your key leaders and your middle leadership level, you are keeping succession and you are building [leadership capacity]. (Michael)

Rita helped Di to imagine herself into headship (see Wenger, 1998):

> I was having a crisis because of the extra responsibility and I was ill at the beginning of the week. There were many things and I didn't know if I could actually cope with this. [...] Rita was very, very supportive as she always is. She said 'you will get through this, you are going to be a deputy one day and you will be a head one day' and she said 'if that is what you want' and that was it. (Di)

Temporary leadership roles were opportunities for junior colleagues to see school leadership differently:

they all comment on how much they understand the school better as a result of sitting with people who understand the school and sitting in meetings when [leadership] issues are discussed. [...] they have talked about their opening eyes to the situation and what Rita does and how instrumental she is. (Lawrence)

Enabling colleagues to 'act up' was difficult, 'it is tough to cover for somebody who's leaving you now at a really high level' (Rita). Nevertheless, opportunities to exercise leadership at a senior level were seen to enhance leadership learning (MacBeath 2007). There were opportunities to lead and participate in multiple working groups (Hodkinson and Hodkinson 2005).

CONVENING ONE-TO-ONE REFLECTIVE MEETINGS

Reflection on leadership practice was encouraged (Hodkinson and Hodkinson 2005). Weekly one-to-one meetings ensured priorities were agreed and acted on. The agenda was set by *learning-leaders*:

that slight bit of trepidation like going to meet with Rita and thinking: 'What have I done?' did force me to think – yeah I have got this in my overview; I wasn't going to do it till next week but I think I better get kicked off. So it keeps the pace of your work up, keeps Rita fully engaged with it but also just let me have my space. (Diana)

One-to-one reflective conversations were challenging. Rita 'challenged me constantly' (Jessica). Michael, Lawrence and Di referred to 'hard talk' once they became senior leaders. Nevertheless, each constructed these spaces for reflective practice as learning opportunities. Lawrence valued the questioning of priorities:

she will push you really hard in one to one conversations, in meetings. She will ask you really challenging questions about why we are doing certain things and it might be quite clear that it is the right thing to do. She really wants you to think through why you are doing it, what you are doing it for and whether it fits with the bigger picture in the school. (Lawrence)

Differentiated working practices accounted for varying constructions of one-to-one meetings. Samantha was ambivalent. She recounted 'painful' conversations that Rita saw as, 'robust conversation[s]' (Samantha).

Samantha reflected on her leadership approach, 'I have learned through Rita that I am too protective of staff that I manage' (Samantha, adapted from Fuller 2015: 184). Rita's shaping of Samantha's leadership caused discomfort. Rebecca constructed one of these conversations as questioning her 'as a person' (Rebecca, adapted from Fuller 2015: 183). It so undermined her sense of self as a leader that she left the school (see below). *Learning-leaders'* individual positions, dispositions and capital as well as the power relations of headship are discussed further below (Hodkinson and Hodkinson 2003, 2004b, 2005; McGregor 2003).

Expanding Leadership Repertoires

SUPPORTING LEADERSHIP LEARNING OPPORTUNITIES OUTSIDE SCHOOL

External leadership learning opportunities consisted of a variety of experiences, 'She really does push visits [to] other schools, meeting other people, going and seeing experiences as opposed to just simply [attending] the course' (Michael). Visiting schools and listening to others was important for Rita as a continuing learner (MacBeath 2007). Colleagues were expected to integrate their learning in school. *Learning-leaders* were challenged to take risks in developing leadership outside their comfort zone. Di and Michael spoke at professional conferences and provided school-to-school support. Di described her trepidation:

> She gets us to do presentations to visiting people, teachers or on a national level and she takes you entirely out of your comfort zone. I hate doing them; I really, really dislike doing them but recognise the fact that it is something that will develop you further. [...] afterwards I feel a lot better and I know it has contributed to my development in some way, but I never look forward to them. (Di)

Talks at other schools were not always received well. Michael built up resilience as well as presentation skills:

> We used to do the circuit of going to schools [...] you may as well stand in front of a dart board because you can see the venom and the hatred about [saying] 'this is what

we do' [...] We used to do the circuits and I built up my confidence and experience and all [the] technical skills. (Michael)

Professional identities were further developed by crossing boundaries inside and outside school (Hodkinson and Hodkinson 2005). Engagement in system leadership was demonstrated by committing staff to supporting other schools in the improvement of teaching and learning for young people more widely (Hopkins and Higham 2007). A 'virtuous circle' approach meant *learning-leaders* were expected to emulate Rita in bringing back ideas. The articulation to others of successful practice increased staff self-confidence:

> they've got something that's special that people want to know about. So again, that helps create a climate and a culture of 'We're doing something good.' I know it's hard work – because it is hard work here – you do have to step up when you come here, but they feel, you know, that sort of positive moral purpose. (Rita)

Learning-leaders were encouraged to attend specific courses necessary to the school's management and organisation as well as for their development. Michael attended an aspiring headteacher's programme; his learning about Ofsted inspection preparation impacted on his line management of temporary assistant headteachers in school, talks to deputy headteacher audiences in other local authorities and to audiences visiting the school through its work with the National College. *Learning-leaders* constructed a wide range of leadership learning opportunities (Hodkinson and Hodkinson 2005). Lucy's secondment to the local authority broadened her perspective. Di's articulation of good teaching and learning practice was developed by mentoring student teachers in partnership with a local university. Samantha represented the school with respect to professional support services. Each of these experiences afforded an opportunity to think differently about leadership and/or the leadership of learning (Hodkinson and Hodkinson 2005).

ROTATING ROLES AND RESPONSIBILITIES

Learning-leaders in substantive senior posts expanded their leadership repertoires by rotating roles and responsibilities. These opportunities went beyond school or government priorities (Hodkinson and Hodkinson 2005). In Rita's opinion, Lucy had been side-lined before Rita was appointed,

> She was the only woman, and she was of course doing community. So we brought her back in and gave her a curriculum [role]. (Rita)

Diana took on a head of year role to expand her pastoral leadership. Rita made decisions about leadership responsibilities with *learning-leaders'* development in mind as well as the school's needs:

> if you look at the jobs and roles she has given people within the curriculum team and within SLT you can see that it's not always the jobs that you would naturally give someone because it is not their strength. It is often a developmental issue … Rita and I were deciding which [responsibilities] to give [heads of year], it was a very careful thought about what do they need to do? What do they need to show they can do to progress at the next level? Or what do they need to do to improve as a head of year and assistant headteacher in the future? (Lawrence)

Michael expected to offer colleagues at his new school 'a leadership portfolio' (Michael) that would provide training and experience to enable their progression within and outside the school. He would replicate what he gained by working with Rita. These practices pre-dated approaches to succession planning promoted by the National College (Barnes 2010) and extended beyond the school's or government's priorities (Hodkinson and Hodkinson 2005).

Working Beyond the School

MENTORING FORMALLY AND INFORMALLY THROUGH NETWORKS

Similarly, networking between local schools was established before New Labour's second term of government[3] promoted collaborative working

3   New Labour were in power in the United Kingdom between 1997 and 2010. The second term of government was 2001–5.

in a way that resonates with Rutherford and Jackson's (2006) account. Knowledge was exchanged between schools when *learning-leaders* provided support to schools and other school staff were invited to Alan Road. There was collaborative working between Alan Road School and schools led by Lucy and Diana as well as schools in geographical and national networks.

Lucy, Diana and Jessica spoke of socialising outside work with women as former and current colleagues. Coleman (2010) reported women-only networks benefit women in providing informal mentoring and coaching as well as role models for junior women. That was Jessica's experience. It was a space Rita used to transmit her educational values with respect to her passion for children's education.

Lucy had a close longstanding relationship with Rita that extended beyond working at Alan Road School:

> She is a woman's woman [...]. I think there are probably few friendships in my own case in terms of where it is actually a work colleague, a fellow head. I would say there [are] only Rita and one other where I feel that total trust; total you know. Because I think people are quite wary really [...]. There is always that support; there is never that fear of competition. (Lucy)

Men were excluded from this network but Michael reflected on leadership practice when he socialised with colleagues (women and men) following school-to-school support visits.

Discussion

It is easy to construct the SLT at Alan Road School as a community of practice with Rita as 'full participant'; the *learning-leaders* gradually gaining more authority from legitimate peripheral participation to become 'full participants' as headteachers themselves (Lave and Wenger 1991). There is evidence of alignment with the dominant leadership discourse, imagination of headship, and engagement with the Alan Road School leadership discourse (Wenger 1998). The features of an expansive learning environment might be matched to a set of everyday SLT working practices (Hodkinson and Hodkinson 2005). However, that would confine this account of headteacher preparation to a labelling exercise (O'Neill 2003). Critical leadership scholarship requires an exploration of *learning-leaders'* positions, dispositions and capital (Hodkinson and Hodkinson 2004b) as well as the power relations of headship (McGregor 2003).

Learning-leaders were disposed to being open-minded, challenged and thoughtful. They constructed a broad range of experiences (including painful ones) as opportunities for learning. The practices that marked out their preparation for headship as extra-ordinary were Rita's commitment to rehearsing them in leadership conversations (coaching); creating spaces for reflection on leadership priorities and practice; and expanding the leadership repertoire by providing opportunities to take on temporary senior leadership roles, to rotate roles, and access external facing leadership roles. The level of challenge offered and the less positive responses of two *learning-leaders* (Samantha and Rebecca) bear further consideration.

Positions, Disposition and Capital

Educational theorists have used Bourdieu's social theory to consider educational policy (Blackmore 2010a; Thomson 2005), knowledge production (Gunter 2002, 2003, 2006a) and school leadership (Lingard and Christie 2003; Thomson 2010; Fuller 2013) as well as gender (McLeod 2005), social class (Reay 1995) and race (McKnight and Chandler 2012). Hodkinson and Hodkinson (2003, 2004a, 2004b, 2005) draw on Bourdieu's notion of habitus or disposition to argue that learning environments need to become more expansive in order to maximise 'the potential for effective learning, and the likelihood that more teachers will avail themselves of the opportunities that are available' (2005: 128).

In this expansive leadership learning environment, the importance of position, disposition and capital featured large in Samantha's account of leadership preparation. As deputy headteacher, she enjoyed the benefits of external facing work the status afforded her (see above). Automatic access to meetings for someone deputising formally for the headteacher contrasted with barriers for a bursar or business manager (see Woods 2009 for further discussion of school business managers). Samantha loosened the boundaries of her non-teaching senior leadership role by volunteering to take on additional aspects of school leadership work. Her responsibilities included financial, personnel and site management, school development planning, health and safety, and Building Schools for the Future (BSF) project work. Despite previous management experience in further education, Samantha did not aspire to headship for three main reasons. First, as a member of non-teaching staff she constructed herself as lacking embodied disposition and cultural capital. Headteachers in England have not needed a teaching qualification since 2001. PricewaterhouseCoopers (2007) recommended the extension of the National Professional Qualification for Headship (NPQH) (not mandatory since 2012) to staff without Qualified Teacher Status (QTS). In her words, lack of QTS placed Samantha on 'dodgy ground' (Samantha); it meant she 'struggle[d]' (Samantha) to manage pupil behaviour. The school's performance was judged on teaching and learning outcomes and she was unable to advise teachers about improving practice. She felt 'nervous' and 'uncomfortable' (Samantha) in taking a lead on school development planning as a non-teaching leader. However, no one questioned her ability to take on a SLT position 'so it is probably all in my head but that is still the way you feel isn't it?' (Samantha). Second, she desired 'some form of another life' (Samantha). A heavy workload had been re-negotiated and managed. A non-teaching contract meant Samantha was not entitled to teachers' holidays. Rita encouraged her to take time off in lieu and agreed to time off during term-time. Such flexibility was unusual. Samantha recorded additional hours worked but that was not requested. She stopped taking work home preferring to start early, finish late and leave work behind. Nevertheless, she worked beyond the 48 hour European Working Time Directive, as do headteachers (Halliday-Bell et al. 2008). Third, Samantha was overawed by the size of a headteacher's job and Rita's capacity for it. Rita's attention to detail and flexibility were admired:

> She might be talking to a teacher about [...] that they need to improve something in
> their lessons for example one minute and then walking round the school telling the

caretaker that the bins need emptying more frequently. And she can do that breadth, and I can't do that to the level that she does it. I have never seen anybody able to do that and keep all those things in her head at any one time. (Samantha)

She denied having capacity to cover such breadth but also described her role being concerned with unblocking toilets as well as strategic planning.

For Rebecca, a single incident led to a change of direction. The dialogue with Rita in a one-to-one reflective meeting was interpreted as a challenge to her commitment:

[Rita] changed the way she treated me perhaps in some respects and questioned some of the things I'd done, and perhaps she didn't agree with the way that she'd done that. (Rebecca)

Others noted a change in Rita's approach when they joined the SLT. The coaching conversation was seen as 'questioning me as a person actually' (Rebecca, adapted from Fuller 2015: 182), in a way that others did not interpret such conversations. It was sufficiently upsetting for Rebecca to seek reaffirmation of her ability from others. Eventually she asked Rita:

'Do you still want me working here?' And she said she did and she was very upset I think about the effect it had had on me. And perhaps realised the mistake she had made. [...] I lost confidence in myself and so I just carried on and then just thought maybe it's time for a change. (Rebecca)

Subsequently Rita resourced external coaching sessions for Rebecca as an attempt to resolve the situation. These enabled Rebecca to re-examine the incident and her career from alternative perspectives.

Rebecca chose the next school carefully and was content to work in a different SLT where she was a driving force. She constructed the move as an opportunity to extend her leadership repertoire in a way that had not been possible at Alan Road School. This construction of a restrictive learning environment contrasted with the experience of role rotation described by others as normal practice. It may indicate Rebecca's different disposition, her restricted access to opportunities or lack of recognition by Rita of what she needed in her leadership development.

Power Relations of Headship

Blackmore's (1989) feminist reconstruction of leadership has been used to consider women's and men's leadership discourse regarding the use of power to empower or the use of power to control (Fuller 2013). Rita's leadership drew on multiple feminist discourses as well as the dominant educational policy discourse to ensure the school was judged to be effective (Fuller 2015). Aspects of her leadership also resonated with a masculinist construction of leadership. The unequal power relations of headship were evident in accounts of 'hard talk' (see above) and of Rita's 'intransigence around nonnegotiable practices' (Fuller 2015: 185). Michael described mutual frustration, 'you want to strangle each other after meetings, oh God [...]. It is never a bed of roses with Rita' (Michael). There was a sense of *learning-leaders* being differently adept at working round Rita with some fully aware of their own compliance and thwarted challenges to Rita's authority by others. Jessica espoused Rita's educational values whilst working in the school but reverted to managerial approaches adopted in a previous career that were learned from her father's experience in industry.

The negative impacts of headship power relations were clearly articulated by Samantha and Rebecca. In Samantha's account there was an acute awareness of the power located in Rita as headteacher. Samantha successfully challenged the school's development planning and target setting practices to secure change (see above). She felt confident to lead the school in Rita's absence. However, Rita's aversion to bureaucracy led Samantha to state:

> That is always the key, working out whether Rita is going to like it or not, you know. Because there were some times where there are occasions that I would have done things in a different way, but the buck stops with her. It is painful occasionally when we don't agree, it is quite painful for both of us actually but we have got a lot better on that. I have a tendency, when I'm stressed, to ramble and then what happens is that she can misinterpret what I've said because I'm actually exploring things in my head. I am not actually very clear necessarily. [...] and then she will get frustrated with me or annoyed with me because she thinks what I am saying is rubbish. And then it gets very messy. (Samantha)

Although she was not 'scared' of conflict Samantha described these confrontations as 'painful' (Samantha) on four separate occasions and feelings of discomfort three times. She described Rita as 'frustrated', 'pissed off', 'unhappy' (Samantha), and concerned staff saw some safeguarding practices as 'a waste of time' (Samantha). Responsible for ensuring the school was compliant with statutory regulations for first aid training, Samantha sought a compromise regarding staff training for the use of EpiPen injectors during school visits:

> Well it's not a compromise because we've based it [*sic*] around until Rita is happy, because I was happy before. [...] it depends how you interpret [the guidelines]. I've found we've got to do it, we are supposed to do it and the head is going round saying: 'I'm not having people doing it; it is a complete waste of their time'. And in some schools it just wouldn't have been done, because ultimately you always bow to the head don't you, so we just would have ended up without training probably in some situations. (Samantha)

The conversation had not been 'easy' (Samantha). It was what Rita called a 'robust conversation' (Samantha) but an example of what was sometimes 'an absolute nightmare' (Samantha) when working relationships with the headteacher were dysfunctional. At the same time Rita was trying to alter Samantha's staff management (see above). Rita's resistance of government policy and excessively bureaucratic practices countered the dominant discourse to which Samantha was trying to conform.

Rita's power relationships extended beyond the school. Despite networking arrangements, Samantha was aware of competition between schools and by extension between headteachers:

> some of the bursars don't appreciate their audience. [...] I am very wary talking to a headteacher [...]. It depends what it is but you do have to be careful don't you? Because we are in a competitive environment, and they all know each other and you don't want to say anything out of turn that is going to get back to anybody. (Samantha)

Samantha was not free to speak openly in meetings designed for collaborative working between schools. Di recognised the extent of Rita's power relations beyond the school through the currency of a reference and recommendation for promotion:

Rita's word will be volumes within the [local authority], [...] I think she would also
have a very big say in which school [Di applied to] because [...] it would matter to
me actually that if she didn't recommend the school that I was going to, that I was
suggesting then it wouldn't be the right one. (Di)

In direct contrast to Rebecca, Di trusted Rita's judgement implicitly about
the direction her career might take.

Conclusion

In this chapter, I have outlined twelve practices that constitute a process
of headship preparation as it occurred successfully in one school. The process was conceptualised as taking place in an expansive leadership learning
environment. I have also demonstrated that position, disposition, access
to capital and power relations impact greatly on an individual's leadership aspirations and achievement of them, even within a senior leadership
team constructed largely as an expansive leadership learning environment.
There was much in Samantha's and Rebecca's accounts that demonstrated
misalignment, lack of imagination and disengagement with Rita's, and the
dominant accepted leadership discourse in the school (Fuller 2015). The
power located in the headteacher was used to empower and enable others
in a way that resonated with multiple feminist discourses (Fuller 2015). It
was also used to control *learning-leaders* and shape their leadership in ways
that could be described as a masculinist leadership discourse (Fuller 2013).
A critical approach has revealed that members of the SLT who achieved
promoted posts, including headship, aligned and engaged with Rita's leadership discourse, accommodated it for the duration of their headteacher
preparation, or resisted it with varying consequences for their careers and
well-being. The implications for aspiring headteachers are clear with respect
to securing a SLT post working with a headteacher who prioritises learning
opportunities for leaders.

References

Barton, D., and Tusting, K. (eds) (2005). *Beyond Communities of Practice*. Cambridge: Cambridge University Press.

Blackmore, J. (2010). 'Policy, Practice and Purpose in the Field of Education: A Critical Review'. *Critical Studies in Education* 51 (1), 101–11.

Bush, T. (2011). 'Succession Planning in England: New Leaders and New Forms of Leadership'. *School Leadership & Management: Formerly School Organisation* 31 (3), 181–98.

Coleman, M. (2001). 'Achievement Against The Odds: The Female Secondary Headteachers in England and Wales'. *School Leadership and Management* 21 (1), 75–100.

Coleman, M. (2002). *Women as Headteachers: Striking the Balance*. Stoke on Trentl: Trentham Books.

Coleman, M. (2010). 'Women-Only (Homophilous) Networks Supporting Women Leaders in Education'. *Journal of Educational Administration* 48 (6), 769–81.

Coleman, M. (2011). *Women at the Top*. London: Palgrave Macmillan.

Daresh, J., and Male, T. (2000). 'Crossing the Border into Leadership: Experiences of Newly Appointed British Headteachers and American Principals'. *Educational Management and Administration* 28 (1), 89–101.

Daresh, J., and Male, T. (2001). 'Pluses and Minuses of British Headteacher Reform: Toward a Vision of Instructional Leadership'. Paper presented at the fifteenth annual meeting of the University Council of Educational Administration (Cincinnati, 2–4 November 2001).

Department for Education and Skills (2004). *National Standards for Headteachers*.

Frost, D. (2006) 'The Concept of "Agency" in Leadership for Learning'. *Leading and Managing* 12 (2), 19–28.

Fuller, A. (2007). 'Critiquing Theories of Learning and Communities of Practice'. In J. Hughes, N. Jewson and L. Unwin (eds), *Communities of Practice: Critical Perspectives*, 17–29. London: Routledge.

Fuller, A., and Unwin, L. (2003). 'Learning as Apprentices in the Contemporary UK Workplace: Creating and Managing Expansive and Restrictive Participation'. *Journal of Education and Work* 16 (4), 407–26.

Fuller, K. (2009). 'Women Secondary Head Teachers: Alive and Well in Birmingham at the Beginning of the Twenty-First Century'. *Management in Education* 23 (1), 19–31.

Fuller, K. (2013). *Gender, Identity and Educational Leadership*. London: Bloomsbury.

Fuller, K. (2014). 'Gendered Educational Leadership: Beneath the Monoglossic Façade'. *Gender and Education* 26 (4), 321–37.

Fuller, K. (2015). 'Learning Gendered Leadership: A Discursive Struggle'. In E. Reilly and Q. Bauer (eds), *Women Leading Education across the Continents: Overcoming the Barriers*, 181–6. Lanham, MD: Rowman and Littlefield.

Gee, J. (2000). 'New People in New Worlds: Networks, the New Capitalism and Schools'. In B. Cope and M. Kalantzis (eds), *Multiliteracies: Literacy Learning and the Design of School Futures*, 43–68. London: Routledge.

Grogan, M., and Shakeshaft, C. (2011). *Women and Educational Leadership*. San Francisco: Jossey-Bass.

Gunter, H. (2002). 'Purposes and Positions in the Field of Education Management: Putting Bourdieu to Work'. *Educational Management and Administration* 30 (2), 7–26.

Gunter, H. (2003). 'Intellectual Histories in the Field of Education Management in the UK'. *International Journal of Leadership in Education: Theory and Practice* 6 (4), 335–49.

Gunter, H. (2006). 'Knowledge Production in the Field of Educational Leadership: A Place for Intellectual Histories'. *Journal of Educational Administration and History* 38 (2), 201–15.

Gunter, H. (2005). *Leading Teachers*, London: Continuum.

Halliday-Bell, D., Jennings, D., Kennard, M., McKay, J., Reid, H., and Walter, N. (2008). *Mission Possible: Strategies for Managing Headship*. Nottingham: National College for School Leadership.

Hammersley-Fletcher, L., and Brundrett, M. (2005). 'Leaders on Leadership: The Impressions of Primary School Head Teachers and Subject Leaders'. *School Leadership and Management: Formerly School Organisation* 25 (1), 59–75.

Hodkinson, P., and Hodkinson, H. (2003). 'Individuals, Communities of Practice and the Policy Context: School-Teachers' Learning in their Workplace'. *Studies in Continuing Education* 25 (1), 3–21.

Hodkinson, H., and Hodkinson, P. (2004a). 'Rethinking the Concept of Community of Practice in Relation to Schoolteachers' Workplace Learning'. *International Journal of Training and Development* 8 (1), 21–31.

Hodkinson, P., and Hodkinson, H. (2004b). 'The Significance of Individuals' Dispositions in Workplace Learning: A Case Study of Two Teachers'. *Journal of Education and Work* 17 (2), 167–82.

Hodkinson, H., and Hodkinson, P. (2005). 'Improving Schoolteachers' Workplace Learning'. *Research Papers in Education* 20 (2), 109–31.

Holden, G. (2008). 'Knowledge-Building and Networking: The Leadership for Learning Case'. *School Leadership and Management: Formerly School Organisation* 28 (4), 307–22.

Hopkins, D., and Higham, R. (2007). 'System Leadership: Mapping the Landscape'. *School Leadership and Management: Formerly School Organisation* 27 (2), 147–66.

Hughes, J., Jewson, N., and Unwin, L. (eds) (2007). *Communities of Practice: Critical Perspectives*. London: Routledge.

Lave, J., and Wenger, E. (1991). *Situated Learning: Legitimate Peripheral Participation*. Cambridge: Cambridge University Press.

Lingard, B., and Christie, P. (2003). 'Leading Theory: Bourdieu and the Field of Educational Leadership. An Introduction and Overview to this Special Issue'. *International Journal of Leadership in Education: Theory and Practice* 6 (4), 317–33.

MacBeath, J. (2007). 'Leadership as a Subversive Activity'. *Journal of Educational Administration* 45 (3), 242–64.

McGregor, J. (2003). 'Collaboration in Communities of Practice'. In N. Bennett and L. Anderson (eds), *Rethinking Educational Leadership*, 113–30. London: SAGE.

McKnight, D., and Chandler, P. (2012). 'The Complicated Conversation of Class and Race in Social and Curricular Analysis: An Examination of Pierre Bourdieu's Interpretative Framework in Relation to Race'. *Educational Philosophy and Theory* 44 (S1), 74–97.

McLeod, J. (2005). 'Feminists Re-Reading Bourdieu: Old Debates and New Questions about Gender Habitus and Gender Change'. *Theory and Research in Education* 3 (11), 11–30.

Møller, J. (2009). 'Learning to Share: A Vision of Leadership Practice'. *International Journal of Leadership in Education: Theory and Practice* 12 (3), 253–67.

Morley, I., and Hosking, D.-M. (2003). 'Leadership, Learning and Negotiation in a Social Psychology of Organizing'. In N. Bennett and L. Anderson (eds), *Rethinking Educational Leadership*, 43–59, London: SAGE.

O'Neill, J. (2003). 'Understanding Curriculum Leadership in the Secondary School'. In N. Bennett and L. Anderson (eds), *Rethinking Educational Leadership*, 143–56. London: SAGE.

Paechter, C. (2003). 'Learning Masculinities and Femininities: Power/Knowledge and Legitimate Peripheral Participation'. *Women's Studies International Forum* 26 (6), 541–52.

Paechter, C. (2006). 'Power, Knowledge and Embodiment in Communities of Sex/Gender Practice'. *Women's Studies International Forum* 29 (1), 13–26.

PricewaterhouseCoopers (2007). *Independent Study into School Leadership*. DfES.

Reay, D. (1995). '"They Employ Cleaners To Do That": Habitus in the Primary Classroom'. *British Journal of Sociology of Education* 16 (3), 353–71.

Rhodes, C., and Brundrett, M. (2006). 'The Identification, Development, Succession and Retention of Leadership Talent in Contextually Different Primary Schools: A Case Study Located Within the English West Midlands'. *School Leadership and Management: Formerly School Organisation* 26 (3), 269–87.

Rhodes, C., Brundrett, M., and Nevill, A. (2009) 'Just the Ticket? The National Professional Qualification and the Transition to Headship in the East Midlands of England'. *Educational Review* 61 (4), 449–68.

Ribbins, P. (2007). 'Interviews in Educational Research: Conversations with a Purpose'. In A. Briggs and M. Coleman (eds), *Research Methods in Educational Leadership and Management*, 207–23. London: SAGE.

Rutherford, D., and Jackson, L. (2006). 'Setting Up School Partnerships: Some Insights from Birmingham's Collegiate Academies'. *School Leadership and Management: Formerly School Organisation* 26 (5), 437–51.

Shields, C., and Edwards, M. (2005). *Dialogue is Not Just Talk*. New York: Peter Lang.

Simkins, T. (2009). 'Integrating Work-Based Learning into Large-Scale National Leadership Development Programmes in the UK'. *Educational Review* 61 (4), 391–405.

Stoll, L., Bolam, R., McMahon, A., Wallace, M., and Thomas, S. (2006). 'Professional Learning Communities: A Review of the Literature'. *Journal of Educational Change* 7 (4), 221–58.

Thomson, P. (2005). 'Bringing Bourdieu to Policy Sociology: Codification, Misrecognition and Exchange Value in the UK Context'. *Journal of Education Policy* 20 (6), 741–58.

Thomson, P. (2010). 'Headteacher Autonomy: A Sketch of a Bourdieuian Field Analysis of Position and Practice'. *Critical Studies in Education* 51 (1), 5–20.

Waterhouse, J. (2008). 'Raising Aspirations Within School Communities: The Learning Catalysts Project'. *School Leadership and Management: Formerly School Organisation* 28 (4), 369–84.

Wenger, E. (1998). *Communities of Practice: Learning, Meaning and Identity*. Cambridge: Cambridge University Press.

Wenger, E., McDermott, R., and Snyder, W. (2002). *Cultivating Communities of Practice*. Cambridge, MA: Harvard Business School Press.

Wise, C. (2003). 'Leaders of Subject Communities'. In N. Bennett and L. Anderson (eds), *Rethinking Educational Leadership*, 131–42. London: SAGE.

Woods, C. (2009). 'Remodelling and Distributed Leadership: The Case of the School Business Manager'. In C. Chapman and H. Gunter (eds), *Radical Reforms: Perspectives in an Era of Educational Change*, 80–90. Abingdon: Routledge.

Woods, P., Bennett N., Harvey, J., and Wise, C. (2004). 'Variabilities and Dualities in Distributed Leadership: Findings From A Systematic Literature Review'. *Educational Management Administration & Leadership* 32 (4), 439–57.

Yin, R. (2009). *Case Study Research Design and Methods*. London: SAGE.

MARY CUNNEEN AND JUDITH HARFORD

Gender Matters: Women's Experience of the Route to Principalship in Ireland

Introduction

Research suggests that school leadership globally remains a male dominated arena and that the image of the leader continues to remain effectively vested in the masculine (Coleman 2003, 2011; Fitzgerald 2015). This situation obtains despite the fact that teaching is a profession which, in many countries, is dominated by women. In the Irish context, men continue to hold a disproportionate number of senior posts across all sections of education (Lynch, Grummell and Devine 2012) with men twice as likely as women to accede to the position of post-primary school principal (Department of Education and Skills 2012).[1] Why then is a profession dominated by women promoting a disproportionate number of males to the ranks of its leadership? This is a complex field involving the intersection of a range of influences of a cultural, societal, organisational and personal nature and it

---

1   Post-primary education in the Republic of Ireland is executed through the medium of three sectors; the voluntary secondary sector, the community and comprehensive sector and the Educational and Training Boards. The origins of these sectors are historically, culturally and religiously defined. Churches of both Catholic and Protestant persuasions, having once owned and managed the majority of schools, have extended influence over voluntary secondary schools via Boards of Management and Trusteeships. They constitute the bulk of post-primary education. The state owned Community and Comprehensive sector are managed by Boards of Management of differing compositions including a share by religious denominations. The ETBs are vocational state established schools, providing a variety of state examination options to all levels.

is in the analysis of 'what lies between' (Acker 1992: 142) as opposed to the scrutiny of any one variable that new knowledge and understanding will be gleaned. Over recent decades, feminist researchers (notably Coleman 1996; Evetts, 1994; Fitzgerald 2003; Fuller 2009; Hall 1996; McLay 2008; Shakeshaft 1987; Sperandio 2010; Smith 2011a) have attempted to identify the impediments to principalship accession, with a particular emphasis on the perceived enabling and constraining influences. This scrutiny paves the way for a closer inspection of women's interpretation of principalship and the actions they take when forging a career path.

Building on the pioneering work of Marianne Coleman, in the area of gender and educational leadership, this chapter contributes to this research agenda. It reports a study undertaken from a life story perspective, in the life history tradition, of the perceived enabling and constraining influences which a cohort of twelve women principals articulate as informing their career pathway to principalship in Ireland. It is not suggested that these influences have an objective status; rather, they constitute one set of perspectives that exist alongside others in order to, in the fullness of time, provide a more comprehensive picture of the situation. Ireland constitutes a good site for engaging in such research as while it represents international trends, it also has an idiosyncratic dimension; up until the demise of nuns in Catholic girls' schools, women religious (nuns) dominated the principalship in girls' religious-order run schools.

Theorising Women's Relationship with Teaching

The feminisation of the paid work force across the twentieth century as well as the introduction of gender equity policies led to an expectation that demographic changes would emerge (Fitzgerald 2015). Despite their numerical advantage within teaching ranks and their successful leadership of teachers at middle management level (MacRuairc and Harford 2011), there is a dearth of female school leaders across many countries. This has implications not only for women themselves and for the advancement of their careers within education but also raises issues for those being taught, irrespective of their gender (Cubillo and Brown 2003). As Hall (1999: 159) cautions:

> Analysts of education management acknowledge the disparity between women's numbers in the teaching profession and their representation at senior levels. We have all become sophisticated in interpreting and explaining these figures. We are less proactive in rigorously thinking through the consequences of this disparity for the educational and employment opportunities of girls and boys, men and women.

The lack of attention to gender balance at leadership level within schools has, as noted by Coleman (2002), implications for social interpretation and resulting consequential reproduction of the hegemonic norm. While disquiet has been voiced at the low number of males inhabiting the teaching ranks at both primary and post-primary levels, the same concentration of concern has not been evident when considering the significant lack of meaningful female representation at senior management level in schools (Coleman and Fitzgerald 2008).

Historically, women's relationship with teaching has been a complex one. Teaching was one of the first occupations considered respectable for middle-class women viewed in many ways as an extension of the nurturing role (Redmond and Harford 2010). Much of the rhetoric surrounding women's admission to university education internationally throughout the late nineteenth and early twentieth centuries emphasised the idealised and romanticised role which women would play as teachers (Harford 2008). At various intervals single women teachers were valued over married and *vice versa*. The discourse surrounding the premium placed on single *versus* married women teachers testifies to the way in which women's marital status has been historically viewed as central to their identity as teachers. It also reflects the tension between the 'image of true womanhood' and women's position as paid members of the labour force (Prentice and Theobald 1991: 6). Newman (1994: 193) suggests that teaching offers women 'quasi-familial roles and identities around a core of male hierarchies and privileges'. The so-called 'caring' dimension which teaching requires and/or provides has been the focus of considerable scrutiny by scholars (Acker 1995; Drudy 2009). Acker and Feuverger (1996: 402) caution, however, that an over-emphasis on caring detracts from a deeper understanding of the other core dimensions of the role and may 'discourage women from expressing emotions that might be at odds with the caring script'. This tendency to equate women with the more caring aspects of the teaching role has meant that women have tended to occupy the more pastoral roles at middle management levels (Cubillo and Brown 2003). Sexual stereotypes and gendered occupational structures have thus shaped the experiences of women teachers internationally throughout the twentieth century (Redmond and Harford 2010).

Interrogating the Terrain: The Perceived Challenges and Enablers Women Identify in their Journey towards Principalship

Much of the scholarship on gender and educational leadership has engaged with the issue of barriers for women (Blackmore 1999; Coleman 2001; 2005; Kellerman and Rhode 2007; Coleman and Fitzgerald 2008; Lynch et al. 2012). In interrogating the perceived impediments for women to educational leadership roles, a number of scholars have pointed to the significance of socialisation and stereotyping (Cubillo and Brown 2003). Schmuck (1986) cautions against the adoption of this 'deficit' approach, while Smith (2011b) points to the importance of recognising women's agency. Eagly and Carli (2007) argue that within the working environment, men are perceived as more agentic than women, thereby acceding to and attaining a greater number of leadership positions. Women, they note, are constrained by the double bind which frowns on assertive and strategic pursuit of career goals on one hand, while at the same time lauding more traditional feminine behaviours. Other scholars have focused on issues around women's lack of confidence, lack of competitiveness and a fear of failure (Cubillo and Brown 2003). McGregor and Elliot (2005) have noted that fear of failure, a trait considered as curtailing leadership ambition among women, is a result of childhood socialisation, informing one's general perception of self. Coleman (2002) too has highlighted the role which self-confidence plays when considering headship application. She notes that women often consider their gender an inhibiting factor leading to a decreased sense of confidence. More recently scholars have drawn attention to how traits such as conflict avoidance and diplomacy can help women to be more successful, effective leaders. Although the leadership styles of men and women are not mutually exclusive (Gronn 1999; Keohane 2010), women leaders tend to demonstrate more democratic and collaborative leadership behaviours than men (Eagly and Carli 2007).

A model which takes account of the various complexities of this subject is one which examines the issue at a macro socio-political, meso organisational and micro individual level. The interweaving of the macro (cultural/socio-political), meso (societal/organisational) and micro (societal/personal) (Cubillo and Brown 2003) elements which inform career trajectories allows for a richer understanding of why women choose to pursue a path towards principalship and the perceived enabling and constraining influences which they meet on that journey.

Analysis of the macro level (cultural/socio-political dimensions) which has an impact on women's careers focuses on the hegemonic traditions and culture of a particular country or region which women must negotiate (ibid.). Considering this specifically in relation to the Irish experience, the promise and potential of Irish independence did not provide the opportunities for women that many had expected. The decades immediately following the establishment of the Irish Free State (1922) saw the development of a gendered ideology that, apart from females in religious life, placed women firmly within the home sphere through an alliance between the state and the Catholic Church (Redmond and Harford 2010). According to Dunn (1988: 89), Irish society under the Free State government was 'deeply rooted in a complex and apparently inseparable mixture of nationalism and Catholicism'. The established values and ethos of the Catholic Church were thus placed at the centre of the nascent political system (O' Donoghue and Harford 2011). The merging of a national identity deeply rooted in a Catholic tradition had a deep and lasting impact on Irish society and was especially restrictive of the role and freedom of women. The one exception in this regard was nuns as principals of schools run by female religious orders up until the early 1970s. Although Catholic Ireland fostered a conservative society which placed women firmly within the domestic sphere, at the same time it provided leadership opportunities for women religious who played key roles in education and health, disrupting the wife/mother binary and subtly challenging the male hegemonic norm (O'Donoghue and Harford 2014).

Analysis of the meso-level (societal/organisational dimensions) allows for a focus on power relations within organisations and the often hierarchical and paternalistic nature of educational institutions (Cubillo and Brown 2003). In relation to education in Ireland, Lynch et al. (2012) note that with the rise of neo-liberalism as a global political ideology, it has increasingly become market driven, fostering a 'for-profit' mentality at the expense of caring and nurturing. Such commodification of education has created a climate in schools concerned with measurable outcomes, one that dissuades and discourages potential principal applicants.

Primarily it is still women who attend to the majority of domestic and familial duties (Keohane 2011). The inherent basic assumption that domestic responsibilities are largely taken care of by an-other is therefore propagated and reproduced (Hall 1996). Having a career and a family or other dependents, poses challenges for those who work outside of the home. On this, both Coleman (1996; 2002) and Shakeshaft et al. (2007) have noted from reassessment surveys concerning research they had earlier conducted in the British and American contexts that the structures governing domestic responsibilities did not alter very much over time. While changes have occurred which show that men now participate more in the execution of domestic responsibilities, it is the female who still bears the greater burden, placing her in the difficult position of having to execute many roles; wife, mother, daughter or carer to others who rely on her for support (Coleman 2002). Coleman's study of headteachers in England and Wales in 2005, found that male headteachers typically had more children than their female counterparts and relied to a considerable extent on their partners to care for them (Coleman 2005). Female headteachers, on the other hand, relied typically on 'childminders, nurseries and relatives' (ibid.: 21). Many women who became headteachers had, at some stage, put their own careers on hold or had worked part-time prior to obtaining the post of headteacher, leaving the male partner freer to pursue his career goals.

More broadly, Keohane (2011: 9) summarises the conflicts faced by females who inhabit work and non-work spaces succinctly when she notes:

> Few organisations (or nation states) have workplace practices that support family-friendly life-styles including high quality, reliable, affordable child-care facilities, flexible work schedules while children are young, and support for anyone with a sick or aging parent [...] it does take two committed partners, healthy children, lots of stamina, enough of money to pay for good childcare and housekeeping, strategic planning worthy of a mid-size firm-and a fair amount of luck.

Finally, interrogation of the micro level (societal/personal dimensions) shines the spotlight on such variables as levels of confidence and the significance of role-models. More women than men lack confidence in their ability to become a headteacher (Coleman 2002; Young and McLeod 2001; Shakeshaft et al. 2007). On this, Coleman found that women are far more likely than men to feel insecure in relation to applying for principalship and locate this insecurity in a lack of confidence relating to personal issues. She cautions that 'confidence is very important for successful promotion and lack of confidence has been particularly linked to women' (Coleman 2002: 15). Shakeshaft (1987: 84) suggests that women may lack self-confidence in situations which are unfamiliar to them observing: 'we see that women have self-confidence in areas in which they have experience (private sphere functions). Whereas men have self-confidence in areas in which they have been allowed to participate (public sphere functions)'.

Those who lack self-confidence to make the initial steps in application for headship are defined by Smith (2011b) as protégées who depend on colleagues to highlight their strengths. They exhibit a reluctance to put themselves forward for promotion unless encouraged to do so by more senior members of staff, on whose advice and support they depend for career guidance (ibid.). In this way, more senior colleagues can be a determining force for the protégée, informing the decision – making process and the ultimate attainment of occupational advancement. Such colleagues can act as informal mentors and offer solace and counsel when applications for headship have not been successful, thus supplying the impetus for pursuing the desired career objectives even when success seems elusive (ibid.). At the same time, Smith cautions that 'by soliciting direction from senior colleagues the protégée to an extent abdicates responsibility for her career development' thus not extending her personal agency to its capacity (ibid.: 20).

Currently, the role of mentors and role models is considered to be of great importance to potential school leaders. On this, Coleman (2002) advocates the importance of mentoring and considers the lack of role models for aspiring headteachers to be a critical issue. The proliferation of men in headship posts at post-primary level suggests that women need to draw on other sources of inspiration and motivation to encourage career development. Addressing this, Keohane (2011: 9) notes that men are more likely to be mentored in organisations than women and that if senior women are unwilling to assist their younger female colleagues 'and the men aren't sympathetic, you don't get mentored'. Coleman (2011: 63) sums up the imperative of this argument for mentors and role models for women when she notes that 'mentoring, coaching and the existence of role models are vital tools for the support and development of women who are attempting to access senior positions'.

Methodology

The remainder of this chapter details a study undertaken on a life story approach. Life story was the chosen research methodology for this study for as Dimmock and O'Donoghue (1997: 25) note, a greater understanding of the role of principal is obtained by 'examining the socialisation influences relevant to the formation of the principal over the full life experience'. In seeking to give voice to those women who became principals in the Republic of Ireland, life story approach offers a platform which 'accentuates subjectivity' (Casey 1993: 11) while simultaneously situating the informant in the wider cultural and political sphere. It goes beyond statistical and anecdotal evidence to produce 'a generative space for understanding not only the complexity of women's lives but how women construct a gendered self through narrative [...] how they talk about their lives' (Munro 1998: 5).

Life story research in the life history tradition has particular appeal for those who do not have a public outlet for expressing their views. The case for situating professional and personal lives side-by-side and examining them in tandem is made by Weiler (1997: 47) when she states:

> Women teachers' narratives and the descriptions of their lives by contemporary observers both draw upon existing representations of what it means to be a teacher and what it means to be a woman. The descriptions of outside observers tend to draw upon dominant representations to give meaning and shape to the lives they describe, while in their own accounts women teachers represent themselves both through dominant discourses and through counter memories.

The narratives upon which the exposition provided in the rest of this chapter is based approximates the approach of Weiler (1997) and Smith (2011b) who note that life story research written in the life history tradition does not exclude mitigating circumstances but rather forefronts and provides the space to articulate the complexities which inform career trajectories.

Taking cognisance of Goodson and Sikes' (2010: 23) observation that 'adequacy is dependent not upon quantity but upon the richness of the data', the number of participants in this particular study was small and there is no intent to generalise from the study to all women. Rather the study sought insights to produce tentative generalisations which can be tested in larger scale studies, both quantitative and qualitative. Twelve women principals working across a range of schools in the Republic of Ireland were solicited for interview. Those selected were drawn from the four provinces of the Republic of Ireland (Ulster, Munster, Leinster and Connaught) and represented all post-primary educational sectors (voluntary secondary, community/comprehensive and vocational). All of the women taught for a significant number of years (average of 20.4 years). All twelve enjoyed leadership experience prior to taking up the post of principal, while nine of the twelve had a further post-graduate qualification in a related area. Seven of the twelve are married and all of those have children. The participants were sought initially *via* the teacher unions then *via* snowballing (Goodson and Sikes 2010).

Table 1: Principal Cohort

Name	Age	Number of Years Teaching	Number of Years as Principal	Subject Specialism	Posts of Responsibility Occupied	Postgraduate Qualifications	Sector	Urban Rural	Marital Status	Number of Children
Hilda	45–50	22	4	History German	Acting Deputy Principal Deputy Principal	Diploma in Special Needs Diploma in Educational Management	Voluntary Secondary Single Sex	Urban	Married	3
Paula	47	24	1	Religion English	B post, A post Deputy Principal	N/A	Voluntary Secondary Mixed	Rural	Single	N/A
Irene	40–50	22	1	Home Economics	Year Head Home School Liaison Coordinator	Master's in Counselling and Psychotherapy	Voluntary Secondary Mixed	Urban	Married	2
Jane	50–60	27	1	Maths Science	B Post A Post	Master's in Educational Management	Voluntary Secondary Single Sex	Urban	Married	4
Lara	35	10	1	Irish Geography	Deputy Principal	Master's in Education	Comprehensive/ Community	Rural	Single	N/A

Name	Age			Subjects	Position	Qualification	School Type	Location	Marital	Children
Barbara	49	16	13	English French	Home School Liaison Officer	MA in Education	Voluntary Secondary Single Sex	Urban	Married	2
Jennifer	Late 30s	12	2	Art	A Post TY Coordinator	N/A	ETB	Urban	Married	1
Lily	50	14	6	Religion History	B Post Acting Deputy Principal Deputy Principal	Master's in Educational Management	ETB	Rural	Married	2
Breda	40–50	22	2	English History	A Post	Diploma in Psychotherapy Master's in Education	Voluntary Secondary Mixed	Rural	Single	N/A
Maria	Late 40s	24	2	Maths Economics	Acting Deputy Principal Deputy Principal	Diploma in Special Needs Diploma in educational Leadership	Voluntary Secondary Single Sex	Rural	Married	N/A
Natalie	58	32	3	Geography	B Post A Post Deputy Principal	N/A	Community/ Comprehensive	Rural	Married	2
Emma	50–60	20	13	French English	B Post Acting Principal	Diploma in Educational Management	ETB	Rural	Married	4

Data and Discussion

Almost without prompting, the women in this study envisioned their experience of the route towards principalship in terms of a binary – the obstacles they encountered and the enablers which assisted them. While there were subtle differences between what constituted obstacles and enablers for these women, there were obvious commonalities, many of which map to the common themes found across scholarship in this field more broadly, and some of which were shaped by the particular exigencies and circumstances of Irish society. The perceived obstacles and enablers, as articulated by this cohort of women, were as follows:

Perceived Obstacles

- Cultural expectations around who should occupy leadership roles, especially in Catholic-run schools
- Perspectives that organisational cultures did not support childcare-friendly practices
- A neoliberal policy agenda which was at odds with a social justice agenda

Perceived Enablers

- Perspectives on supportive partners and/or family members
- Perspectives on mentors and role models

Cultural Expectations Around Who Should Occupy Leadership Roles, Especially in Catholic-Run Schools

The majority of women in this study were aged forty or over. Their childhoods coincided with a growing appetite for choice and freedom of expression internationally, features of Irish society which had yet to be attained to any significant degree. During their formative years, the Catholic Church enjoyed a close relationship with the government of the day and had done so for decades (O'Donoghue and Harford 2011). This enabled and assisted the promotion of a conservative Irish society concerned with land inheritance, anti-intellectualism and a hierarchical bestowal of power (Lynch et al. 2012). The associated value system promoted the view that women, unless they became nuns, belonged in the private arena of home, carrying out domestic duties and engaging in care responsibilities. In exercising control over education, the Catholic Church ensured, initially, that the role of school principal was occupied by a religious, male or female. With the fall in vocations, the Church then controlled who attained the post of principal through trusteeships and appointments to boards of management. Although post-primary schools in the Republic of Ireland are now answerable to more numerous stakeholders, the legacies of Church control remain.

All of the women spoke at length about the cultural norms in which they worked as teachers and cultural expectations around who should occupy leadership roles. For those working in Catholic-run schools, the expectation they held was that leadership positions in the school would fall to a male, even when it involved nuns handing over the principalship of all-girls' schools. Maria was the first female principal of an all-boys' school in rural Ireland. Her comments reflect the legacy of male religious control of the school which had lasted from the school's foundation in 1923 until 2001. On this she stated:

> When I started first, we had a Brother who was Principal and then he was succeeded by the first lay principal, a man. Men dominated the management structure in the school for many years. Women did the teaching, men did the management. When management roles did come up, I found myself saying – they are all men. How would a woman fit in with that structure?

Maria went on to state that the school was part of a trusteeship to provide Catholic education in the tradition of its male founder. By eventually seeking the deputy-principalship and then the post of principal, Maria tried to incrementally gain access to a leadership role in a school which historically had valued men and side-lined women.

Jane too noted the legacy of patriarchal religious control of her school until very recently. When the religious order retired from direct management of the school in 1986, the first lay principal, a man, was appointed and Jane was appointed to the position of deputy-principal. On this she observed:

> I definitely would have felt it was an interesting time. There had never been a female in senior management [...] there had hardly been a female in senior management in the whole enterprise [...] and I definitely would have felt that there were a few men on the board for my interview for Deputy-Principal who were less trusting of the fact that I was a woman and probably felt that a man would have done the job better.

Historically Breda's school was an all-male boarding and day school under the auspices of the local Catholic bishop. While she conceded that the male religious principal was keen to employ women teachers, she noted that it was 'simply understood' that women should not entertain ideas of leadership within the school. The first lay appointee to the role of principal was a male and Breda noted that it took considerable time and courage for her to even consider applying for a leadership position once one became available in the school.

Cullen (2003: 150) notes the 'uneasy dialogue' that exists between culture and religion. She argues that religion can be a potent force in shaping societal culture, particularly if it enjoys a powerful position within it. While over the last decade, efforts have been made to provide for a pluralistic model of governance across Irish education, the Catholic Church continues to control the vast majority of schools and there is a particular social caché associated with attendance at Catholic schools, particularly elite fee-paying post-primary schools. The testimony of the female principals in this study confirms the deep-seated cultural influence which the Catholic Church has enjoyed in the sphere of education for decades and how this hegemony has restricted the advancement of women.

Perspectives that Organisational Cultures Did Not Support Childcare-Friendly Practices

Organisational practices take their cues from organisational culture, a derivative of national cultural modes of management. Lynch et al. (2012: 151) note that 'organisational culture is a key factor governing the experience of senior management across the education sector'. The participants in this study held that the organisational culture within schools they themselves had attended, schools in which they subsequently carried out their teaching practice and schools in which they were ultimately employed as teachers, all acted as informing agents for their career trajectories. They concurred with the view that motherhood was a significant factor in influencing women teachers and headteachers' career choices and paths (Coleman 2002; Smith 2015). They also concurred with the findings of Smith (2015: see p. 83) who has argued convincingly that 'it is particularly striking that, despite societal and legal changes, an enduring constant is the unquestioned and unspoken assumption that women will take primary responsibility for childcare'.

All of the women principals who had children commented on the lack of an organisational culture which supported childcare-friendly practices. This was particularly acute for those women who succeeded a religious principal. On this Barbara commented:

> Being the first lay principal was very challenging because you had a whole convent that was running a school and suddenly here am I, a young woman [...] with small children and there was no concept, there was nothing to bridge that, suddenly I was supposed to do everything. But I also had a life and my family but that never would have come into it [...] and I suppose the staff were spoiled over the years because they'd seen these people who didn't have to look after children or pay bills or worry or commute [...] but I just knew that I have a job to do it so who else is going to do it?

Other comments from Barbara amplified the toll which she felt principal-ship took on family life:

> The children spent so much time here with me [...] I never really had holidays [...] I always worked. And when you were doing things with the children, school was always in your head so you were actually never free, ever [...] they would see the school as theirs, they would have spent their childhood here, under the desk often, playing in the classrooms or on the corridors.

Another participant, Emma, initially held a teaching position in the voluntary secondary school sector. She chose to job share when the option first became available. However the timetable was unconducive to her family's needs and this prompted her departure from the sector:

> I travelled to Stoneside five days a week for classes scheduled first thing in the morn-
> ing and last thing in the evening, with gaps of hours in between [...]. I think that's
> when I finally realised I can't keep doing this. I loved the school ... but I just thought
> I can't keep doing this. While job share seemed like an obvious way of juggling both
> my career and my family's needs, my childcare situation was not taken into account
> when the senior management was drafting the timetable. I may have been working
> part-time but I ended up paying for full-time childcare.

Emma's subsequent move to the Educational and Training Board sector
(ETB) proved an effective career move as this sector promoted on the
basis of merit and not on seniority. Working in the ETB sector, Emma was
afforded opportunities to gain experience in middle management. This
experience then provided her with the self-confidence to apply for principalship once the position became available. She noted that her children
were of an age that facilitated the uptake of the post, and this had been a
significant factor in prompting her application:

> My children were at an appropriate age. I had twins in sixth class and they were going
> on to secondary school and I had two others in secondary school so it was a good
> stage, it was an appropriate stage in my life to take it on.

Family obligations and commitments to children in particular were identified by all of the twelve women as an issue they reflected on when mapping
out their career path. For those women without children of their own in
the study, they were nonetheless keenly aware of how difficult it would
have been to try to juggle children with the role of principal. Breda noted
'there is no way I could go home to children. I don't know how they do
it'. She continued:

> I mean I know if I had children, I would be saying to myself I can't do this. I cannot
> go home at 9 o'clock at night three or four evenings a week. I cannot be out until 11
> o'clock at night or driving down from Dublin at 1 o'clock in the morning because
> you know children are not accessories and they shouldn't necessarily suffer for one's
> career path [...]. I have spoken to one or two women at training who have children
> and I really do not know how they do it.

Maria reflected on the added pressures faced by women principals with
children:

> Women have to take time off to have their families and they are missing a lot of time because kids might be off sick and it is inevitably nearly always the mother that has to stay at home with them [...] or has to go to the doctor, the appointments, stuff like that.

The lack of a sustainable organisation culture which supported childcare-friendly practices and the sacrifices this cohort of women were forced to make in order to juggle principalship with family life was readily apparent.

A Neoliberal Policy Agenda Which Was At Odds with a Social Justice Agenda

The move away from a 'theocentric paradigm' (O'Sullivan 1992) towards a more mercantile one in Irish education has led to a more market driven model, concerned with building a knowledge economy (O'Donoghue and Harford 2011; Drudy 2009). The demands for accountability and performativity which have pervaded wider socio-economic policy have had a significant impact on the educational landscape, resulting in significant pressure for those working in leadership positions across education. On this, Eagly and Carli (2007) contend that organisational demands in terms of time and commitment act as an impediment to the career advancement of many women. Long hours and a willingness to be ever present to the organisation is now an accepted norm: 'At the highest levels, hours can become very long and therefore difficult to reconcile with family responsibilities' (ibid.: 141). Coleman too found that the demands of principalship allowed little time for family life: She noted (2003: 47) 'It does appear that a large proportion of the younger, in particular, were making a choice to remain childless in view of the demands of the job ... only about two-thirds of the women were married, and divorce and separation were much more common among the women'.

Reflecting on the Irish context, Lynch et al. (2012: 134) have commented on the 'all-consuming' nature of senior management across all sectors of education in the Republic of Ireland. Each of the women in this study commented at length about the impact of a growing culture of performativity and accountability on their work practices and professional identity. Each also observed how such an agenda conflicted with their rationale for becoming a school principal, which had been closely informed by a social justice agenda and a desire 'to make a difference in kids' lives' (Breda). Awareness of the administrative policy agenda and the impact it would have on the execution of the role of principal was a consideration for some of the group in their deliberations over whether or not to apply for principalship:

> The amount of paperwork, the level of administration, the stress of all of that [...] it made me think very carefully about it, and reflect very carefully on it. (Irene)

The complexity of the role, the multiplicity of tasks and the administrative burden these women then faced was clearly in evidence:

> I just am very aware that in recent times it has become so multifaceted and there is so much responsibility from child protection to [...] responsibility of new programmes ... the admin, the financial end of it [...] you need to be an expert in everything which no one person can possibly be [...] I am double, triple checking everything to ensure that I am following the correct practice and doing the right thing. (Paula)

> I think the admin [...] it's monstrous and because there are constantly evolving circulars from the Department of Education and things are constantly changing [...] the hours are long; you would work three Saturdays a month easily. (Breda)

The hidden roles which principals are expected to play in ensuring the daily smooth running of schools was also problematic for some of the women in this study:

> There are also roles which principals have to take responsibility for that no one ever thinks about or prepares you for. Some of these roles, I found more difficult as a woman, because I felt I lacked the skill-set and also I felt I was taken less seriously because I was a woman. I am thinking, for example, about having to interact with plumbers and electricians, and even at the beginning I found it a bit tricky when dealing with the male caretaker. (Lara)

Some women alluded to the importance of a supportive staff who helped to alleviate the anxiety that surrounded the multiplicity and complexity of the workload:

The need to constantly respond to policy change, to provide evidence that we were always engaging with change and open to scrutiny and inspection at any time, often caused me sleepless nights [...]. Once we had one issue sorted, then there was inevitably another we had to put our energies into. The only consolation was the staff [...] at least I knew they were always behind me, you know no matter what. (Emma)

Dissatisfaction articulated by this cohort of women in relation to workload, administrative tasks and bureaucracy maps to concerns voiced internationally regarding the increasing challenges of school leadership.

Perspectives on Supportive Partners and/or Family Members

Family obligations, both to immediate and extended members coupled with domestic responsibilities have been cited extensively as an obstacle to women in the pursuit of leadership positions (Coleman 2002; 2011; Kellerman and Rhode 2007; Keohane 2010; Lynch et al. 2012; Smith 2011a). On this, Kellerman and Rhode (2007: 11) contend that 'ironically the home is no more an equal opportunity employer than the workplace [...] women are and are expected to be the primary caregivers, especially of the very young and the very old. In principle most men support gender equality – but in practice they fail to structure their lives to support it.'

Lynch et al. (2012) concluded from their study of new managerialism on the application for senior management posts across the primary, post-primary and tertiary sectors in the Irish context, that only women who have a supportive partner or do not have children or women whose children are older pursue a management position in education. These conclusions echo those of Coleman (2002) who noted the difficulties faced by women, especially younger women, who had opted to pursue principalship. She noted that over 50 per cent of her respondents had opted to remain childless or have only one child. Men in the same position and in the same age bracket did not face the same perceived challenges.

The group of women principals in the study being reported here identified the range of supports they drew on in juggling family responsibilities with the role of principal. Some noted the role played by childminders in providing much needed assistance, while others noted the role of spouses and parents. All those with children had in some way found a way of negotiating their public and private roles, weaving a path which permitted participation of both spheres.

Those participants with children had delayed their ascent to senior management until their children were older and less directly reliant on their mothers. Those who availed of child-minding facilities noted that they had been solely responsible for identifying this service and they remained uniquely responsible for managing issues in relation to childcare, despite the presence of a partner or spouse. Each of the women cited long hours and shortened holidays as a constituent of the role. Husbands, partners and family members, especially parents, all appeared centre-stage in supporting them in the execution of their role. What was also evidenced as each told her story was the necessity for the other partner in the relationship to modify his career aspirations at least until the children of the relationship had reached a certain level of self-sufficiency.

Emma, whose children were in secondary school, noted that the 'stage I took up the role of principalship was key. I look at people now with small children and I think how do you do that?' Irene reflected on the necessity to rely on after-school activities and neighbours to ensure the smooth running of her domestic responsibilities. Her husband was a teacher and that had made the decision to apply for principalship a lot more palatable:

> He's understanding of my job, I think that was the kind of critical thing around it, he knew what was involved for me [...] he knows why I have to put in the extra time, he knows the ins and outs of how a school operates. And the fact then, that he was going to be home earlier, would have made a huge difference because without his support, I couldn't do this.

Emma too acknowledged the role played by both outside carers and family members in assisting her to pursue her career path when her children were young:

> That was a busy time, there was no doubt. I was always lucky [...] we had two people that came to the house and they stayed with me all along [...] and my mother was there

[...] so she was a huge influence as well [...] having said that Sean was self-employed he collected the [...] kids from the school bus and if they were sick he was there ... I really would never have missed school for any reason [...] because I had such support and that doesn't happen in every situation.

Natalie noted the practical arrangements which were formulated to facilitate the pursuance of both careers simultaneously. Care for her children had been organised by her. She retained the same childminder for a long number of years whom she considered 'probably kinder to the kids than I was'. She acknowledged that her husband was always prepared to do what had to be done, whether with household chores or childcare:

I was a really nervous mother so he definitely would have been hugely involved [...] it was the culture of the time that the guys would have Friday evening off and gone drinking at 5 o'clock [...] and I said I don't see the point of my working all week if you are going to pub it at a weekend [...] but he wouldn't have been the kind of fella to do it either but I was particularly lucky he was the kind of fella to muck in at home in a big way, manage his girls.

She reflected on the career decisions of the men and women on her staff and the factors which guided their career paths:

Some of our females are non-family, without family as in without children of their own and they are career ruled [...] and there are some in the middle who are mixing both well. And I've got some guys who are very driven [...]. So I can see women and men who are madly ambitious. But I think the ladies, most of them have to fit in with family, and for that reason there are not as many pursuing management positions.

Coleman (2011: 98) concluded from her study of women in leadership, both within and outside education, that 'there is no doubt that the complications of combining family life with a demanding job are seen by the interviewees as the biggest potential obstacle to the career success of females'. The principals in this study concluded that without the emotional and material support provided by family and friends, the likelihood of them being successful in their careers would have been seriously diminished. In citing the supportive role of partners and parents, especially mothers in providing both childcare assistance and encouragement to pursue career goals, as well as the backing of friends, the women in this study echoed the findings of Hall (1996) who concluded that there was a small cohort of critical others in the lives of her interviewees who facilitated career attainment and actualisation.

Perspectives on Mentors and Role Models

Coleman (2011: 39) notes that 'a lack of female role models is not helpful to women who aspire to leadership'. In the Republic of Ireland only 35 per cent of those who hold the most senior management positions at post-primary school level are women (DES: 2012). Cultural definitions of how women ought to be play a large part in how women internalise their role in society. On this, Keohane (2011: 6) notes how femininity is constructed and enacted in modern society damages a 'convergence towards parity'. In rarely depicting women in leadership in a positive light, popular culture, she notes, is responsible for assisting in keeping the numbers of women who reach leadership positions at a lower level than their male counterparts. It is therefore imperative that female role models exhibit actions which do not deny their femininity, but rather augment it in ways which showcase women as assertive and confident, independent and comfortable in their own skins.

The principals in the study being reported here who identified a role model in their lives noted both positive and negative aspects which ultimately informed their career decision-making processes and their management style. Jane emphasised the influence of a former religious sister who had been principal at the school which she had attended. Jane's own family circumstances were difficult and this nun supported Jane through her schooling and continued to play a key role in Jane's personal and professional formation:

> She supported me and nourished me and pushed me and you know pushed me again [...] and really made me achieve the maximum that I could achieve [...].

Hilda noted the negative impact of a principal she had worked under as a teacher and how this management style had shaped Hilda's own sense of effective leadership:

> Certainly the first principal I worked for was the one I would have felt had many flaws, a very nice woman but in leadership very flawed and I think even as a young person I could see this wasn't the way to do business. She left a very acrimonious atmosphere and she enabled a really big rift to happen amongst the staff [...] this was you know a kind of a negative bit of role modelling.

Irene noted the ethic of hard work modelled by her mother, a trait that characterised Irene's own drive and ambition:

> And my mum would have worked far too hard. And Dad was an intellectual who read, who loved history, who loved politics, who wasn't a businessman. So Mum really had to take over [...] we could have ended up on the street, there's no question about it. Had she not had that brainpower and she had a business background in her own family [...] and we in turn took on helping her with the business [...] Mum was the real driver behind it.

Lara noted the significance of informal group mentoring for her own professional development:

> I started with the most wonderful bunch of industrious teachers and we are still great friends today. One of them is principal of a school now, another one is deputy-principal in another school, another one is an A post holder [...] we are products of our own motivation. We all got involved [...].

She also commented on the work ethic demonstrated by her grandmother and how this influenced her own development:

> She had her own family company [...] now she did this by herself [...] she travelled the country [...] so in terms of being self-driven I am very close to my grandmother.

The importance of role models for women has been identified as a crucial facilitating element for career development. Kellerman and Rhode (2007: 78) note that the lack of role models has 'meant that few women have thought about leadership as an appropriate women's role'. Coleman (1996, 2002) too considered that the lack of visible role models in leadership for female teachers, coupled with a neglect of mentoring, discouraged aspirations to principalship for women teachers.

Concluding Thoughts

In this exploratory study, we have identified the perceived enabling and constraining influences articulated by a cohort of twelve women working as principals in the Republic of Ireland. Key findings indicate that the perceived challenges women principals in the Republic of Ireland have encountered include the cultural expectations around who should occupy leadership roles, especially in Catholic-run schools, organisational cultures which do not support childcare-friendly practices and a neoliberal policy agenda which is considered to be at odds with a social justice agenda. Perceived enablers include supportive partners and/or family members as well as the significance of mentors and role models. This study indicates that gendered norms and cultural expectations continue to limit women's full engagement with leadership in education and beyond. Gallos (1989: 118) reminds us that 'phases of development for women do not have the linear and predictable quality that male life patterns suggest, nor is the process of evaluating life choices as straightforward or as singularly focused on work and career'. While public policy debates in Ireland continue to engage with the issue of gender equality in education, a fundamental disconnect between the level of rhetorical engagement and any impact on the ground remains.

Acknowledgements

We are grateful to Marianne Coleman and Tom O'Donoghue for comments on a previous draft of this chapter.

References

Acker, S. (1992) 'Creating Careers: Women Teachers at Work'. *Curriculum Inquiry* 22 (2), 141–63.

Acker, S. (1995). 'Carry On Caring: The Work of Women Teachers'. *British Journal of Sociology of Education* 16 (1), 21–36.

Acker, S., and Feuverger, G. (1996). 'Doing Good and Feeling Bad: The Work of Women University Teachers'. *Cambridge Journal of Education* 26 (3), 401–22.

Blackmore, J. (1999). *Troubling Women: Feminism, Leadership and Educational Change*. Buckingham: Open University Press.

Casey, K. (1993). *I Answer with my Life: Life Histories of Women Teachers Working for Social Change*. New York and London: Routledge.

Coleman, M. (1996). 'Barriers to Career Progress for Women in Education: The Perceptions of Female Headteachers'. *Education Research* 38 (3), 317–32.

Coleman, M. (2001). 'Achievement against the Odds: The Female Secondary Headteachers in England and Wales'. *School Leadership* and *Management* 21 (1), 75–100.

Coleman, M. (2002). *Women as Headteachers: Striking the Balance*. Stoke on Trent: Trentham Books.

Coleman, M. (2003). 'Gender and Educational Leadership'. In M. Brundett, N. Burton and R. Smith (eds), *Leadership in Education*, 36–51. London: SAGE.

Coleman, M. (2005). *Gender and Headship in the Twenty-First Century: Project Report*. National College for School Leadership, Nottingham.

Coleman, M. (2011) *Women at the Top*. Basingstoke: Palgrave Macmillan.

Coleman, M., and Fitzgerald, T. (2008) 'Gender and Leadership Development'. In J. Lumby, G. Crow and P. Pashiardis (eds), *International Handbook on the Preparation and Development of School Leaders*, 119–35. London: Routledge.

Cubillo, L., and Brown, M. (2003). 'Women into Educational Leadership and Management: International Differences?' *Journal of Educational Administration* 41 (3), 278–91.

Cullen, S. (2005) *Religion and Gender*. Dublin: Veritas.

Department of Education and Skills (DES) (2012). <www.departmentofeducationand skills/statistics>.

Dimmock, C., and O'Donoghue, T.A. (1997) *Innovative School Principals and Restructuring: Life History Portraits of Successful Managers of Change*. Abingdon: Routledge.

Drudy, S. (2009). 'Education and the Knowledge Economy: A Challenge for Ireland in Changing Times'. In S. Drudy (ed.), *Education in Ireland: Challenge and Change*. Dublin: Gill and Macmillan.

Dunn, S. (1988). 'Education, Religion and Cultural Change in the Republic of Ireland'.
    In W. Tulasiewicz and C. Brook (eds), *Christianity and Educational Provision
    in International Perspective*. London: Routledge.
Eagly, A.H., and Carli, L.L. (2007). *Through the Labyrinth*. Cambridge, MA: Harvard
    Business School Publishing.
Evetts, J. (1994). *Becoming a Secondary Headteacher*. London: Cassell.
Fitzgerald, T. (2003). 'Changing the Deafening Silence of Indigenous Women's
    Voices in Educational Leadership'. *Journal of Educational Administration* 41
    (1), 9–25.
Fitzgerald, T. (2015) 'Venturing into the Habitat of the Powerful: Women Leaders
    in Higher Education'. In K. Fuller and J. Harford (eds), *Gender and Leadership:
    Women Achieving Against the Odds*, 209–225. Oxford: Peter Lang
Fuller, K. (2009). 'Women Secondary Headteachers: Alive and Well in Birmingham
    at the Beginning of the Twenty-First Century'. *Management in Education* 23
    (1), 19–31.
Gallos, J. (1989). 'Exploring Women's Development: Implications for Career Theory,
    Practice and Research'. In Arthur, M.B., Hall, D.T., and Rousseau, D. (eds),
    Handbook of Career Theory, 110–31. Cambridge: Cambridge University Press.
Goodson, I., and Sikes, P. (2010) (eds). *Life History Research in Educational Settings*.
    Buckingham: Open University Press.
Gronn, P. (1999) *The Making of Educational Leaders. Management and Leadership
    in Education*. London: Cassell.
Hall, V. (1996). *Dancing on the Ceiling: A Study of Women Managers in Education*.
    London: SAGE
Hall, V. (1999). 'Gender and Education Management: Duel or Dialogue?' In T. Bush,
    L. Bell, R. Bolam, R. Glatter and P. Ribbins (eds), *Educational Management:
    Refining Theory, Policy and Practice*. London: Paul Chapman.
Harford, J. (2008). *The Opening of University Education to Women in Ireland*. Dublin:
    Irish Academic Press.
Kellerman, B., and Rhode, D.L. (2007). 'The State of Play'. In B. Kellerman and D.L.
    Rhode (eds), *Women and Leadership: The State of Play and Strategies for Change*.
    San Francisco: Jossey Bass.
Keohane, N.O. (2010). *Thinking about Leadership*. Princeton: Princeton University Press.
Keohane, N.O. (2011). 'The Future of Women's Leadership: Address to Rhodes Schol-
    ars'. Rhodes House, Oxford. 1 November.
Lynch K., Grummell, B., and Devine, D. (2012). *New Managerialism in Education:
    Commercialisation, Carelessness and Gender*. Basingstoke: Palgrave Macmillan.
McGregor, H.A., and Elliot, A.J. (2005). 'The Shame of Failure: Examining the Link
    Between Fear of Failure and Shame'. *Personality and Social Psychology Bulletin*
    31 (2) 218–31.

MacRuairc, G., and Harford, J. (2011). 'Teacher Leadership: Awakening the Sleeping Giant'. In B. Hudson and M. Meyer (eds), *Beyond Fragmentation: Didactics, Learning and Teaching*. Opladen: Verlag Barbara Budrich.

McLay, M. (2008). 'Headteacher Career Paths in UK Independent Secondary Coeducational Schools: Gender Issues'. *Educational Management Administration and Leadership* 36 (3), 353–72.

Munro, P. (1998). *Subject to Fiction: Women Teachers' Life History Narratives and the Cultural Politics of Resistance*. Buckingham: Open University Press.

Newman, J. (1994). The Limits of Management: Gender and the Politics of Change. In J. Clarke, A. Cochrane and E. McLaughlin (eds), *Managing Social Policy*. London: SAGE.

O'Donoghue, T., and Harford, J. (2011). 'A Comparative History of Church-State Relations in Irish Education'. *Comparative Education Review* 55 (3), 315–41.

O'Donoghue, T., and Harford, J. (2014). 'The Conception, Construction and Maintenance of the Identity of Roman Catholic Female Religious Teachers: A Historical Case Study from Ireland'. *Teachers and Teaching: Theory and Practice* 20 (4), 410–26.

O'Sullivan, D. (1992) 'Cultural Strangers and Educational Change: The OECD's Report Investment in Education and Irish Educational Policy'. *Education Policy* 7 (5), 445–69.

Prentice, A.L., and Theobold, M.R. (1991). *Women who Taught: Perspectives on the History of Women and Teaching*. Toronto: University of Toronto Press.

Redmond, J., and Harford, J. (2010). 'One Man, One Job: The Marriage Ban and the Employment of Women Teachers in Irish Primary Schools'. *Paedagogica Historica: International Journal of the History of Education* 46 (5), 639–54.

Schmuck, P.A. (1986) 'School Management and Administration: An Analysis by Gender'. In Hoyle, E. and McMahon, A. (eds), *The Management of Schools*, World Yearbook of Education 1986. London: Kogan Page.

Shakeshaft, C. (1987). *Women in Educational Administration*. Thousand Oaks, CA: SAGE.

Shakeshaft, C., Browne, G., Irby, B.J., Grogan, M., and Ballenger, J. (2007). 'Increasing Gender Equity in Educational Leadership'. In S. Klein (ed.), *Handbook for Achieving Gender Equity through education* (2nd edn), 103–29. Mahwah, NJ: Lawrence Erlbaum Associates.

Smith, J.M. (2011a). 'Aspirations to and Perceptions of Secondary Headship: Contrasting Female Teachers' and Headteachers' Perspectives'. *Educational Management, Administration and Leadership* 39 (5), 516–35.

Smith, J.M. (2011b). 'Agency and Female Teacher's Career Decisions: A life History Study of 40 Women'. *Educational Management Administration and Leadership* 39 (1): 7–24.

Smith, J.M. (2015). 'Motherhood and Women Teachers' Career Decisions: A Con-
    stant Battle'. In K. Fuller and J. Harford (eds), *Gender and Leadership: Women
    Achieving against the Odds*, 83–114. Oxford: Peter Lang.
Sperandio, J. (2010) 'Modeling Cultural Context for Aspiring Women Leaders'. *Journal
    of Educational Administration* 48 (6), 716–26.
Weiler, K. (1997) 'Reflections on Writing a History of Women Teachers'. *Harvard
    Educational Review* 67 (4), 635–58.
Young, M.D., and McLeod, S. (2001). 'Flukes, Opportunities and Planned Interven-
    tions: Factors Affecting Women's Decisions to become School Administrators'.
    Educational Administration Quarterly 37 (4), 462–502.

JILL SPERANDIO AND JENNIFER POLINCHOCK

Roads Less Travelled: Female Elementary School Principals Aspiring to the School District Superintendency

Introduction

Marianne Coleman's quest to expose the gender inequalities in educational leadership in the UK and to seek to help women aspiring to be leaders to confront and overcome the barriers facing them has inspired and supported similar research in other nations of the world. Discussing women's access to leadership, she noted 'There are two types of women: ones who perceive there is not a problem – they are wearing blinkers; they tend to pull up the drawbridge – then there are women who admit there are issues, but also see that there are lots of things that can be done' (Coleman 2011: 18) Coleman believed that making women aware of the perceptions and biases that limit their selection for positions of educational leadership would empower them to find the things that can be done, including developing career paths and strategies to counter discrimination. Knowledge of the patterns of gender discrimination allows women to position themselves to take on the roles for which they are well qualified and to which they bring fresh perspectives and leadership styles. This chapter presents research that indicates one group of women – elementary school principals in the USA – are doing this, by forging non-traditional paths to the top leadership position in US school districts, that of the district superintendent.

The underrepresentation of women in school and district leadership positions in the USA has been well documented, and persists to this day (Aud et al. 2011; Brunner 1999, 2000; Brunner and Grogan 2007; Glass 2000; Glass, Bjork and Brunner 2000; Grogan 1996; Grogan and

Shakeshaft 2011; Kim and Brunner 2009; Kowalski, McCord, Peterson, Young, and Ellerson 2011; Riehl and Byrd 1997; Shakeshaft 1989; Sherman 2005; Tallerico and Blount 2004; Young and McLeod 2001). Across the nation in 2010, the proportion of female superintendents was 24.1 per cent (Kowalski et al. 2011). Women represent 75.5 per cent of the teaching force but occupy slightly higher than 50 per cent of principalships and less than 25 per cent of superintendencies (Kowalski et al. 2011). Given their prevalence in teaching, women have not reached equitable representation in educational leadership positions, particularly as superintendents.

Just as in the UK (Coleman 2011), studies have revealed several factors contributing to the phenomenon around women's inequitable representation in educational administration in the USA. These factors include women's experiences with internal and external barriers and perceptions about their leadership abilities. Internal barriers such as self-perceptions about job readiness or adequacy (Grogan 1996; Gupton and Slick 1996; Howley, Andrianaivo and Perry 2005; Mahitivanichcha and Rorrer 2006; Sherman 2005; Tallerico 2000a; Young and McLeod 2001), responsibility to the nuclear or extended family (Brunner and Grogan 2007; Loder 2005; Shakeshaft 1989), and individual agency in career aspirations (Brunner and Grogan 2007; Eckerman 2004; Riehl and Byrd 1997; Ruhl-Smith, Shen, and Cooley 1999; Young and McLeod 2001) have had a chilling effect on women's aspirations to upper-level administrative positions. External barriers such as limited sponsorship or mentorship opportunities (Bjork 2000; Daresh 2004; Grogan 1996; Orr 2006; Sherman 2005; Young and McLeod 2001), preferred experiences in educational leadership (Brunner and Kim 2010; Grogan and Shakeshaft 2011; Mahitivanichcha and Rorrer 2006; Ortiz 1982; Tallerico 2000a, 2000b), normative gatekeeping practices (Chase and Bell 1990; Kamler 2009; Newton 2006; Newton, Giesen, Freeman, Bishop and Zeitoun 2003; Riehl and Byrd 1997; Tallerico 2000a, 2000b), existing power structures (Adkison 1981; Grogan 1999, 2000; Mahitivanichcha and Rorrer 2006; Ortiz 1982; Sherman 2005; Tallerico and Blount 2004), and gender-based stereotyping (Brunner, 2000; Burkman 2011; Grogan 1996, 1999; Mahitivanichcha and Rorrer 2006; Rusch and Marshall 2006; Skrla 2000; Skrla, Reyes, and Scheurich 2000; Shakeshaft 1989; Tallerico 2000b) limit women's access to networks that promote and provide access to the superintendency. Perceptions by school board members as well as the public about women's leadership abilities as lacking fiscal acuity and organisational management skills perpetuate a belief that women are ill-suited for the superintendency (Chase and Bell 1990; Brunner and Kim 2010; Brunner and Grogan 2007; Kamler 2009; Mahitivanichcha and Rorrer 2006; Mountford 2001; Tallerico 2000a, 2000b). For women who experience these barriers and perceptions, the superintendency may be unappealing and inaccessible.

Another factor which has contributed to women's inequitable representation in the superintendency is the nature of their career pathways. A career pathway is an established, hierarchical sequence of commonly held positions that leads to increased visibility and scope of responsibility (Ortiz 1982). One conceptualisation of a typical career pathway includes a route that flows from teacher, to principal, to central office administrator, to superintendent (Kim and Brunner 2009; Shakeshaft 1989). The notion of a typical career pathway derives from the routes successfully used by men to access the superintendency (Brunner and Kim 2010; Shakeshaft 1989). Male superintendents traditionally followed a career pathway that moved vertically and directly from a high school principalship to a superintendent position.

Men have traditionally also dominated assistant high school principal and high school principal positions, while women in educational leadership have been best represented as elementary assistant principals and principals. Thus women who aspire to the superintendency and who are in elementary education are outside the typical career pathway. If they are committed to achieving their goal, they must envision and pursue new career paths to obtain their objectives. A recent survey of the career paths of superintendents indicates that 58 per cent of women started their leadership careers in elementary schools, suggesting that new paths have indeed been found.

The Study

The aim of our study (Polinchock, 2014) was to explore how female aspirants to the superintendency who are outside the typical career pathway do in fact envisage and pursue potential routes to the superintendency within the context of one US state, Pennsylvania. We sought to find out what proportion of female elementary principals in Pennsylvania aspired to the superintendency and how these aspirations were developed; how they envisaged their career pathways to the superintendency; and how they perceived their ability to access other school and district leadership positions.

Research Site

Pennsylvania has 500 public school districts (Pennsylvania Department of Education [PDE], 2013a). The percentage of female teachers and principals approximates national percentages (PDE 2013b); during the 2011–12 school year, 45.4 per cent of public school principals were women with 56.7 per cent of women serving as elementary principals (PDE 2013b). In 2012, Pennsylvania had 28.2 per cent female superintendents (PDE 2013b), which is slightly higher than the national percentage of female superintendents – 24.1 per cent (Kowalski et al. 2011). By locale, the highest percentage of female superintendents were in city school districts – 41 per cent and the lowest were in suburban school districts – 24 per cent (PDE 2010). Thirty per cent of female superintendents were in small and mid-size school districts whereas 23 per cent were in large school districts. In Pennsylvania, women occupied superintendencies in small and mid-size school districts in urban locales whereas men occupied superintendencies in large school districts in suburban and rural locales.

Research Design

Our study used a convergent parallel mixed methods design which involved the concurrent collection of quantitative and qualitative data, the independent analysis of data from both strands, the merging of results from both strands, and the interpretation of the merged results (Creswell and Plano Clark 2011). Quantitative data from a researcher developed survey (Polinchock 2014) was used to determine the relationship between female elementary principals' aspirations to the superintendency and their perceived ability to access positions in school and district leadership. Qualitative data from the open-ended questions on the survey and interviews from three case studies was used to explore how female aspirants to the superintendency envision their career pathways. The reason for collecting quantitative and qualitative data was to compare and corroborate the results from the two types of research strands to develop a more complete understanding of female elementary principals' career aspirations and perceived access to career pathways.

Participants

The participants in the quantitative strand included a simple random sample of eighty-nine female elementary principals from a sample frame of 251 potential participants in the population of 938 female elementary principals (PDE 2013b). Participants in the qualitative strand included a purposeful, critical case sample of two female aspirants, separate from the random sample in the quantitative strand, and one female superintendent. The three case study samples represented women in educational leadership positions who would, or have already experienced the phenomenon of accessing the superintendency from outside the typical career pathway to the superintendency.

Methods of Data Collection and Analysis

The method of data collection included the concurrent collection of quantitative and qualitative data. Quantitative data was collected using a survey instrument comprised of eleven questions and administered electronically through Survey Monkey to a sample of 300 female elementary principals. The survey instrument included multiple choice questions about demographics, career aspirations, and perceived accessibility to positions and multiple choice ranking, and open-ended questions about potential career route development. Qualitative data was collected from three case studies through individual, face-to-face, semi-structured interviews using an interview guide and a record review of résumés and curricula vitae. The interview guide consisted of nine open-ended questions developed around themes from the literature which included career aspirations, sources of motivation, career decision-making processes, and career planning. Interview sessions were tape recorded, transcribed, and stored in a database.

The quantitative and qualitative data results were analysed separately. The methods for quantitative data analysis included quantitative procedures for analysing responses to the survey using descriptive statistics. The researcher determined frequencies for the responses to the categorical questions. Response frequencies were compared among aspirants and non-aspirants and by age groups. The methods for qualitative data analysis included qualitative procedures for analysing the open-ended responses from the survey and interview transcripts from the case studies. The recorded case study interviews were converted into written interview transcripts. The interview transcripts and open-ended responses were read for: (a) memos, or short statements; (b) recurring statements within the interview; (c) significant statements; and (d) statements or terms that coincided with the literature in the conceptual framework. Each data set was coded and analysed for emergent patterns and themes and combined into a matrix which included a priori categories. The results from the record review were used to develop a descriptive profile of the case study participants.

The quantitative and qualitative data results were merged using procedures described by Creswell and Plano Clark (2011) that involve: (a) reducing the quantitative and qualitative data; (b) transforming the qualitative data quantified units; (c) correlating and comparing the quantitative and quantified qualitative data in a category matrix; (d) integrating the combined data for analysis; and (e) interpreting the results of the merged data.

A comparative method was used to interpret the merged results to address the research questions in the study. The researcher identified themes from the merged results and compared them to the demographic characteristics of the survey participants and the case study participants. This analysis involved comparing participants' age with aspirations to the superintendency, envisioned career routes to school and district leadership, and perceptions about the ability to access these positions. The interpretation of the merged data results involved reviewing the quantitative and qualitative data results separately for additional information and connecting merged data results with emergent patterns and themes.

Results

Summary of Survey Results Regarding Career Planning

The percentage of female elementary principals in the total sample who had an interest in the superintendency was 24 per cent. Among the sub-set of elementary principals who planned to pursue another position in school or district leadership, the percentage of female elementary principals with interest in the superintendency increased to 72 per cent. Female elementary principals aspiring to the superintendency indicated they planned to use a career route that included only positions in the school district central office, such as district curriculum coordinator, director of community and student services and director of assessment which gave them knowledge and understanding of how the school district operated, and experience leading initiatives and working with personnel in all schools within the district. The most common rationales for pursuing district-level positions included (a) having an interest in the position (b) having the necessary professional experience, and (c) believing the position was attainable. The perceptions about the accessibility of positions in school and district leadership differed among female elementary principals by age. While the district leadership positions were the most frequently reported accessible positions among the total sample, female elementary principals, forty years of age or younger, also perceived secondary school leadership positions to be accessible in greater proportion to those forty-one years of age or older, suggesting changes in the nature of these positions had made them more accessible to women.

Case Study Profiles

Loretta – Elementary Principal

Loretta has been an elementary principal in a suburban school district in southeastern Pennsylvania for four years. Prior to her appointment to the elementary principalship, she served as a supervisor of gifted instruction for three years and as a gifted education specialist and primary teacher for eighteen years in the same school district. Loretta received a master's degree in educational leadership with a K-12 Principal certification early in her teaching career. She decided to wait until her children were in high school before actively pursuing administrative positions. During her tenure as a teacher, she was actively involved in leadership roles within the teachers' association, serving as the head advocate for the teachers' association and as the association president. Loretta developed her aspirations to the superintendency once she became an elementary principal. Loretta intends to move from the elementary principalship to a district-level director or assistant superintendent position as the next position in her career pathway.

Abigail – Assistant Superintendent

Abigail is an assistant superintendent in a suburban school district in central Pennsylvania. She began her career as an elementary teacher in a neighbouring state where she taught primary and intermediate grades for ten years. During this time, she became involved in curriculum and professional development as a teacher-leader. Prompted by principals and assistant principals who served as influential role models, she pursued a master's degree in educational administration and became an elementary assistant principal. After two years, she became the principal of another elementary school within the county-based school system in this state. After three years as an elementary principal, Abigail moved to Pennsylvania to assume the principalship of an elementary school where she served for eight years. When the director of curriculum and instruction position became available within the district, she moved into that position. After serving as the director of curriculum and instruction, Abigail was promoted to her current position as assistant superintendent in the same district. Since this promotion two years ago, Abigail completed her doctoral work and anticipates pursuing the superintendency in her current district or possibly a neighbouring district.

Rebecca – Superintendent

Rebecca began her teaching career as a primary and intermediate elementary teacher in another state. She immediately pursued a master's degree in educational administration and aspired to become a principal. After moving back to her home town, she worked for a social services agency and developed relationships with the school district. She joined the district as an intermediate elementary teacher and filled a one-year vacancy for the director of curriculum who was on leave. From this position, she became an elementary principal and high school assistant principal in the same district for three years. During this time, she began her doctoral studies. She was able to move back to the director of curriculum position and served in that position for eleven years. During the search for a permanent superintendent within the district, she was approached by the acting superintendent and select school board members to apply for this position. Rebecca was named superintendent, and she has served in this position for six years.

Open-Ended Survey Respondent Profiles

Fifteen female elementary principals completed the open-ended survey question regarding their rationale for the career route they planned to pursue from the elementary principalship to the superintendency. Twelve of the respondents were over forty-one years of age. Nine of the respondents had completed graduate study beyond a master's degree with two respondents holding a doctoral degree. Four of the respondents were pursuing the next position in their career pathway to the superintendency.

Common Threads

The open-ended survey responses contained two common threads: (a) participants perceptions and identification of key positions they must access for their envisioned career pathway; (b) participants perceptions of their need to gather knowledge and experience. First, the women expressed that the next position they planned to pursue mirrored the pathway used by superintendents in their district or by whom they knew. Sixty percent of the respondents identified the positions in their planned career pathways as key positions needed to access the superintendency. Three respondents commented on the available positions within their district, which suggests an intention to remain within their current district.

Second, the respondents noted that their planned career routes would allow them to gain experience for the superintendency. One responded stating that she would gain 'the requisite skills for the superintendent position' by following her planned career pathway. While the respondents to open-ended questions did not elaborate within their responses, these two threads weaved into the emergent themes developed through the case study interviews.

Emergent Themes

The results of the case study interviews and open-ended survey responses revealed two emergent themes about how women with experiences as elementary principals envision their career pathways to the superintendency. *Developing a career pathway* focuses on how the women processed and contextualised their experiences and the influences that led them to pursue the superintendency. *Accessing positions in school and district leadership* focused on the indicators of career development that could lead to successfully attaining the superintendency.

Developing a Career Pathway

EXPERIENCES AND CAREER ASPIRATIONS

The narratives of the case studies revealed that as each woman successfully attained a position in school or district leadership, she developed confidence in her leadership skills as well as her knowledge of instructional pedagogy and organisational systems. Each woman's discourse included reflections on how the experience in past positions helped her to prepare for a more challenging position. Loretta described her experience as gifted education specialist as an area where she developed a broader understanding of developmental learning and scheduling a building. Loretta also reflected on her experience as the teachers' association head advocate as a critical experience by working with administrators and supporting teachers' professional growth. Abigail described how she viewed her progression from an assistant elementary principal, to elementary principal, to director of curriculum and instruction, to assistant superintendent as moving from 'impacting an entire building' to focusing on 'what's happening in all our classrooms, all our environments' to 'the greatest level of moving an entire district.' Loretta's and Abigail's self-efficacy developed as they gained confidence in their knowledge base and leadership skills within their respective roles.

Once a sense of self-efficacy developed from these experiences, the women sought other positions that could broaden their scope of responsibility and influence over the school systems. Learning how to balance the facets of leadership from feelings of isolation, to confronting personnel and legal issues, to resolving complex conflicts within the organisation is a crucial aspect for being successful in of top-level leadership positions. Each woman spoke about how she resolved this balance in her professional life. Specifically, Loretta and Rebecca identified collaboration with trusted colleagues and seeking the advice of experts as strategies for resolving the challenges they experienced in their leadership roles.

Yet, in considering the superintendency, the women expressed resolve in balancing the challenges of leadership for the opportunity to exert greater influence over the organisational system to promote student learning and achievement. Abigail summarised her career aspirations by stating:

> So it really was with doing what I really loved and wanted ... and then opportunities became available and were offered to me. And I think with each job that I have had, I have loved even more. So it's really, I think, my focus is just where I can make the most significant difference. If that's where I am supposed to be, then that's where I need to be.

Abigail's aspirations to the superintendency represented her sense of 'calling' to a position where she could make a positive impact on students. Along a similar vein, Rebecca described her reaction to a school board member's question about her candidacy for the superintendent position. Rebecca stated that if she was not the successful candidate for the position, she would 'go right back and be in the curriculum office because I really love curriculum.' Rebecca continued with, 'I think I am making a good difference. But I think, that by being a superintendent, I can make those curriculum things happen too.' Abigail's and Rebecca's aspirations to the superintendency developed from a lens of servant leadership. Both women expressed that the source of their motivation was grounded in their work for schools and with students and was not dependent upon a position title.

EXTERNAL INFLUENCES ON CAREER ASPIRATIONS

In their career development narratives, each woman recounted how endorsement and encouragement from a supervisor were important influences over their decision to pursue school and district leadership positions. Abigail recalled how a conversation with the assistant superintendent when she was a teacher led to her first position as an assistant elementary principal:

> The district, at that time, chose to come in and do climate surveys of some select people in regard to what was happening in the building, and where they felt they really needed to take the building and make some movement. So, at that point in time, I was doing interviewing with the area superintendent, and he was asking questions such as, 'What do you think could happen within the building to better help us to establish collaboration, environment, of teamwork, focus on achievement [...]'. And

at the end of the interview [...] he said to me, 'Where are you in terms of the leadership programme?' And I said, 'Well, I've completed it all, and I just transferred to this school as a second grade teacher. I'm very happy.' And he said, 'I'm putting your name forward to become, to be part of the administrative pool in terms of leadership academy in the district.' And I thought, 'Well, that's very kind of you [...] thinking, well maybe in a few years when they call, and if I'm ready, then you know, what a nice compliment.' So, I ended up going home that night to share with my husband and I'm like [...] oh, they put my name in the leadership pool. I had a great interview with a phenomenal area assistant superintendent. We had this great dialogue about how could really turn this school around. And a week later I got a phone call for an interview as the [...] for an assistant principal position in an elementary school. And I thought, 'Isn't that interesting. Oh [...] OK [...] I will probably be a few years, but I'll go ahead on the interview and it will be good skill building.' And interviewed and was called the next week. They said we're appointing you for the Board [...] at the [...] at the school board meeting.

At that time, Abigail did not recognise the opportunity to share her vision for the school with the assistant superintendent was a career-defining moment. Abigail's experience coincided with how the other women in the case studies either entered or advanced in educational administration. These formal or informal, serendipitous or strategic, conversations with supervisors and mentors led to opportunities for recognition or advancement. For each woman, the recognition by supervisors and their subsequent promotion led to the opportunity to apply for, and ultimately attain, administrative positions.

The encouragement of colleagues and friends was also noted as well as the support of family members to pursue leadership positions. The women identified mentors whom they relied on for career advice as well as for assuming their leadership roles. Loretta shared how she relied on her sister who is an assistant superintendent in another state for advice as well as other colleagues in district leadership positions. Rebecca remarked on her relationship with her superintendent when she was a curriculum director. The superintendent exposed her to the functions of central office that extended beyond curriculum development into areas such as managing school finance and working with constituencies. Having role models whom they could emulate helped the women assume their leadership roles and develop their aspirations to advance in educational administration.

INTERNAL FACTORS AND CAREER ASPIRATIONS

Each woman situated her aspirations to school and district leadership within her leadership orientation. Loretta expressed her keen focus on 'doing what's best for kids'. Abigail spoke about the role of collaboration with teachers and other administrators in developing curriculum and implementing effective instructional practices. Rebecca shared examples that resonate with a leadership for learning orientation as described by Grogan and Shakeshaft (2011). Rebecca stated that:

> And, you know, I really think that the […] that understanding how kids learn and how you have to teach is really what matters most regardless of what administrative position you're in. You can learn the management things. Or, you have enough support staff to help you in terms of the management of things. But if you don't have a clear idea of what the instructional design in a classroom should look like. How to really weave reading and writing into every content area. If you haven't studied those standards. If you haven't done that stuff, having all those other things, is meaningless in comparison. So where I always try to concentrate my efforts, even in terms of course work and those kinds-of things. You have to take the school law and you have to take some of that other stuff. But what I always … what I really wanted to understand what should be going on in that classroom. That that's where it really mattered. And so that any administrative position I would be in would be about knowing, learning, understanding the classroom. So, I'd say that was … that was really tried to keep my focus.

Rebecca's vision about leadership involved maintaining a sharp focus on effective instruction and student learning.

Career goals developed from internal sources of motivation to develop school systems that resonated with core beliefs about effective school systems. The women sought the superintendency to extend their influence over the organisation system focused on student learning and achievement. None of the women expressed seeking the position for its own sake. Abigail was adamant about a potential superintendency:

> If they, philosophically, met my set of beliefs. The kids really come first, and it would really need to be a cohesive, collaborative team where we empower each and every person regardless of who they are to really collectively move a district forward.

For Abigail, seeking the superintendency depended on a philosophical match. She values her beliefs about effectiveness leadership; therefore, she would be selective about the existing conditions of a district she would choose to lead. Each woman shared a commitment to student learning and a self-awareness of her leadership orientation. These two factors not only influence their career aspirations, but also the types of organisations they would seek to lead.

Accessing Positions in School and District Leadership

MAKING CAREER DECISIONS

Each woman could identify a specific career decision in her career pathway that served as an entry port to school and district leadership. First, each woman connected her involvement in teacher leadership roles, such as writing curriculum and delivering professional development, to a foundational experience for developing aspirations to formal leadership roles. Loretta explained how she decided to become a gifted education specialist so that she could broaden her knowledge of curriculum and instruction across the elementary continuum. Abigail spoke of her experiences in writing curriculum and delivering professional development as additional roles that demonstrated her potential leadership qualities to her supervisors. Rebecca spoke of her involvement in a student assistance programme with an outside agency forging her relationship with school district leaders. The decision to enter school leadership developed from their experience in teacher-leader roles. In order to access their first administrative positions, these women promoted their burgeoning leadership skills, which gained the attention of their school and district leaders.

Second, assuming positions in district-level curriculum leadership afforded each woman the opportunity to develop a K-12 perspective on teaching and learning, leadership experience at elementary and secondary levels, and proximity to central office leaders. Abigail explained how she approached the curriculum director position:

> My goal was to prove to these secondary folks that I did know instruction. I wasn't just a little elementary person. I can relate to you. It's not about content as much as it's about what we're doing in the classroom environment to really to promote higher level thinking and what not.

Coming from an elementary background, Abigail actively worked with secondary teachers and principals to establish her credibility. Loretta shared how her experiences as a K-12 gifted supervisor helped her to learn the functions of the district office as well as how the leadership skills necessary at this level differs from the skills needed for school leadership. Rebecca focused on her work with programme implementation and district initiatives as a curriculum director as a position where she learned about managing complex change in school systems. By building relationships with school leaders, the teachers' association, parent and community members, and the superintendent, she learned how to modulate her leadership approach. Rebecca believed this experience allowed her to develop the competencies needed for the superintendency. Throughout their narratives, each woman identified a district-level curriculum leadership position as one of the sentinel position in their career development.

DEVELOPING PROFESSIONAL PREPARATION

Throughout their discourse, the women reflected on how each position in their career pathway allowed them to gain leadership experience, to hone their professional acumen, and to feel efficacious in their leadership roles. The most significant preparatory position for each woman was district-level leadership experience in K-12 curriculum. Loretta shared how a supervisory position is 'tremendous because it gives you the opportunity to go to every building that's in your district.' Abigail spoke of 'having that experience as the K-12 director of curriculum and instruction was critical, just to see the alignment.' Abigail reflected on the sum of her experiences as they related to her, or anyone's, preparation for a superintendent position from an elementary principalship:

> [...] would I have been ready to jump from a building principal to an assistant superintendent from elementary, I never would have done it. I would have thought why

would I do that without enough experience? I need to immerse myself in the secondary programme. I need to know the curriculum. I need to know what makes
the high school tick. I need to know the all dynamics of it. I need to know [...]. So
I felt that I would [...] I would [...] I would hope that anyone would see where their
lack of experiences are and try and immerse themselves in them before they would
get to another level.

For Abigail, she would not have felt prepared for her current role as an
assistant superintendent, nor would she have believed she was ready for a
superintendent position without her experience as a district-level director.

Along a similar vein, Rebecca spoke of how her experiences as a principal and as a curriculum director influenced her expectations for the principals as effective, instructional leaders in her district:

> [...] you would sit in meetings with folks who you knew didn't know. And it was
> so easy to pull the wool over anybody's eyes. If you know what's going on in that
> classroom you can really help those teachers improve. You can. And that's your job.
> A big part of your job is to help people improve. So how are you going to help them
> improve if you don't know what they're doing [...]. It was not just making teachers
> better, but was making those administrators better. So they could speak with author-
> ity about things to teachers. So they could sit in parent meetings and be a viable
> member of the team [...]. Those principals have to be able to speak with authority
> about what's happening in the classroom.

Rebecca's perspective on the role instructional leadership developed from
her experiences working with principals as a curriculum director. In her
work as a superintendent, she recognised the principals' need for professional growth as instructional leaders. Because of her experience in curriculum and instruction, she was able to establish an expectation for principals'
competency as instructional leaders as well as for providing training and
support as a superintendent.

In the context of effective leadership knowledge and experience for
the superintendency, Abigail and Rebecca identified their district-level
director positions in curriculum as the position where they gained the most
knowledge about effective instruction and student learning at all levels,
an understanding of organisational structures of elementary and secondary schools, and access to the superintendent and other key positions in

district-level leadership. Superintendents need to have a deep knowledge base about curriculum and instruction as it affects student learning, models of professional development for teachers and administrators, and organisational leadership within schools and school systems.

Another critical area of professional preparation involved developing effective communication and interpersonal skills. Building trust within the organisation and with the outside community requires adeptness in various modes of communication. With personnel, school and district leaders need to foster a trust among their colleagues to support how messages are communicated as well as received. This requires asking questions and assessing the climate before, during, and after communicating a message or directive. Loretta spoke of her growth in effective communications:

> I think that you need to understand, and I'm not sure I fully did when I started this position, that you never finish everything. And that you're never, no matter what you, going to make everybody happy. Always [...] whatever [...] I think, I wish that I knew, and I know now, you need to be careful with [...] it's not always good to put something out there unless you run it by someone you can trust. Because things that you say, or you have an understanding of ... you want to make sure that someone who isn't in the same place as you also understands it. Because you can put out an email and say this is what I want to do, and if the person who's reading it doesn't get it, it can cause a major meltdown in your faculty. That's an important thing [...] you need to find someone you can trust.

Loretta's comments demonstrated how learning to communicate to a faculty requires a thoughtful and methodical process for ensuring the message is clearly received and understood by the faculty.

In a broader sense, communication skills are a critical component of effective relations between the superintendent and school board. Rebecca shared how she communicates with her school board members, faculty, and community. She established a set of norms for communication with the school board that ensured they are continually informed. These norms extended to how she manages recommendations from individual school board members and redirects them to the appropriate venues for discussion and action. When communicating with the faculty on sensitive issues such as school district consolidation, she shared how she acknowledged their emotional responses to reassignments and provided clear goals for the purpose and rationale behind administrative decisions. When communicating with parents and community members, she provided a context for administrative actions. Rebecca spoke from the perspective of being 'the head advocate for kids'. Her communications from her office reflect this stance:

> And sometimes you have to come across not [...] 'You know, we have to shut down your school.' That doesn't sound like I'm advocating. But the reality is, if we don't shut down that school with seventy kids in it, we're gonna have classes of forty, and I can't do that. So I have to advocate for the big picture here. And I'm bringing your kids to a lovely school, where there's going to be twenty-two in their class. They're gonna have more opportunities because it's a bigger campus with more things. And so, I want you to see that really, this is an exercise in advocacy because I have to look at this big picture. I try to do things too ... like I started this year; it's been really, very positive I do a positive phone call thing. So the buildings give me across the gamut, and I call, and just leave messages, you know, about [...]. So it's that effort of trying to make the superintendency not just a ... it's not just about being an administrative walk. It's about being a real person who really cares about the education that [...] that [...] and if they can really believe that [...].

In Rebecca's communications about difficult and controversial issues, she established rapport through empathy, maintained a focus on students, and delivered information with honesty. In particular, Loretta and Rebecca shared examples of how they developed effective communication skills through their experiences that enabled them to feel successful in their respective positions. Furthermore, their understanding of internal and external constituencies worked to mitigate the pitfalls dealing with multiple perspectives and misconceptions faced within organisations.

Another area of professional preparation included using networking skills from within and outside the district. Each woman shared that finding a trusted colleague within the organisation was essential to a successful tenure. By attending professional learning seminars, school and district leaders stayed abreast of current research and practices as well as engaged in collegial discussions about how other leaders and school systems manage similar issues. Networking provided a venue to make professional contacts and extend one's reputation in circles outside the school district. Abigail spoke about networking as an 'opportunity to see and learn the strengths from people outside your own little world and to be able to put them all

together to add your own strengths.' By remaining informed and developing relationships with colleagues outside the district, these women could
open avenues to positions in other districts.

CONFRONTING EXTERNAL FACTORS

External factors affected how the women access school and district leadership positions. Recognising how opportunities for upward mobility,
access to decision makers, and perceptions about elementary experience
influenced the career decisions these women made. Each woman attained
a school or district leadership position from within the district. The wom-
en's performance in their current roles, demonstrated leadership skills
and knowledge base, and anticipated success influenced how supervisors provided them with opportunities for upward mobility within the
organisation. When asked about her perceptions about moving into the
superintendent position if it becomes available in her district, Abigail
responded with the following:

> I do. This will be my fourteenth year here. So, and certainly, I think, just what I've
> been able to demonstrate in terms of school improvement, dedication, commitment,
> motivation, innovativeness, to the Board from serving for in multiple roles. I've been
> a principal for eight years, two years as director of curriculum, and these years here, I
> think that will give me access to then say [...]. Certainly when they open it up, they
> understand my track record of commitment, and my track record of what I've been
> able to do in the district as well too.

Abigail believed that she has the potential to move into the superintendent position because of her demonstrated performance and experiences
in school and district leadership.

Rebecca shared a similar experience with her appointment to the superintendent position. During the superintendent search, the interim superintendent identified her to the school board as their candidate. Although she
had not yet applied, the interim superintendent recognised that Rebecca's
performance as the curriculum director and her history with the district
made her the most qualified candidate for the position. At major points in
their career pathways, having access to gatekeepers benefited the women's

advancement. In many instances, these individuals functioned as mentors who identified the women as potential candidates for positions or encouraged the women to pursue these positions.

However, when opportunities for upward mobility do not exist, the women expressed that looking outside the district could be an option. Another external factor the women confronted was the perceptions by supervisors and gatekeepers within in the organisation about elementary experience. Loretta expressed that her district is 'male dominated' in top leadership positions coupled with a lack of elementary representation in district leadership. She continued:

> So I think that as much as I hate to say it, elementary administrators, elementary personnel, for sure, are not looked at with the same level of, perhaps, knowledge base that middle school and secondary are. So I think that could hold people back. So from that perspective, you'd almost have to go [...] if you were looking at that route, you'd have to go [...] you may end of having to do the route of the district office of an elementary curriculum coordinator and them move up from there to a bigger position, which shows you've earned your stripes and you know what you're doing.

Loretta expressed that despite her demonstrated performance, her elementary background would prevent her from accessing the assistant superintendent position without intermediary experience as a director or similar experience in another district. Abigail echoed similar concerns; however, in recognising her lack of experience in the secondary level, she approached the director of curriculum and instruction position as an opportunity to broaden her range of experience. While the women believed that their elementary teaching and principalship experience was vital to their professional preparation for the superintendency, they acknowledged that hiring bodies prefer secondary experience and/or a broader range of experiences.

RECOGNISING PERSONAL CHARACTERISTICS

The women's discourse included reflections and beliefs about age, gender and personality as factors that can promote and inhibit access to school and district leadership positions. First and foremost, the women were cognisant of their personal identities outside their professional life. These identities guided their career pathways decisions, but also influenced their perceptions about readiness for school and district leadership positions. In particular, Abigail focused on the breadth of experience that is necessary to be an effective leader:

> And I think that what you really see is the kind of folks that want the role. They want the title, and they're OK with 'I'm the leader in charge and I lead by my title and I'm not concerned with knowing every aspect everything going on around me because I'm just going to delegate that and someone else will take care of it [...]'. I've also seen folks who are [...] just really young folks. You know, they're in their early or late thirties or early forties saying, 'That's it. I want to be the superintendent.' And I value every year of my twenty-eight years to say, 'You know what, I want all different positions. I did all different things. I've taught in different schools. I've taught in [...] different leadership positions. I really tried to stay on the cutting edge in every way I can, so I didn't jump too quickly.'

For Abigail, chronological age was not as critical a factor for readiness for the superintendency as was the professional experience and maturity that comes with age.

The women reflected on gender as a factor in accessing school and district leadership positions. The women were not gender-bound; rather, each woman expressed how she used her female identity to empower her. When asked about why people may not be attracted to top leadership positions in school districts, Rebecca focused on the nature of the positions. She found that many principals thrived in a similar role as did teachers:

> And I think that if you don't, and you like a black and white world, which I think a lot of teachers like a black and world. So, you really look at principals come out of the teacher ranks, what do the teachers like? What time am I supposed to be there? And what am I supposed to bring? You know, they like structure. They like it. That's why a lot of them stay as teachers because they like structure of school.

Rebecca did not differentiate between men's and women's attraction to district leadership. Rather, she believed that aspirations to top positions in district leadership attract individuals who are comfortable being autonomous and self-directed in positions that exist in a continuous state of flux and lack of resolution. When asked specifically about why few women aspire to top leadership position, Rebecca focused on how women interact with one another in leadership roles:

> One of the things that I tried to do here is also, and I think that all women in positions, should try to do, is advocate for one another. And, you know, that's been one of maybe, in sometimes, one of the most disheartening thing has been that some of your, and I don't wanna say toughest critics, because I'm not afraid of criticism, but unwarranted criticism come from other females. I guess that the only other thing that I'd say is I try to build a culture [...] and that's what you're doing, you're changing the culture; you're doing these things, of women being in roles of advocacy for other women. That we're here to support [...] to support good work we have her. And, and not to say we don't support males either, but just to say that ... that we know that sometimes women will not support other women just because they're women. And that, that it is disheartening [...] that is very disheartening to me. So that's something that in an effort to try to say, 'How do we build this culture where we as females, we support one another in these things?' Where we don't do this? Where we're a little more cautious even with this 'behind the back' stuff. Or the 'mean girl' stuff [...] has [...] has no place if you're gonna be in positions like the principalship, like the directorship, like the superintendency. But, the 'mean girl' stuff's gotta go. And that you'll still have some people, at times, who will try to function in that realm, and that that can be [...] can be a difficult area too.

Rebecca spoke candidly about her experience with women in educational leadership. Significantly, as women's representation in leadership positions increases, her call to promote advocacy for women, among women, exemplifies how barriers to accessing top positions may also be attributed to detrimental behaviours that promote negative stereotypes about women.

While acknowledging a lack of female role models, the women shifted the focus to promoting quality leaders. The emphasis on women supporting one another as leaders and not reifying stereotypical behaviours were ways to increase women's representation in top leadership positions. Ultimately, personality is the crux of leadership aspirations leading to accessing school and district leadership positions. Finding balance between their professional and personal lives was a constant struggle. Along a similar vein, Rebecca described the nature of district leadership as a circuitous flow without a defined end or point of accomplishment. She postulated that many teachers and principals who thrive in a professional environment that have a product or task orientation are not attracted to district leadership positions, such as curriculum or the superintendency, where the environment has a process orientation dictated by managing change, external forces and response to crises.

Summary

The two themes that emerged through the case studies of women with elementary principal backgrounds, two women aspiring to the superintendency and one female superintendent, were *developing career pathways* and *accessing school and district leadership positions*. Throughout their narratives, the women identified how their experiences in district-level positions in curriculum promoted their aspirations to pursue the superintendency. These positions served as professional preparation for the superintendency by developing their interpersonal communication skills with multiple constituencies, knowledge of organisational systems, and K-12 instructional leadership. Accessing positions in school and district leadership resulted from the recognition and endorsement of supervisors and mentors who promoted their demonstrated and potential leadership skills. While acknowledging the continuous struggle to balance all facets of leadership in their professional lives, the women expressed self-awareness of their leadership orientation and commitment to student learning. Aspirations to the superintendency developed from their motivation to promote a positive culture of learning as well as their resiliency to confront the internal and external factors that make the superintendency a challenging and demanding position.

Key Findings

The merging of the findings from both the survey and the three case studies result in a number of key findings that encompass the role of district-level positions in women's career pathways in educational administration, influential factors in women's career development, and professional practices that enhance women's career development.

DISTRICT-LEVEL POSITIONS

District-level positions provide superintendent aspirants with opportunities to develop their communication skills with broader internal and external constituencies. In district-level positions, these women learn to balance the various facets of organisational leadership such as school finance, curriculum development, professional development, personnel, and student services. In terms of preparation for the superintendency, the women's' proximity to critical stakeholders such as the superintendent and school board members grants them access to complex functions involved managing and leading public school districts. Recognising that they confront unique barriers to accessing the superintendency as a result of their elementary experience the women in the study use, or anticipate using district-level positions as a career route that leverages their expertise in the foundations of teaching and learning. In doing so, female superintendent aspirants can enhance their credibility and mitigate assumptions about the deficits in their professional background. While deepening their understanding of instruction and curriculum across the K-12 spectrum, the women validate their leadership orientations.

Female superintendent aspirants identify the district-level position as the next position in their career route to the superintendency as well as the most accessible position from the elementary principalship. They strategically select district-level positions because they recognise the importance of preferred professional experience. In this milieu between accessible positions and preferred experience, the women enterprise from the opportunity for career advancement and exert agency over their career decisions. Female superintendent aspirants' perceptions about access to district-level positions extend beyond resignation to the only career route available to them. They modulate their access to these positions into an opportunity to prepare for a superintendent position where they can actualise their career commitments to student learning and achievement and broaden their influence over school systems.

CAREER DEVELOPMENT

Career development theory (Ortiz 1982) suggests that internal and external factors influence women's career opportunities, decisions, and aspirations and the broader factors that influence women's career aspirations to school and district leadership positions. The traditional model of women's career development in the field of education espouses that women enter teaching because it is a socially acceptable profession that conforms to society's expectations about women's gender roles as nurturing caregivers. Women's slow progress into educational administration has been attributed to normative gatekeeping practices that inhibit women's access to positions that lead to the superintendency. The lack of preferred professional experience in school leadership, such as the high school principalship and the use of non-traditional career pathways in educational administration have created a nexus between the traditional view of women as potential school and district leaders and their internal motivation to pursue school and district leadership positions.

Women seek positions in school and district leadership that conform to their career commitments and that align to their intrinsic motivation and self-efficacy, the willingness to seek and conquer new challenges while experiencing autonomy over one's self-authored goals. Female superintendent aspirants who are guided by career commitments to improve student learning and advance school systems seek positions where they can exert their influence over these career commitments as opposed to positions that are narrowly defined by a traditional hierarchy. By rejecting the status quo of the traditional hierarchy, female superintendent aspirants create career pathways that provide continuous meaning to their work in school systems. This study reveals that women view their career pathways to the superintendency as a series of equally challenging and critical professional experiences that concurrently prepare them for the superintendency. Their positional goals are rooted in having influence as opposed to having a title; in the experience gained through the position as opposed to the benefits of having the title.

MENTORS AND ENDORSEMENT

Mentors and endorsement have a profound influence over women's career development. Women actively pursuing the superintendency are purposive in selecting their career routes and responsive to endorsement. These women attribute their career route decisions to their mentors and the endorsement they received. Furthermore, mentors and endorsement bolster women's confidence in their leadership abilities. The effect of mentors and endorsement becomes a transformative moment of realisation, enhancing motivation to pursue and achieve a career goal.

MAKING CAREER DECISIONS

A decision-making point in a career pathway is the confluence of internal and external factors that lead to the individual consciously and deliberately choosing to remain in a position or to pursue a different position. This study reveals that the internal factors that influenced their career decisions include a desire to have a broader effect on student learning and achievement and the school system. As the women became confident in their leadership abilities through successful practice and efficacious in their leadership orientation, they developed aspirations to positions in district-level leadership and the superintendency. The external factors that influenced their career decisions included endorsement from supervisors and mentors and opportunities for internal mobility within their school districts.

Figure 1 illustrates how female superintendent aspirants experience two decision-making points. The first decision-making point is entering educational administration. A majority of women's entry ports, such as the elementary principalship, are outside of the traditional career path to the superintendency. The second decision-making point is envisaging and pursuing a school or district leadership position as a path to the superintendency. The influence of these internal and external factors converged in the women's second decision-making point when they pursued positions that highlighted their expertise as instructional leaders and that potentially lead to the superintendency. From their entry ports as elementary principals, female superintendent aspirants are attracted to district-level positions because they are accessible and advantageous to their career development.

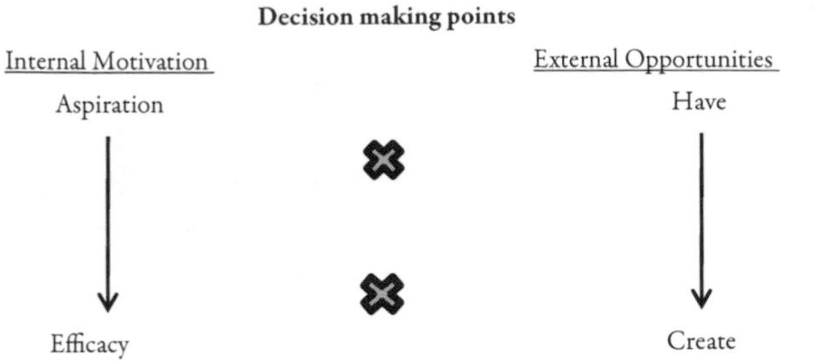

Decision making points

Internal Motivation   External Opportunities

Aspiration   Have

Efficacy   Create

Figure 1:   Concurrent factors in women's decision-making points

Women's aspirations to the superintendency develop as they gain confidence in their leadership abilities, experience success in their current positions, embrace their leadership orientations, and reinforce their career commitments. Female superintendent aspirants career decisions evolve as they develop self-efficacy and goal achievement. Their aspirations extend to broaden their influence of student learning and achievement and school systems. While the superintendency is the goal, female superintendent aspirants are not motivated by the title of the position. Rather, they are motivated to achieve their career goals as they relate to their career commitments. The fulfilment of the innate need to have an impact on student learning and achievement leads to consciously setting career goals and making career decisions that align to their career goals. The concomitant of their career goals and career decisions are influenced by their self-efficacy derived from their professional experience.

IMPLICATIONS FOR PROFESSIONAL PRACTICES

The implications of this study on professional practices include the re-visioning of women's career development in educational administration and the development of professional networks for potential female superintendent aspirants. First, women's career pathway development differs from the traditional career pathway to the superintendency. The corpus of literature around women and educational administration (Glass and Franceschini 2007; Shakeshaft, Brown et al. 2007) identifies the internal and external barriers women confront in aspiring to and pursing school and district leadership positions. Because of their limited access to positions within the traditional career pathway to the superintendency, female superintendent aspirants pursue alternative career routes via district-level leadership positions. However, these positions do not diminish women's professional experience or credibility. Rather, these positions serve as a vehicle to expanding their leadership development through valuable experiences in the management and leadership functions of public school districts. If school boards and search consultants are committed to finding qualified candidates with a breadth of knowledge and experience focused on student learning and achievement, they should consider female candidates who have diverse experiences in building-level and district-level leadership.

Second, professional networks can provide female teachers and administrators with opportunities to explore the positions in district-level leadership. Since a majority of the women in the field of education are concentrated at the elementary level, networks should market to potential candidates. Professional organisations can provide opportunities for learning about the role of curriculum and instructional leadership in school districts. District-based programmes that offer formal mentorships and apprenticeships allow teacher leaders to develop their leadership skills and confidence in their abilities as well as expose them to the alignment of these positions to their existing career commitments. By understanding that women's career development and aspirations to school and district leadership positions evolves as they develop confidence by experiencing success and endorsement, professional networks and programmes should adapt to women's proximal zone of readiness to consider positions in school and district leadership that may lead to the US superintendency.

References

Adkison, J.A. (1981). 'Women in School Administration: A Review of the Research'. *Review of Educational Research* 51 (3), 311–43.
Aud, S., Hussar, W., Johnson, F., Kena, G., Roth, E., Manning, E., Wang, X., and Zhang, J. (2011). *The Condition of Education 2012* (NCES 2012–045). US Department of

Education, National Center for Education Statistics, Washington DC. <http://nces.ed.gov/pubs2011/2011033.pdf> accessed 10 January 2013.

Bjork, L.G. (2000). 'Introduction: Women in the Superintendency – Advances in Research and Theory'. *Educational Administration Quarterly* 36 (1), 5–17.

Brunner, C.C. (1999). *Sacred Dreams: Women and the Superintendency*. Albany: State University of New York Press.

Brunner, C.C. (2000). 'Unsettled Moments in Settled Discourse: Women Superintendents' Experiences of Inequality'. *Educational Administration Quarterly* 36 (1), 76–116.

Brunner, C.C., and Grogan, M. (2007). *Women Leading School Systems*. Lanham, MD: American Association of School Administrators.

Brunner, C.C., and Kim, Y. (2010). 'Are Women Prepared To Be School Superintendents? An Essay on the Myths and Misunderstandings'. *Journal of Research on Leadership Education* 5 (8), 276–309.

Burkman, A. (2011). 'Gender and Related Issues in Elementary School Leadership'. *National Forum of Educational Administration and Supervision Journal* 28 (1), 64–77.

Chase, S.E., and Bell, C.S. (1990). 'Ideology, Discourse, and Gender: How Gatekeepers Talk About Women School Superintendent'. *Social Problems* 37 (2), 163–77.

Coleman, M. (2011). *Women at the Top: Challenges, Choices and Change*. Basingstoke: Palgrave Macmillan.

Creswell, J.W., and Plano Clark, V.L. (2011). *Designing and Conducting Mixed Methods Research* (2nd edn). Thousand Oaks, CA: SAGE.

Daresh, J. (2004). 'Mentoring School Leaders: Professional Promise and Predictable Problems?' *Educational Administration Quarterly* 40 (4), 495–517.

Eckman, E.W. (2004). 'Does Gender Make A Difference? Voices of Male and Female High School Principals'. *Planning and Changing* 35 (3–4), 192–208.

Glass, T.E. (2000). 'Where Are All The Women Superintendents?' *The School Administrator* 57 (6), 28–32.

Glass, T.E., Bjork, L., and Brunner, C.C. (2000). *The Study of the American School Superintendency 2000: A Look at the Superintendent of Education in the New Millennium*. Arlington, VA: American Association of School Administrators.

Glass, T.E., and Franceschini, L.A. (2007). *The State of the American Superintendency: A Mini-Decade Study*. Lanham, MD: American Association of School Administrators.

Grogan, M. (1996). *Voices of Aspiring Women to the Superintendency*. Albany: State University of New York Press.

Grogan, M. (1999). 'Equity/Equality Issues of Gender, Race, and Class'. *Educational Administration Quarterly* 35 (4), 518–36.

Grogan, M., and Shakeshaft, C. (2011). *Women and Educational Leadership*. San Francisco, CA: Jossey-Bass.

Gupton, S.L., and Slick, G.A. (1996). *Highly Successful Women Administrators: The Inside Stories of How They Got There*. Thousand Oaks, CA: Corwin Press.

Howley, A., Andrianaivo, S., and Perry, J. (2005). 'The Pain Outweighs the Gain: Why Teachers Don't Want To Become Principals'. *Teachers College Record* 107 (4), 757–82.

Kamler, E. (2009). 'Decade of Difference (1995–2005): An Examination of the Superintendent Search Consultants' Process on Long Island'. *Educational Administration Quarterly* 45 (1), 115–44.

Kim, Y., and Brunner, C.C. (2009). 'School Administrators' Career Mobility to the Superintendency: Gender Differences in Career Development'. *Journal of Educational Administration* 47 (1), 75–107.

Kowalski, T.J., McCord, R.S., Peterson, G.J., Young, I.P., and Ellerson, N.M. (2011). *The American School Superintendent: 2010 Decennial Study*. Lanham, MD: Rowman & Littlefield.

Loder, T.L. (2005). 'Women Administrators Negotiate Work-Family Conflicts in Changing Times: An Intergenerational Perspective'. *Educational Administration Quarterly* 41 (5), 741–76.

Mahitivanichcha, K., and Rorrer, A.K. (2006). Women's Choices Within Market Constraints: Re-Visioning Access to the Participation in the Superintendency'. *Educational Administration Quarterly* 42 (4), 483–517.

Mountford, M. (2001). 'Motives and Power of School Board Members: Implications for School Board-Superintendent Relationships'. *Educational Administration Quarterly* 40 (5), 704–41.

Newton, R.M. (2006). 'Does Recruitment Message Content Normalize the Superintendency as Male?'. *Educational Administration Quarterly* 42 (4), 551–77.

Newton, R.M., Giesen, J., Freeman, J., Bishop, H., and Zeitoun, P. (2003). 'Assessing the Reactions of Men and Women to Attributes of the Principalship'. *Educational Administration Quarterly* 39 (4), 505–31.

Orr, M.T. (2006). 'Learning the Superintendency: Socialization, Negotiation, and Determination'. *Teacher's College Record* 108 (7), 1362–403.

Ortiz, F.I. (1982). *Career Patterns in Education: Women, Men and Minorities in Public School Administration*. Boston, MA: Bergin Publishers.

Pennsylvania Department of Education (PDE). (2010). *Urban-Centric and Metro-Centric Locale Codes 2007–2008* [data set]. <http://www.portal.state.pa.us/portal/server.pt/community/data_and_statistics/7202/school_locale/509783> accessed 10 January 2013.

Pennsylvania Department of Education (PDE). (2013a). *Pennsylvania's School Districts and Intermediate Units* [map] <http://www.dot.state.pa.us/Internet/Bureaus/pdPlanRes.nsf/infoBPR_Education_PA_Intermediate_unit> accessed 10 January 2013.

Pennsylvania Department of Education (PDE) (2013b). *2011–2012 Professional personnel summary public school final* [data set] <http://www.portal.state.pa.us/portal/server.pt/community/professional_and_support_personnel/7429> accessed 15 May 2013.

Polinchock, A.J. (2014). 'Female Elementary Principals' Perceptions about Access to Potential Career Routes to the Superintendency in Pennsylvania'. Unpublished dissertation, Lehigh University.

Riehl, C., and Byrd, M.A. (1997). 'Gender Differences Among New Recruits to School Administration: Cautionary Footnotes to an Optimist Tale'. *Educational Evaluation and Policy Analysis* 19 (1), 45–64.

Ruhl-Smith, C.D., Shen, J., and Cooley, V.E. (1999). 'Gender Differences in Reasons for Entering and Leaving Education Administration: Discriminant Function Analysis'. *The Journal of Psychology* 133 (6), 596–604.

Rusch, E.A., and Marshall, C. (2006). 'Gender Filters and Leadership: Plotting a Course to Equity'. *International Journal of Leadership in Education: Theory and Practice* 9 (3), 229–50.

Shakeshaft, C. (1989). *Women in Educational Administration* (3rd edn). Newbury Park, CA: Corwin Press.

Shakeshaft, C., Brown, G., Irby, B.J., Grogan, M., and Ballenger, J. (2007). 'Increasing Gender Equity in Educational Leadership'. In S. Klein, B. Richardson, D.A. Grayson, L.S. Fox, C. Kramarae, D. Pollard and C.A. Dwyer (eds), *Handbook for Achieving Gender Equity through Education* (2nd edn), 103–29. Florence, KY: Lawrence Earlbaum.

Sherman, W.H. (2005). 'Preserving the Status Quo or Renegotiating Leadership: Women's Experiences with A District-Based Aspiring Leaders Program'. *Educational Administration Quarterly* 41 (5), 707–40.

Skrla, L. (2000). 'The Social Construction of Gender in the Superintendency'. *Journal of Education Policy* 15 (1), 293–316.

Skrla, L., Reyes, P., and Scheurich, J.J. (2000). 'Sexism, Silence, and Solutions: Women Superintendents Speak Up and Speak Out'. *Educational Administration Quarterly* 36 (1), 44–75.

Tallerico, M. (2000a). *Accessing the Superintendency: The Unwritten Rules*. Thousand Oaks, CA: Corwin Press.

Tallerico, M. (2000b). 'Gaining Access to the Superintendency: Headhunting, Gender, and Color'. *Educational Administration Quarterly* 36 (1), 18–43.

Tallerico, M., and Blount, J. (2004). 'Women and the Superintendency: Insights from Theory and History'. *Educational Administration Quarterly* 40 (5), 633–62.

Young, M.D., and McLeod, S. (2001). 'Flukes, Opportunities, and Planned Interventions: Factors Affecting Women's Decisions to Become School Administrators'. *Educational Administration Quarterly* 37 (4), 462–502.

TANYA FITZGERALD

Venturing into the Habitat of the Powerful: Women Leaders in Higher Education

Introduction

The subject of women in leadership has received increasing attention as more women occupy senior roles in politics, business, community organisations and across the public sector. Continuing evidence indicates that significant obstacles remain for capable women who aspire to these key leadership roles (Bagilhole and White 2011; Coleman 2011). Numerous studies have highlighted how women might effectively respond to these challenges and their struggles as newcomers to the terrain of leadership (Burke and Nelson 2002; Coleman 2010; Davidson and Burke 2004; Hayward 2005; Morley 2013). A fundamental difficulty that remains is that the image of the leader is resolutely masculine. As Sinclair (1998: 109) points out 'even before they open their mouths or act, men are likely to be endowed with power and the potential for leadership'. It is this masculinity of power (Charles and Davies 2000) that reinforces gendered organisational hierarchies that preserve leadership as the prerogative of men.

Women appointed to senior positions in organisations are highly visible and highly scrutinised. Very much the numerical minority in these roles across the public and private sector (Coleman 2011; Fitzgerald 2014; Morley 2013), women experience both vertical and horizontal segregation. One of the consequences is that women are frequently exposed to gendered expectations that serve to limit opportunities for leadership (Gherardi and Poggio 2007). The significant absence of women in senior posts is a recurrent theme across public policy debates, and despite sustained attention there is a remarkable persistence of inequities (Coleman 2011). Furthermore, for those women who do succeed they are regularly the subject of media attention and backlash (Banyard 2010; Woodfield 2007). An immediate conclusion would be that 'women at the top' (Coleman 2011) are unable to shatter the male enclaves of power.

Women in senior leadership roles must reconcile two equally difficult demands. In the first instance they are expected to adjust to the behavioural style typical of the roles and positions they occupy. Secondly, they are required to restore the gender order disrupted by their entrance. This involves undertaking repair work and deploying strategies to mediate their femininity while at the same time mobilising their femaleness to engage in care work (Fitzgerald 2014). Paradoxically, there is a reluctance to openly discuss the discriminatory structures, attitudes or practices women encounter within organisations as they may well be labelled as troublemakers and provoke a structural backlash (Sinclair 1998; Wajcman 1998). Perceived as possessing 'softer' or more feminine skills (Coleman 2002, 2007, 2010, 2011), the underpinning assumption is that women must upgrade their skills in order to meet the standards set by their masculine colleagues.

Stepping out of and away from traditional or perceived conventional roles can be risky and unfamiliar work for women (Gherardi 1996). Responses to their presence may range from being simply ignored or excluded, regarded as less than competent, or weighed down by the weight of expectations (Acker 2010). Remedial approaches to this positioning may involve women adopting tough and masculine management approaches, trying to blend in as 'one of the boys' while simultaneously being given the message that they are subordinate and inferior (Fitzgerald 2014; Grummell, Devine and Lynch 2009). There appears to be no retreat from scrutiny and criticism and any perceived failure can expose women to high levels of rebuke and criticism (Ryan, Haslam and Postmes 2007). Women leaders are doubly scrutinised; by their female and male peers. On the one hand senior women struggle to be recognised for their talents and abilities and on the other, their female colleagues carry expectations that they will represent the interests of all women. Thus, there are two equally unappealing options presented; manage like a man (Bryans and Mavin 2003; Collinson and Hearn 1996), or risk a level of condemnation by not conforming to preconceived ideas about 'women leaders' (Fitzgerald 2014).

Women leaders are caught in the institutional spotlight as they mediate and negotiate their own roles and institutional authority and are exposed to gendered expectations about how they ought to lead and manage (Coleman 2011; Gherardi and Poggio 2007). These expectations include behavioural norms, unwritten rules surrounding notions of respectable and constrained ways of working as well as conformity to dominant and gendered images of the 'woman leader'. The double bind here is that women can behave as women and in doing so accentuate their 'otherness' or they can comply with masculine norms thereby provoking disapproval as they are then regarded as women trying to act as men.

In many ways, senior women are organisational transgressors (Fitzgerald 2014). They dare to venture into the 'habitat of the powerful' (Corsun and Costen 2001: 4) and consequently their very presence is a challenge to the organisational status quo (Saunderson 2002). Women therefore occupy a deeply ambiguous position. Leadership work requires an outward demonstration of masculinity and a simultaneous suppression of femininity (Eagly and Carli 2007; Sinclair 2004).

In this chapter I draw on the work of Marianne Coleman to complicate 'leadership' and tease out the ambiguities, silences and contradictions of women's lived leadership lives. In particular, my attention is turned to women leaders in higher education and to contribute to the debates highlighted in Marianne's 2011 work *Women at the Top*. For the majority of her academic career, Marianne's focus was women headteachers (see for example Coleman 2002, 2007), and her recent attention to the challenges women leaders across the workforce encounter is a welcome addition. Importantly, in the concluding chapter of *Women at the Top*, Marianne notes the slow pace of change, the impact of work environments on women's careers as well as the persistent and untenable dominance of 'one sex in positions of power' (2011: 175). It is this point that I pick up across this chapter and interrogate leadership in higher education as the 'habitat of the powerful' (Corsun and Costen 2001: 4).

Outsiders and Insiders

The feminisation of the paid work force in the twentieth century stimu-
lated a level of optimism that demographic changes would occur. Despite
the introduction of gender equity policies, affirmative action practices
and equal employment legislation (Blackmore and Sachs 2007; Probert
2005), challenges and negotiations remain for women in higher education (Cotterill, Jackson and Letherby 2007). Notably the imbalance of
women in senior roles in higher education is an enduring and seemingly
unbreakable pattern.

At present 13 per cent of leaders in higher education institutions in
Europe are women. A bleaker statistic is that only 9 per cent of research-
intensive universities with a female head (Enders and de Weert 2009).
However, in Sweden where there has been sustained attention to gender
equity and gender mainstreaming policies and practices, 43 per cent of
Vice Chancellors (VC), 60 per cent of Deputy Vice Chancellors (DVCs)
and 31 per cent of Deans are women (Peterson 2011; White, Carvalho
and Riordan 2011). Iceland, Norway, Finland and Israel also have high
numbers of female rectors (VCs) while in Jordan, Morocco, Denmark,
Cyprus, Lithuania, Luxembourg and Hungary there are currently no women
VCs (Morley 2013). In South Africa 17 per cent of VCs are women and in
Portugal only 7 per cent of VCs are women. In Malaysia, there are three
female VCs (15 per cent) across the 20 public universities, and in India 3
per cent of women are VCs, the majority of whom are in women-only colleges (Morley 2013). Across the 39 public universities in Australia, women
comprise 40 per cent of the Pro Vice-Chancellors (PVC), 34 per cent of
DVCs, yet only 18 per cent of VCs (White et al. 2011). In 2014, Professor
Margaret Gardiner was appointed as the VC of Monash University, a
research-intensive university. She was the third woman VC of a Group
of Eight, or research-intensive, university (previous women VCs were
Professor Fay Gale, University of Western Australia from 1990 to 1997, and
Professor Mary O'Kane, University of Adelaide, from 1996 to 2001). In
May 2015 it was announced that Professor Louise Richardson was nomi-
nated as the next Vice Chancellor of Oxford University. To take up the

appointment in January 2016, Richardson, born in the Republic of Ireland, will be the first woman VC at this university, a marked achievement given that it has taken over 800 years for this to occur.

In Ireland men occupy 85 per cent of university management roles and are eight times more likely to be in positions at the level of Dean and above and five times more likely to be promoted to the professorial level (O'Connor 2008). Breakwell and Tytherleigh (2008) determined that in Britain VCs were likely to be white, male and with an average age of 57.76 years and typically had either undergraduate or postgraduate degree from Oxford or Cambridge universities. The majority of VCs in the UK and Australia have backgrounds in science, technology, engineering and maths [STEM] (Blackmore 2014; White et. al. 2011). Similarly, in Ireland and Portugal VCs are more likely to have backgrounds linked with stereotypical male-dominated industries (O'Connor and Carvalho 2014). The immediate problematic with the over-representation in the STEM disciplines is that there is a lack of career experiences, lack of disciplinary differences, and a perceived absence of a leadership habitus but rather the presence of a positivist disposition at senior levels. Cultural capability, interdisciplinary understanding, and ontological perspectives are therefore more rigidly defined in the absence of gender equality and diffusion of disciplinary paradigms (Fitzgerald and Wilkinson 2010).

In Hong Kong, men outnumber women six to one and there are currently no women VCs (Aiston 2014). In New Zealand there has only been two women VCs; Judith Kinnear appointed to Massey University (2003–2008), and Harlene Hayne appointed to the University of Otago in 2011 (Fitzgerald 2014). In the United States, four of the eight Ivy League universities have had women presidents: Ruth J. Simmons at Brown in 2001, the first Black leader of any Ivy League institution, Drew Gilpin Faust at Harvard (2007), Shirley M. Tilghman at Princeton (2001), Judith Rodin at the University of Pennsylvania in 1994 whose successor was Amy Gutmann in 2004. It would seem that while there may be subtle differences across various countries, the global trend is that women are not present in equitable numbers. Thus, the gendered pattern that emerges is that where status and power exist, women's presence is almost non-existent. But perhaps the focus on the numerical picture is misplaced and attention should be shifted to examining organisational culture and practices that perpetuate gender divisions and gendered patterns of behaviour.

Despite the advancement women have made in terms of their participation rate as undergraduates, this has not translated into success in breaking the academic glass ceiling (Coleman 2011). Masculinity and power are intertwined in such a way that men represent the standard. Simply put, men represent the norm against which the performance of women is measured. Notwithstanding decades of affirmative action strategies and equity policies, the dearth of women at senior academic levels such as associate professor and professor continues (Acker 2012; Fitzgerald and Wilkinson 2010). A professorial position is part of the academic pipeline to senior management and it is those who benefit most who participate in the construction of the ideology of meritocracy and standards of academic performance. Standards of merit and excellence are presented as precise, neutral and objective measures and imply that success can be individualised, itemised and counted. The construction of excellence, whether at an individual or institutional level, accumulates advantage for men and produces substantial inequalities for women (van den Brink and Benschop 2012).

Inequities are intensified if selection processes, search committees and promotion policies are predicated on a normative view of what counts as a good leader and good leadership. An almost unrelenting emphasis on STEM is further reinforced through university agendas that focus on global rankings, research performance, productivity and income, entrepreneurial activities and the generation of prestige and esteem. These allegedly neutral and objective indicators of research excellence grounded in performative measures systematically support and reproduce multiple inequalities (Fitzgerald and Wilkinson 2010).

The privileging of STEM in terms of strategic direction and priorities has ramifications for humanities and social sciences; disciplines that traditionally have high numbers of women academics (van den Brink and Benschop 2012). The likelihood of women from a Humanities or Social Sciences background taking up a prestigious role such as VC, or even DVC Research is less possible if the prevailing culture is to 'think-manager-think-male' (Schein and Davidson 1993) *and* there is high value placed on STEM disciplines. A further unintended consequence of this less than inclusive management culture is that the university itself, concentrated in the STEM areas, is potentially undermining its own liberal mission. The strategic question ought to be: what should a contemporary university look like? Arguably an emphasis on STEM and a high concentration of men in senior management roles is less defensible if the core intention is to promote a university with a liberal mission and critical responsibility.

This statistical picture that I have depicted in this chapter is somewhat gloomy. The clear indication is that the pace of change is glacial. The stark reality is that women are a visible minority and simultaneously part of the managerial fabric of the organisation yet marginalised on the basis of their gender. As interlopers in a predominantly male world, women are expected to be managerial (read masculine) enough to be acknowledged as managers, yet feminine enough to display a different set of work practices (Gherardi 1996).

For those women who do succeed, senior management can be a lonely and isolating experience. In many ways, they are the institutional 'Other' (Gherardi and Poggio 2007) and in order to succeed must manage their otherness (Probert 2005). Unlike their male colleagues, women must visibly and overtly demonstrate that they possess credible leadership skills, knowledge and dispositions; skills, knowledge and dispositions linked with masculinity and men (Collinson and Hearn 1996; Wajcman 1998). Consequently, women who are seen to display masculine behaviours no longer 'fit' into prevailing stereotypes or conform to expectations held by either men or women. 'Think-manager-think-male' (Schein and Davidson 1993) is a powerful metaphor that has withstood the passage of time. And although managerialism promotes increased transparency, documentation and data, it is precisely this evidence that in turn shines a light on gender imbalances across institutions. Managerialism is somewhat of a fig leaf as it can be used to justify institutional logics that safeguard an accumulation of advantages for those at the top.

Venturing into the habitat of the powerful (Corsun and Costen 2001) can mean that strong and authoritative women face accusations that they have become 'one of the boys' (Keller and Moglen 1987), are adept at mimicking successful men or are 'playing a game' (Bryans and Mavin 2003). Women are criticised for adopting hegemonic masculine ways of leading

(Kerfoot and Knights 2004; Mavin and Grandy 2012) and face a degree of censure for their apparent infiltration of the management, and masculine, world of men. Successful women may well feel indeed that they are part of a game, or playing a game, as pressure is exerted to modify their behaviour and become more like men (Wajcman 1998). Yet, if women deploy aspects of femininity and show a more collaborative, relational and caring form of leadership, they stand accused of being too 'soft' (Blackmore and Sachs 2007; Sinclair 1998).

There is an uncomfortable dilemma at work here. On the one hand, women can either behave in stereotypical ways that further accentuate their 'otherness'. In this scenario, women can face a level of resistance and condemnation precisely because they do not conform to established stereotypes. On the other hand, women who are perceived to adopt masculine norms provoke a level of peer disapproval because they are seen as women trying to act like men (Itzen and Newman 1995; Schein 2007). The risk here is that if women surrender to these norms they are positioned as conciliatory and submissive (Blackmore 2014; Due Billing 2011) and in the eyes of their female colleagues, neither likeable nor nice. The reductionist assumption that inevitably surfaces is that women are either 'queen bees' or 'wannabees' (Mavin 2008). Queen bee, as a derogatory term, accentuates the seemingly incompatibility between gender identity and the masculinity of power (Charles and Davies 2000). Wannabees are those women seen as 'good girls' (Gallop 1995) who seek to conform to the managerial habitus.

The agonising reality is that 'management incorporates a male standard that positions women out of place' (Wajcman 1998: 2). Women are caught between dominant masculinist images of leaders and leadership. There seems to be a widening chasm between what is expected, the realities of the role and the tasks and activities to be accomplished. In many ways women are caught in the institutional spotlight between discursive binaries positioning them as being both in and out of control (Fitzgerald 2014). Based on their gender, women are strangers in the world of male leaders; they are simultaneously outsiders on the inside and insiders on the outside. As Coleman (2011) has shown, women who do not succeed are frequently deemed the problem precisely because they have not successfully adapted to male patterns of behaviour.

Women's presence in the world of men is conditional on their willingness to 'fit in', adapt to the prevailing culture and modify their behaviour and become more like men (Gherardi 1996; Wajcman, 1998). Put simply, women must lose their exaggerated visibility in order to 'fit in' (Bryans and Mavin 2003), and at the same time distance themselves from their female colleagues. The more senior a woman becomes in an organisation, the more she may be viewed as an outsider by her female colleagues. Inherently problematic in the use of the outsider/insider binary is that it suggests that there is a desirable inside to which women seek admittance. Less scrutinised are the gendered boundaries and borders of the gendered university that reinforce and reproduce divisions (David 2014).

Challenges and Change

Morley (2005) has argued that women's entry into senior management in universities may not necessarily serve women's collective and long-term interests. Although new managerialism has opened up opportunities for women to move into senior management, all is not what it seems. The majority of women in mid-senior levels of university management as Deans, PVCs and Executive Directors predominantly perform the toxic labour of management that requires adherence to performative regimes and practices (Blackmore and Sachs 2007; Charles and Davies 2007; Morley 2013). Immersed in roles shaped around managerial objectives such as audit, accountability, quality assurance, performance management and student satisfaction, women have unconsciously adopted institutional housekeeping portfolios (Fitzgerald 2014). It is these roles frequently linked with teaching and student support that are inward-looking and less prestigious in terms of the portfolios, reporting structures and institutional hierarchy.

Managerial positions shaped around organisational compliance and performative demands deceptively offer women an opportunity to ascend the management career ladder (Acker 2014; Deem and Ozga 2000). Furthermore, as the statistics presented in this chapter highlighted, these are not the positions that directly lead to career opportunities at the DVC and VC level. In a myriad of ways, institutional housekeeping roles are adjunct rather than top-level leadership roles. The hidden message here is that the managerialised, neo-liberalised, globalised and highly masculinised culture of higher education is unattractive and risky for women leaders (Fitzgerald 2014).

There are a significant number of studies that have drawn attention to the multiple systemic barriers that have slowed women's progress into senior leadership roles (see for example Acker 2010; Aiston 2014; Bagilhole and White 2011; Blackmore and Sachs 2007; Coleman 2011; Fitzgerald and Wilkinson 2010; O'Connor and Carvalho 2014). A number of studies have pointed to inequities in employment and promotion processes (Probert 2005), the unequal responsibilities women carry for home and family (Grummell, Devine and Lynch 2009) as well as the emotional well-being of colleagues (Acker 2010) and the absence of access to role models and mentors (Coleman 2010, 2011). The gendered effects of increasingly corporatised and managerial environment of higher education have highlighted the invisible systemic and structural discrimination women face (Blackmore 2014; Fitzgerald 2014). Although the numerical increase in women's representation at senior levels is frequently taken as evidence that barriers have dissolved, the reality is that women remain at a relative disadvantage. Sinclair (1998) theorised that this cumulative problem provoked four particular responses:

1) *Denial*: The numerical absence of women in senior management is not regarded as a problem;
2) *The problem is women*: Women do not have the necessary skills, abilities or dispositions to be managers and therefore must learn and adopt masculine ways of working;
3) *Incremental adjustment*: The solution rests on targeted appointments of token women who already possess the necessary track record and therefore not 'high risk';
4) *Commitment to a new culture*: The exclusion of women is seen as evidence of deeper systemic problems that require new ways of thinking.

These four stages suggest that organisations move from 1) to 4) in a seamless way and that an inclusive culture can be created as various adjustments are made. In effect, Sinclair has prompted a rethinking of the problematic of the absence of women in senior management whereby the organisation is cast as the problem, not women. There is no suggestion that strategies of intervention, improvement and inducement are required to 'change' the relative status of women. Rather, the imbalance of women in management is depicted as a fundamental organisational problem and the commitment to a new organisational culture (step 4) is not possible unless inequities are challenged (Ely and Meyerson 2000). The focus then is not requiring women to 'fit' in to improve their 'functioning' in an organisation, but that questions are raised about the 'fit' of the university and whether there is systemic discouragement of aspirant leaders (Currie, Thiele and Harris 2000).

Curiously universities trumpet their roles as critics and conscience of society yet as institutions continue to legitimise gendered structures and processes. It seems to be that universities are incapable of self-scrutiny and institutional logics reinforce visible masculinist practices and beliefs as 'the way things are' (Meyerson and Tompkins 2007: 308). Seemingly, change is difficult, but it is not impossible. It is in the less visible spaces that women can quietly mobilise and agitate for change. As Meyerson and Tompkins (2007) suggest, localised strategies can stimulate a wider momentum for change. What is needed is a bottom-up approach; that is, women in less senior roles collectively building connections and arousing support for institution-wide change. The power for change rests not with individuals but with the collective group. For senior women, their visibility in the organisation ostensibly places them in a risky position. Paradoxically, the more senior their role is in an institution, the greater the potential exists to pressure for change. Yet, the more senior the role, there is a corresponding intensity of pressure to conform to institutional norms and practices.

Fundamentally, what is at stake here is that the nature and role of the university and the norms about what constitutes leadership in higher education ought to be questioned more closely. Asking questions about the relative absence of women is not the place to begin. The question becomes whether management's actions are appropriate with respect to what universities ought to be doing (Barnett 2011). The yawning gender equity gap cannot be attributed to the absence of skills, abilities or aspirations of women, but with the changing nature of the university. As Davies and Bansel (2007) have pointed out, there is an increasing reluctance to take up leadership positions. Despite over two decades of equity in employment legislation, policies and practices, there is a continuing lack of diversity in university management or senior corporate roles (Coleman 2011; Fitzgerald 2014; Fitzgerald and Wilkinson 2010).

Coleman (2011) does make the point that gender equity has opened up possibilities for women but that much work remains to be undertaken. Research evidence shows that women who seek leadership positions frequently do so because they see the potential to work as change agents (Acker 2010; Blackmore 2014; Blackmore and Sachs 2007). However, pursuing equity objectives can be difficult if not optimistic and unpopular work. Primarily this work requires interventions that do not necessarily, or immediately, align with corporate strategic plans and which require a dismantling of normative and discriminatory practices. In many ways the organisational strategy and direction require individuals to 'fit' the university, but there is less attention paid to the transformative role of the university and its leaders. The task cannot be simplified to counting women in or encouraging more women into leadership roles with the expectation that they will reform the university (Acker 2014).

The challenges are complex and multidimensional. An important first step is to catalogue the absences, silences and exclusions that have occurred. This work continues to be done through research, advocacy and legacies of academics such as Marianne Coleman who has worked tirelessly to rehabilitate exclusionary practices and raise awareness of the vertical and gendered segregation women face. As Coleman (2011) points out the stark absence of women at senior levels is an institutional problem. Keeping gender on the agenda ought to be an institutional remit; not a problem solely for women to highlight.

The second challenge is to ensure that women in the academic pipeline at associate and full professor levels are supported and encouraged into leadership roles (Blackmore 2014; Morley 2013). This may involve active mentoring (Coleman 2010) as well as the wider transformation of institutional structures, processes and culture (Acker 2014; Deem and Ozga 2010; van den Brink and Benschop 2012).

The third challenge is to lessen the adjunct role that women frequently occupy. This can habitually result in women being corralled to provide either a gender balance on committees (usually in the form of adding one woman to the mix) or being hyper-visible for gender equality purposes. Women are disadvantaged through these disproportionate expectations as well as confined to particular forms of work based on their gender (Fitzgerald 2014). An unintended consequence is that gender imbalances can be further exacerbated if senior women evacuate their roles because of job dissatisfaction or if the personal toll is too high (Acker 2010; Blackmore 2014). Longer term the signal might well be that securing a senior role is neither professionally nor personally rewarding.

The final challenge is to locate a theoretically sophisticated tool to understand the complexities of the positioning of women leaders with regard to exigencies of gender, sexualities, race, class, ethnicity, and spatial location. What is required is a more nuanced understanding of the social relations of gender and how different femininities and masculinities are constructed in relation to each other and in specific contexts. Without this integrated focus, the stories that are told will always be incomplete. The critical questions to ask are—Which women and which men are advantaged/disadvantaged within specific contexts? Which women and which men get to be leaders and why? These certainly are questions that Marianne Coleman has grappled with across her career and are perhaps fitting legacy questions with which to leave the field.

References

Acker, S. (2010). 'Gendered Games in Academic Leadership'. *International Studies in Sociology of Education* 20 (2), 129–52.
Acker, S. (2012). 'Chairing and Caring: Gendered Dimensions of Leadership in Academe'. *Gender and Education* 24 (4), 411–28.

Aiston, S.J. (2014). 'Leading the Academy of Being Led? Hong Kong Women Academics'. *Higher Education Research & Development* 33 (1), 59–72.

Bagilhole, B., and White, K. (eds) (2011). *Gender, Power and Management: A Cross Cultural Analysis of Higher Education*. New York: Palgrave Macmillan.

Banyard, K. (2010). *The Equality Illusion: The Truth about Men and Women Today*. London: Faber and Faber.

Barnett, R. (2011). *Being a University*. Abingdon: Routledge.

Blackmore, J. (2014). 'Wasting Talent? Gender and the Problematics of Academic Disenchantment and Disengagement with Leadership'. *Higher Education Research & Development* 33 (1), 86–99.

Blackmore, J., and Sachs, J. (2007). *Performing and Reforming Leaders: Gender, Educational Restructuring and Organisational Change*. Albany: State University of New York Press.

Breakwell, G.M., and Tytherleigh, M.Y. (2008). 'UK University Leaders at the Turn of the 21st Century: Changing Patterns in their Socio-demographic Characteristics'. *Higher Education* 56 (1), 109–27.

Bryans, P., and Mavin, S. (2003). 'Women Learning to be Managers: Learning to Fit In or To Play a Different Game?' *Management Learning* 34 (1), 111–34.

Burke, R.J., and Nelson, D.L. (eds) (2002). *Advancing Women's Careers*. Oxford: Blackwell Publishing.

Charles, N., and Davies, C.A. (2000). 'Cultural Stereotypes and the Gendering of Senior Management'. *Sociological Review* 48 (4), 544–67.

Coleman, M. (2002). *Women as Headteachers: Striking the Balance*. Stoke on Trent: Trentham Books.

Coleman, M. (2007). 'Gender and Educational Leadership in England: A Comparison of Secondary Headteachers' Views Over Time'. *School Leadership and Management* 27 (5), 383–99.

Coleman, M. (2010). 'Women-only (Homophilous) Networks Supporting Women Leaders in Education'. *Journal of Educational Administration* 48 (6), 769–81.

Coleman, M. (2011). *Women at the Top: Challenges, Choices and Change*. New York: Palgrave Macmillan.

Collinson, D., and Hearn, J. (1996). *Managers as Men: Critical Perspectives on Men, Masculinities and Managements*. London: SAGE.

Corsun, D.L., and Costen, W.M. (2001). 'Is the Glass Ceiling Unbreakable: Habitus, Fields and the Stalling of Women and Minorities in Management'. *Journal of Management Inquiry* 10 (1), 16–25.

Cotterill, P., Jackson, S., and Letherby, G. (2007). *Challenges and Negotiations for Women in Higher Education*. Dordrecht: Springer.

Currie, J., Thiele, B., and Harris, P. (2002). *Gendered Universities in Globalised Econo-mies: Power, Careers, and Sacrifices*. Lanham, MD: Lexington Books.

David, M. (2014). *Feminism, Gender and Universities: Politics, Passion and Pedago-gies*. Farnham: Ashgate.

Davidson, M.J., and Burke, R.J. (eds) (2004). *Women in Management Worldwide: Facts, Figures and Analysis*. Aldershot: Ashgate.

Davies, B., and Bansel, P. (2007). 'Governmentality and Academic Work: Shaping the Hearts and Minds of Academic Workers'. *Journal of Curriculum Theorizing* 23 (2), 5–20.

Deem, R., and Ozga, J. (2000). 'Transforming Post-compulsory Education? Femocrats at Work in the Academy'. *Women's Studies International Forum* 23 (2), 153–66.

Due Billing, Y. (2011) 'Are Women in Management Victims of the Phantom Male Norm?'. *Gender, Work and Organisation* 18 (3), 298–317.

Eagly, A.H., and Carli, L.L. (2007). *Through the Labyrinth: The Truth about how Women Become Leaders*. Cambridge, MA: Harvard Business School.

Ely, R.J., and Meyerson, D.E. (2000). 'Theories of Gender in Organizations: A New Approach to Organizational Analyses and Change'. *Research in Organizational Behaviour* 22, 103–51.

Enders, J., and de Weert, E. (eds) (2009). *The Changing Face of Academic Life: Analyti-cal and Comparative Perspectives*. New York: Palgrave Macmillan.

Fitzgerald, T. (2014). *Women Leaders in Higher Education: Shattering the Myths*. Abingdon: Routledge.

Fitzgerald, T., and Wilkinson, J. (2010). *Travelling Towards a Mirage? Gender, Lead-ership and Higher Education*. Brisbane: Post Pressed.

Gallop, J. (ed.) (1995) *Pedagogy: The Question of Impersonation*. Bloomington: Indi-ana University Press.

Gherardi, S. (1996). 'Gendered Organisational Cultures: Narratives of Women Travel-lers in a Male World'. *Gender, Work and Organisation* 3 (4), 187–201.

Gherardi, S., and Poggio, B. (2007). *Gendertelling in Organisations: Narratives from Male-Dominated Environments*. Liber: Copenhagen Business School Press.

Grummell, B., Devine, D., and Lynch, K. (2009). 'The Care–less Manager: Gender, Care and New Managerialism in Higher Education'. *Gender and Education* 21 (2), 191–208.

Hayward, S. (2005). *Women Leading*. Basingstoke: Palgrave Macmillan.

Itzen, C., and Newman, J. (1995). *Gender, Culture and Organisational Change: Putting Theory into Practice*. Abingdon: Routledge.

Keller, E.F., and Moglen, H. (1987). 'Competition and Feminism: Conflicts for Women Academics'. *Signs* 12, 493–511.

Kerfoot, D., and Knights, D. (2004). *Management, Organisation and Masculinity*. London: SAGE.

Mavin, S. (2008). 'Queen Bees, Wannabees and Afraid to Bees: No More "Best Enemies" for Women in Management?' *British Journal of Management* 19, S75–S84.

Mavin, S., and Grandy, G. (2012). 'Doing Gender Well and Differently in Management'. *Gender in Management: An International Journal* 27 (4), 218–31.

Meyerson, D.E., and Tompkins, M. (2007). 'Tempered Radicals as Institutional Change Agents: The Case of Advancing Gender Equity at the University of Michigan'. *Harvard Journal of Law and Gender* 30 (2), 303–22.

Morley, L. (2005). 'Opportunity or Exploitation? Women and Quality Assurance in Higher Education'. *Gender and Education* 17 (4), 411–29.

Morley, L. (2013). 'The Rules of the Game: Women and the Leaderist Turn in Higher Education'. *Gender and Education* 25 (1), 116–31.

O'Connor, P. (2008). 'The Challenge of Gender in Higher Education: Processes and Practices'. *Proceedings of the 4th International Barcelona Conference on Higher Education, Vol. 3, Higher Education and Gender Equity*. Barcelona: GUNI.

O'Connor, P., and Carvalho, T. (2014). 'Different or Similar: Constructions of Leadership by Senior Managers in Irish and Portuguese Universities'. *Studies in Higher Education*, DOI: 10.1080/03075079.2014.914909.

Peterson, H. (2011). 'The Gender Mix Policy: Addressing Gender Inequality in Higher Education Management'. *Journal of Higher Education Policy and Management* 33 (6), 619–28.

Probert, B. (2005). 'I Just Couldn't Fit It In: Gender and Unequal Outcomes in Academic Careers'. *Gender, Work and Organisation* 12 (1), 50–72.

Ryan, M., Haslam, A., and Postmes, T. (2007). 'Reactions to the Glass Cliff: Gender Differences in the Explanations for the Precariousness of Women's Leadership positions'. *Journal of Organisational Change and Management* 20 (2), 182–97.

Saunderson, W. (2002). 'Women, Academia and Identity: Constructions of Equal Opportunities in the "New Managerialism": A Case of Lipstick on the Gorilla?'. *Higher Education Quarterly* 56 (4), 376–406.

Schein, V.E. (2007) 'Women in Management: Reflections and Projections'. *Women in Management Review* 22 (1), 6–18.

Schein, V.E. and Davidson, M.J. (1993). 'Think Manager, Think Male'. *Management Development Review* 6 (3), 24–8.

Sinclair, A. (1998). *Doing Leadership Differently: Gender, Power and Sexuality in a Changing Business Culture*. Melbourne: Melbourne University Press.

Sinclair, A. (2004). 'Journey Around Leadership'. *Discourse: Studies in the Cultural Politics of Education* 25 (1), 7–19.

Van den Brink, M., and Benschop, Y. (2012). 'Slaying the Seven-Headed Dragon: The Quest for Gender Change in Academia'. *Gender, Work and Organization* 19, 71–92.

Wajcman, J. (1998). *Managing like a Man: Women and Men in Corporate Management*. Cambridge: Polity Press.

White, K., Carvalho, T., and Riordan, S. (2011). 'Gender, Power and Managerialism in Universities'. *Journal of Higher Education Policy and Management* 33 (2), 179–88.

Woodfield, R. (2007). *What Women Want from Work: Gender and Occupational Choice in the 21st Century*. Basingstoke: Palgrave Macmillan.

MARGARET GROGAN AND KLARA WAHLSTER

In Books, on the Screen, and in Games: Leadership and Gender Stereotypes Shape Images of Young Women Leaders

> In the complexity of social relationships that exist in the workplace, stereotypes allow us to make quick and easy judgements of individuals based on the ways in which we categorize people [...] lead[ing]to an emotional response of prejudice [...].
>
> — COLEMAN 2011: 35

Gender stereotypes still exert a great deal of power discouraging or preventing women from pursuing leadership opportunities in education. Marianne Coleman, renowned educational leadership scholar develops this theme in several of her works. This chapter builds on Coleman's work by exploring current images of young women in selected United States book series and their movie versions, games and an Australian book series. The purpose of this limited exploration is to consider whether contemporary young women are being offered less traditional ways of being in the world through fiction than their mothers and older sisters were. This is not an in-depth critique of the selected works. It is, rather, an exploration of the ideas and images that are presented in them. Some questions that guide this exploration include: Are the gender stereotypes identified by Coleman still alive and well in these works? What about the leadership ones? How and where might gender and leadership stereotypes intersect? Are these images likely to influence the next generation of women positively or negatively as they consider leadership options?

Margaret and her daughter, Klara, have had an ongoing conversation about women and leadership for the past fifteen years, ever since Klara was in high school. Like Marianne Coleman, Margaret has been researching women in educational leadership for over twenty years and, no doubt, many dinner table discussions revolved around the topic! However, our interest in what is happening now, has been fuelled by an unusual amount of very recent attention here in the United States on young women protagonists in movies based on books. As a former English teacher and school administrator, Margaret became interested enough to look seriously at this topic when she heard her graduate students, who are principals, assistant principals, coordinators, counsellors, and teachers, talk often about the way adolescents are being depicted in the media today. Class discussions, focused on race and ethnicity, class, gender, sexuality, poverty, language proficiency, and ability yielded strong concerns about the continuing influence of negative stereotypes on students in school. Margaret brought Klara into the conversation by asking her to talk specifically about the ways women are depicted in video games. As an enthusiastic gamer herself, Klara is in an excellent position to understand this medium.

The chapter is organised as follows: First, we look at Coleman's books, *Women as Headteachers* (2002) and *Women at the Top* (2011) to see how she has characterised the effects of stereotyping on women's career paths and leadership roles. Then, we discuss three series of books for young adult readers that feature teenage girls in leadership roles: *The Hunger Games* series by Suzanne Collins, *The Divergent* series by Veronica Roth and *The Tomorrow* series by John Marsden. The first two series have recently been made into major motion pictures and the third is available on DVD. However, while we make some comments about the screen version of the first two series, our main focus is on how the female protagonists, Katniss Everdeen, Tris Prior and Ellie Linton, respectively, have been portrayed in the novels. These particular series have been chosen because they feature women as leaders, and because they have been very successful among the general public, although the third series, set in Australia, has had less exposure than the first two. There are plenty of other memorable female characters in young adult novels (for example, Hermione, in the *Harry Potter* series) but Katniss, Tris and Ellie, are good examples of three women who lead much of the action (however leadership is defined within the context of the works). To address the facts that 42 per cent of Americans regularly play video games and 44 per cent of those are women (Entertainment Software Association 2015), we then turn to an exploratory discussion of how women are portrayed in games and the extent to which women characters in games are seen as leaders either stereotypically or not. Our purpose is to understand whether stereotypes of women and stereotypes of leaders have been challenged enough in fiction and games so that more young women are likely to aspire to leadership and/or be seen as potential leaders in the future.

Stereotypes in the Workplace

Coleman's extensive research of women in leadership, in the United Kingdom, demonstrates the insidious power of gender stereotypes to limit women's leadership aspirations and perceptions of their organisational fit. In her book, *Women as Headteachers* (2002: 79), she argues that stereotypes 'cause barriers to career progress and centre around the unthinking belief that there is a 'natural order' – male leadership and female subordination'. She makes clear that both leadership and gender stereotypes are at work here – what counts as masculine and what counts as feminine interact in complex ways with what is valued as leadership. Moreover, as others' research on women in leadership have shown, these preconceived ideas are amazingly widespread across organisational types, and Western, English-speaking cultures such as Australia, the United States, Canada and New Zealand, as well as the United Kingdom (see for example, Shakeshaft et al. 2007).

Participants in Coleman's studies (2002) remark on how gender stereotypes made progress into leadership positions difficult. Women headteachers commented on how isolated they felt having few other women as close colleagues. Many felt marginalised at meetings where male cultures and attitudes dominated proceedings. The inevitable 'old boys networks' reinforced what Coleman calls the 'prejudice of colleagues' (2002: 81) making women feel very much outsiders in the midst of professional gatherings. Women headteachers stood out among their colleagues often because they were leading co-educational schools, and always because they had domestic responsibilities. The pressure was thus on the women leaders to prove they were as competent as their male counterparts. Having family responsibilities made the women vulnerable to the charge of being un- or less professional. In addition, women suffered from the 'essentialist stereotype' (2002: 84) of being carers rather than managers or administrators. Unfortunately, as Coleman (2002) reported, women leaders often respond to these perceptions by working much longer hours and trying to please everyone – creating another stereotype of superwoman that does not always serve women well.

Another concern Coleman (2002) identified was the contradiction between at least two different negative stereotypes that were associated with women leaders: the belief that a woman cannot make up her mind versus the belief that a woman manager is hard, cold and single-minded. Curiously enough, the latter stereotype appears in the young adult novels, where several women leaders, though not the protagonists, are thoroughly unfeeling and evil.

While *Women at the Top* (Coleman 2011: 35) acknowledges that organisations are changing, Coleman still detected a 'bedrock of stereotypes' operating in various ways. Some she describes as immutable. For instance, one of her participants, a petite woman financier, talked of feeling out of place at gatherings of her taller male colleagues. She'd been told that there were some jobs for which you needed to be six feet tall. Physical attributes like height, weight, and attractiveness together with age can work against women much more than men, 'Stereotypes derived from physical appearances are common both in excluding women from certain jobs and also in controlling or demeaning them' (Coleman 2011: 36). In addition to ingrained beliefs that leadership is somehow associated with size, are beliefs that some behaviours are acceptable from men in leadership positions but not from women. Women participants in Coleman's study spoke of being labelled stubborn and aggressive when they acted directly, in an upfront manner. A particularly damaging effect of the masculine organisational culture that helped perpetuate these stereotypes was that some women internalised the beliefs that they were less competent than their male counterparts.

In summary, Coleman's research clearly identified gender and leadership stereotypes that helped to shape women's experiences as organisational leaders in various ways, but mostly negatively. Stereotypes appear to be surprisingly consistent across organisational types and time. That these stereotypes persist is likely because they are so ingrained in organisational myths and storytelling as well as in leadership theories and 'how-to' management books. For example, the leadership archetype that still greatly influences organisational discourse is the heroic one. Olsson (2006: 197) argues that 'organizational stories reiterate a masculinist paradigm of leadership as archetype'. Regardless of counter stories of leadership as collaborative, collective, or shared, the most dominant storyline expressed in management literature and in the media is still that of the hero. Mythical heroes in the Western canon, serving as the model for such leadership, possessed desirable attributes like courage, initiative, physical strength and skill with weaponry. The ideal corporate executive or leader of schools is still cast as one who acts swiftly and decisively either to save the organisation or to take calculated risks to reach new heights of success. According to Olsson (2006: 197), in this storytelling, women leaders are either absent or anomalies. To counter this prevailing effect, Olsson's project is to challenge the heroic leadership archetype by listening to women's stories and trying to identify a new, female leadership archetype.

Influence of Fictitious Characters

Did the authors of the selected young adult novels have a project similar to Olsson's? Perhaps not as explicitly articulated, but perhaps subconsciously. We are well aware that stories written for young adults are expected to draw upon heroic themes, particularly including adventure and adversity in order to capture the imagination of the young audiences. However, it is not yet commonplace in novels to feature women as the main protagonist. So even if these young women are cast in (male) heroic terms, we wonder whether any of the stereotypical male aspects of the leadership archetype have been modified. To what extent do Katniss's, Tris's and Ellie's characters contribute to a new storyline of female leadership that is not simply women behaving in male heroic ways?

And what about popular video and computer games? In exploring some of these, we are acknowledging that many young adults (and older adults) are being exposed to fictitious women and men behaving in certain ways by interacting with this now prevalent new medium. In the modern age, books and movies now share their influence over how gender is enacted with games. How are women portrayed in the gaming world – only as sex objects and as other negative stereotypes or are there opportunities for women to act in leadership capacities? If so, how? In which contexts?

We argue that one of the most powerful ways young women and men learn how to navigate the world is by exposure to stories in books and movies and by seeing how women and men are depicted in video and computer games. While reading might not be as influential as it once was, it is still high on the list of leisure activities for young adults. A survey conducted by the National Endowment for the Arts (NEA 2008) found that slightly over 50 per cent of eighteen to twenty-four year olds read literature, a 21 per cent increase since 2002. When it comes to video and computer games, in the same year, Lenhart, Jones and MacGill (2008) at Pew Research Center found that more than 50 per cent of American adults and four out of five young adults play games. Therefore it is reasonable to suppose that young adults get ideas about what it means to be leaders by participating in these activities. Of course, since they are leisure activities, and fictional, the strength of their influence is debatable, and it probably differs from individual to individual depending on the extent to which individuals are also involved in leadership opportunities in their schools and communities. Nevertheless books, movies and games certainly excite people's imaginations. As Balaka Basu (2013: 19) notes 'all heroes of young adult fiction – and by extension, their readers – are eventually asked to consider the two great questions of adolescence: "Who am I now? And who do I want to be when I grow up?"'.

Three Novel Series

Of the three series chosen, by far the one most critiqued in scholarly literature (see for example, Broad 2013; Couzelis 2013; Fritz 2014; Gilbert-Hickey 2014; Green-Barteet 2014; McDonough and Wagner 2014; Pharr and Clark 2012; Pulliam 2014) on fiction and literacy, is the *Hunger Games* series. To a much lesser extent, the *Divergent* series has received some attention in the world of literary critique, but the third book in the *Divergent* series was only published in 2013, thus, more critique is likely to be written in the future. The movies made about the *Hunger Games* series and the *Divergent* series have garnered a lot of enthusiasm from young adult audiences in the United States. There are currently two *Divergent* and three *Hunger Games* movies out, with two more *Divergent* coming out in the future, and at least one more *Divergent* to be released next year. Much of the popular critique of these two series focuses on the movies, though we comment primarily on the novels in this chapter. Written earlier than the two US series, *Tomorrow, When the War Began*, was finished in 1999. Initially, the seven novels in the series received attention only in Australia, but they have since been published in other parts of the world. However, we found only one scholarly review of the *Tomorrow* book series (Moore 2011). Like the other two series, the *Tomorrow* series was made into a movie. The Australian film was released in 2010 to huge local acclaim, but never gained an international audience, though it is still available on DVD.

References to the teenage women protagonists as leaders in the narrative help make the case for thinking of these women as leaders, as do the comments by literary critics that suggest they are leaders or heroes. In addition, in these critiques, many scholars mention gender stereotypes that are either reinforced in the novels or challenged. There are also many blogs and other web sites (see for example, Lewit 2012; Lo 2012; Lord 2015; Wetta 2013) that have posted comments on gender and leadership in the novels. We have both read these novels, but Margaret has read them through the lens of leadership theories, particularly those inspired by feminist leadership discourse. Therefore, our interdisciplinary approach, combining literature and leadership frameworks, reveals the nexus between gender stereotypes and leadership stereotypes in the novels and allows us to draw some conclusions about whether or not young adult readers are thus being exposed to positive and encouraging ideas of women leaders in novels that are celebrated for their female heroines.

As mentioned, we will focus our discussion on the three female protagonists from the perspective of gender and leadership stereotypes. All similarly aged about sixteen years, the three young women share some characteristics. In the actual games that are at the centre of the first and second of the *Hunger Games* trilogy, Katniss is depicted as a hunter/warrior who fights to the death many opponents. At the end of the first book in the series, she and her fellow tribune, Peeta, are the only two warriors left standing and both go on to play significant roles in defeating the enemy, the Capitol, though Peeta is captured, drugged and depicted as mentally unstable. Physical fighting also plays a large role in the *Divergent* series from the outset as Tris and all her fellow new initiates compete for membership in the faction, Dauntless. As the name of the faction suggests, courage (or rather, more often than not, foolhardiness) is the primary virtue of the faction. To survive, Tris has to learn how to defeat others in fist fights and to kill enemies with weapons like knives and guns. Ellie, too, in *Tomorrow*, learns how to use guns, explosives and other means to kill enemy soldiers who have invaded Australia. Clearly, to be seen as heroines, all three adopt a male, heroic exterior, which plunges them continuously into often brutal action.

While organisational leaders are not as one-dimensional as the hero archetype suggests, at least not in contemporary organisations, there is still a sense of decisive agency that is often labelled leadership especially in a man. Leaders should certainly display courage, if not physical courage, and should 'fight' for their constituents, stand up for their principles, and generally control the actions of others. Tris, Katniss and Ellie earn the respect of others for these sorts of behaviours to varying degrees. Ellie is the most respected for having courageous ideas that others generally go along with – and her plans are often successful. She sees herself in a leadership role. While Katniss, though often thrust into the limelight as leader of the Rebels, has less agency and decisiveness. Tris is more decisive but is often criticised by others for not thinking her ideas through and for acting impulsively.

As leaders, all three are given stereotypical leadership opportunities to make decisions and to influence others to action. According to educational leadership scholars, Leithwood and Riehl (2003: 2) 'At the core of most definitions of leadership are two functions: *providing direction and exercising influence*. Leaders mobilise others and work with others to achieve shared goals' (italics in the original). All three young women have followers who are inspired by their ideas and cooperate to achieve a desired end. Of the three, Katniss takes the least initiative, but by the end, 'she finally takes full ownership of her image and performance [...] and becomes a galvanizing force' (DeaVault 2012: 197). Tris thinks of leadership as her duty once she joins the Dauntless faction (Basu 2013: 27). And, Ellie 'assumes the role of the major strategist [...] guid[ing] her small band to achieve great success in the war' (Moore 2011: 138).

Without a doubt, the action in all novels revolves around these three protagonists and they are certainly meant to be seen as heroes. A ninth grader, Sabrina C., (2014: n.p.) wrote a blog entry on the Mission Viejo Library Teen Voice blog: 'The Hunger Games and Divergent trilogies have great examples of women who are heroic and brave. They are shown as the person to look up to in their books'. Sabrina goes on to say '[Katniss] was written as a strong character who can fight her own battles and isn't afraid to say or do what she wants [...]. [Tris] is a great role model for people, not because she is a rebel and rulebreaker, but because she is strong and independent' So, some young women, at least, admire courage, strength (physical), and independence in a woman role model. Others pick up on the rebel or 'badass' aspect of the two American heroines. Many Facebook entries and blog posts describe their behaviour as 'badass.' A forum, *Divergent Question*, posted on Goodreads website on 9 April 2012 asked: 'Who do you think is more badass [Tris or Katniss]?' (n.p.). This received nearly seventy responses, including several that argue one or the other is more 'badass' because of her strength, determination and/or independence. Several avoided choosing one over the other as this comment reflects 'I think they're both badass and that's why I like books where girls kick ass' (Goodreads 2012: n.p.). Another commentator on the same site used the phrase 'a force to be reckoned with' to justify her choice of Tris.

Literature scholar, Miranda Green-Barteet also writes about the rebellious subjectivities of Katniss and Tris. She argues that 'The circumstances of their respective worlds have enabled Katniss and Tris to be strong, active young women who willingly challenge authority and even confront injustice when they feel compelled to do so' (Green-Barteet 2014: 35). In Green-Barteet's view, the pair have redefined what it means to be young women. She interprets their rebellious behaviour as a way to discover their own power and agency, which turns them into active subjects instead of passive, stereotypically feminine objects. Thus, young women in real-life are attracted to these heroines' boldness, confidence and autonomy in ways that clearly challenge traditional feminine roles in society. Even Ellie, in the *Tomorrow* series, displays a strong sense of self that is developed through acts of courage and sabotage. *Tomorrow*'s world, though not dystopian in the same way the worlds of the other two series are, is certainly horrifyingly dysfunctional since a ruthless enemy has invaded the country and taken all Australians prisoner. Ellie and her band of teens turned refugees not only must avoid capture if they are to survive, but they are even supplied with sophisticated explosives to create havoc through guerrilla warfare tactics. The adults in this series, like those in the other two series, are portrayed as evil, incompetent or limited by a desire to cling to the past. There are a few morally good, but hopelessly out of touch adults in each series such as Katniss's mother, Johanna Reyes in *Divergent*, Ellie's father, and the commander of the New Zealand armed forces. Thus, the young adults in the novels are forced into taking action that is often unwise, often anti-authoritarian but necessary to create a better future for everyone they love. Masculine and feminine stereotypes are mixed together as zeal replaces socially acceptable behaviours.

One of the most obvious ways Collins, Roth and Marsden have achieved this gender fluidity is through offering their female protagonists at least the male accoutrements of weapons and gender-neutral clothing (although Katniss is made up and arrayed in a variety of outfits that are designed to reduce her to a symbol on the television screens). Contrary to female stereotypes, none of the three women protagonists cares about their appearance, hair, cleanliness, or attractiveness to boys in general, although all three have male love interests. Both Tris and Katniss are described as small in stature and Ellie seems to be relatively short as well. Since most of the novels depict these young women in the male spheres of warfare and public agency, they are rarely seen as particularly feminine though all think about their futures and imagine some kind of life different from the turbulent one in which they act. None of them is nurturing though Katniss looks after her little sister, Tris sacrifices her life for her brother, and Ellie surprises herself by caring about what happens to the children they befriend. DeaVault (2012: 195) argues that 'For Katniss, who is neither overtly feminine nor masculine, the path towards autonomy lies in learning how to channel aspects of both'. The same could be said of the other two.

Using a feminist leadership lens that reminds us how women leaders are often viewed as 'less than' or not as 'competent' as their male counterparts, we can conclude on the one hand the reasons for Katniss's, Tris's and Ellie's success in their fictitious worlds is the blurring of the gender roles. On the other hand, Tris and Katniss derive a lot of their popularity from their rebellion against authority, and against evil. Though not a rebel like the other two, Ellie also uses her intelligence and scheming to bring down the enemy regime. Judging by the responses to the books and movies on the Internet, real young women have responded enthusiastically to the freedom from gendered social constraints that these characters enjoy. It remains to be seen whether or not they want to act like Katniss or Tris in real life. Of course, if real young women play video or computer games, they can become characters like Katniss and Tris and practice behaving like them as we describe in the next section.

Three Popular Games

Video and computer games are not traditionally narrative constructs so the opportunities for characters to enact leadership are limited and less developed than those in novels and movies. However, more recent games have characters, who face challenges, and players who can become those characters. Stories were inserted into games slowly as a way of making them more complex and more marketable. Something strange happened towards the mid to late 1990s, maybe with the advent of 3D graphics, and the fact that game rendering in quality swiftly improved to match that used to animate cartoons on television and in film. Suddenly, games were considered intelligent, narrative entertainment, not just by their creators, but by critics and players alike. Play-time increased, expectations changed, and legitimate, critical analyses of games started to surface (see for example, *Feminist Frequency*'s video series on how women are portrayed in video games). Players now had expectations of wanting to or needing to care about their in-game counterparts while they collected gold coins and threw fire-balls at the bad guys. Since so many people under 35 now play video games and the need for sophisticated narrative entertainment has not dwindled, video games offer more tangible degrees of immersion than books do. For example, as a result of the immersive experience of video games, a player actually needs skills to fight battles as the protagonist, and a player can actually feel scared walking down the dark corridor hearing things that 'go bump in the night' (see Madigan 2010). A player can choose to save the girl or sell her to the bar-keep for that extra fifty gold coins the player needs to buy the scrolls with the right spell on them. Players are attracted to games because they make choices, move the characters around, hear the sounds they hear, and because they become someone else entirely.

One weakness of games is in the lack of diversity of the narratives being offered. Anita Sarkeesian (2015) has identified five common stereotypes of women used in games: Damsel in distress, Ms male character, the fighting f@#k toy, women as background, and the Scythian positive female character. Sarkeesian and others criticise game narratives for appealing exclusively to the male audience. Female gamers have become more vocal. Michelle Starr (2014) writes: 'gamers definitely want the option to be able to play as anything other than the generic brooding white guy hero'. However, more recent games have been lauded as good contributions to gaming. Klara plays the female characters in the following games: *The Last of Us* (*TLoU*), *Tomb Raider*, and *Life is Strange*. The female characters, Ellie (*TLoU*), Lara Croft (*Tomb Raider*) and Maxine or Max (*Life is Strange*) are major playable characters that are very important to the narrative. All have story elements that make them worth exploring in this chapter.

In *TLoU*, the player bears witness to Joel and his charge Ellie as they navigate a zombie-infested, post-apocalyptic world in an attempt to get infection-immune Ellie from the government controlled quarantine zone of metro Boston to the research labs of the anti-government group where she can help in the development of a vaccine against becoming a zombie. Critic Larry Hogue praises *TLoU* as 'the most character-driven game he has ever played', as well as providing an interactive, feminist-sensitive story (Hogue 2014: n.p.). Ellie and Joel have to fight and sneak their way through bands of hostile hunters and other life-threatening hazards until Joel convinces Ellie, in a lie, that the anti-government group has given up on finding a vaccine.

There are examples of group female leadership and group male leadership in this game. The major difference between those two kinds of leadership is that the female groups do not revert to blind, reactionary violence on first contact with Ellie and Joel. The male groups are roving hunter factions, amoral scavengers. Unlike these groups, the female groups are seen as alternative, stable and self-sufficient factions using constructs of civilisation to further their means. When Ellie and Joel approach one of the female groups, the group does not shoot at them on sight, choosing rather to disarm them and question their motives before deciding what to do with them.

The player gets a chance to step into Ellie-as-leader's shoes when she and Joel travel across the country. She demonstrates that she is a capable young woman who not only knows how to take care of herself against a potential rapist, but who also saves Joel's life. She acts with a great deal of agency in both the main game and even more so in the downloadable content (DLC).

Tomb Raider (2013) is an updated version of the *Tomb Raider* game that was created in the 1990s. In this latest version, everything has changed, save for the fact that the character's name is still Lara Croft. Instead of being a greedy, fashionable, kill-happy, sex-doll-like marauder, Lara is now an academic, dressed in fairly modest clothing. She and her team have been shipwrecked and land on an island full of horrors. The game incorporates a lot of positive female modalities, although Lara rescues her team in stereotypically male heroic ways when Lara/the player, is thrown head-first into overcoming murder attacks, human sacrifice, active pagan worship and packs of vicious wolves. A review of the new *Tomb Raider* describes Lara as 'one of the best action heroes, I've ever seen. Not *female* action heroes – *action heroes*, period, full stop' (Chambers 2013: n.p.).

However, Lara is more than a stereotypical action hero. She is allowed to express her fears. Lara is often alone with nothing but her own internal monologue for company – the static of her portable radio crackling with a definite absence of human communication. Players hear her step-by-step narration as she convinces herself to put one foot in front of the other, one-by-one, and march forward despite her perfectly valid misgivings. As Becky Chambers (2013) writes, 'You'd be hard-pressed to find a male action hero shown panting with fear, shaking with cold, holding his best friend's hand reassuringly, or any of the many other emotive things we see Lara do' (Chambers 2013: n.p.). The reviewer points out that it is these human emotions that render Lara such a compelling character. It is not just the realism that is emphasised in the portrayal of Lara's fears, it is also the boon it provides in the form of empathetic game play.

In *Life is Strange*, there are three parallel layers of narratives about microscopic and macroscopic conflict. Many of these conflicts arise as Max attempts to navigate the high school scene at an elite, boarding school for twelfth graders. The game opens with Max falling asleep in class and having a nightmare-like vision about a huge storm and tornado hitting her coastal town destroying everything and everyone in the town. After class, she stumbles into the bathroom, and witnesses a popular boy shoot a girl in the stomach. Her strong emotional reaction to the scene causes her to realise that she can reverse time. After some internal debate, Max uses the opportunity to prevent the girl in the bathroom from being shot. It turns out to be a good thing because the girl Max saved is her estranged childhood friend Chloe. Max tells Chloe about the storm and, at the macro level, the two vow to try to stop it at all costs using Max's power.

At the micro level, the tom-boyish Max is given the opportunity to be a social leader by navigating the high school scene and dealing with the popular Victoria's antagonism. Victoria is a slightly more rounded version of what Sarkeesian (2013: n.p.) calls the 'personality female syndrome.' This is when a character is 'reduced to nothing more than a shallow collection of negative female stereotypes […] vain, bratty, spoiled, and quick to anger' (Sarkeesian 2013: n.p.). As a leader, Max is calmer, more rational, less cold when exercising authority, less catty and bitchy, thus avoiding the stereotype of a young female social leader. Moreover, what makes Max gain the respect of her peers and become a more effective leader than Victoria is Max's empathy and compassion. As Max, the player is offered choices and time to get to know the various girls in the grade, and is able to gain their trust by treating them as a player would treat a sister or friend in real life. During the game, there are plenty of opportunities to engage in petty sniping with Victoria, but the game encourages Max to show kindness and respect even towards those antagonistic to her. This is done through positive social reinforcement. If a player chooses to be the better person in moral terms when offered the option, the players' peers respect her more. What that means in the actual game mechanics is multifaceted: sometimes, it means Victoria makes the player's (and the player's friends') life less miserable in the form of less retaliatory bullying; sometimes that means people who are not the player's friends express respect for the player's ability to keep a secret, or make a good decision, and become allies in achieving a soft objective during the chapter of the game that would have otherwise been harder to achieve. Sometimes it is almost frivolous – the player has a photo album she can fill as the game proceeds (as a secondary, or even tertiary objective) and some of the moments the player wants to photograph may be otherwise impossible to capture.

Despite their diverse universes and goals, and despite the different ways each of them struggles to lead in times of extreme adversity, there are commonalities among the three characters. The commonalities include: experiencing fear while being expected to act as leaders; struggling with the morality of their actions, especially killing; and an empathetic approach to others that moderates their behaviour. It is important to note that these qualities differentiate them from the male-leader stereotype in games and each quality is portrayed as either a flaw in the female character or something that strengthens that character. Reviews suggest that some players find these qualities attractive (see, for example Blackwell 2012; Chambers 2013; Hernandez 2013). On her blog, Hernandez (2013) tells the particularly compelling story of a teenager whose life was profoundly affected by the courage he saw in Lara Croft, 'we see Lara like we never have before. She's hurt, she's bruised, she's vulnerable – and none of that stops her. It's easy to see how the game could inspire someone to be stronger'.

In addition, all three characters are young (Ellie is about fourteen years old, Lara about twenty-one and Max about seventeen). They are physically limited by their relative strength and size, and have little or no chance in physical confrontation with adults/men in their worlds without weapons. Max and Ellie use their wits and intelligence to escape many of their predicaments. Instead of rushing in with brute force, they manage their situations with stealth, surprise tactics, and by being socially empathetic towards their teammates or peers. There are times when both find their smaller stature an advantage in being able to hide in places larger people could not. In general, most of the physical disadvantages introduced by their gender and age are directly negated by or ignored in favor of the advantages they offer. Lara, on the other hand, is less able to turn her strength deficit into advantage though she is very resilient.

Clearly differentiating them from the stereotypical hero, the fears these women experience render them more complex characters than the usual video game character. For example, Ellie is afraid of being left alone for the rest of her life, and when Joel is gravely injured, she is very fearful of having to fend for both of them. She is terrified of her enemy, David, as she scrambles to get away from him in the burning restaurant. In Ellie's shoes, the player understands these fears. Becky Chambers (2013) argues that depth and honesty are largely absent from the stereotypical male protagonist in video games. Ellie is never a coward. There is no swagger, no calm, cool professionalism, only human honesty. Similarly, Max fears making the wrong decisions, and not being able to save the town from the tornado. But she never lets her fears stop her from performing an action. The player truly empathises with her lack of surety under such circumstances. 'Max is no superhero, she's just a girl trying to do right by everybody. But like in the real world, trying to please everyone has consequences, and Life is Strange (sic) lets you know that with a shot to the heart' (Corriea 2015: n.p.). Like Max, Lara's fears do not paralyse her either. Being hunted, suddenly she finds herself in a position of having to murder her foes just to survive long enough to save herself and her friends, not sure always who is friend and who is foe. In one scene, finding herself in an awful, frightening position, Lara is not able to keep her cool. However, she takes a moment to wipe tears from her face and then shoots the guards in order to help her friends. She revels in relief when she succeeds and crumples in anguish when she fails, but she always perseveres. According to Carol Pinchefsky (2013: n.p.), 'The game does an absolutely superb job of balancing [Lara] between inexperience and determination. Lara might be wounded and afraid, but she's going to press on regardless. We do root for her, but she also demands our respect'. Fear is a hugely humanising element of these games – and, unlike male heroic types, these female heroes are allowed to be human and successful.

Conclusions

All in all, these young female protagonists in both the books and the games complicate the picture of young leaders within the circumstances of their worlds. Feminist lenses draw our attention to the negative connotations of some of the qualities we have labelled desirable in a leader. As described above, we view positively the young women's internal reflections that allow us to see their fears, empathy, moral struggles and moments of doubt. We could have critiqued these ruminations as signs of the characters' lack of confidence, weakness, inability to make a decision, immaturity and so on. After all, Katniss is manipulated by others, just as Ellie (*TLoU*), and Max are both manipulated by others and engage in manipulation themselves. Lara Croft plays up her feminine vulnerability in the early stages, and Ellie Linton organises every last detail of each manoeuvre. Above all, expressing emotions, as they all do, is often indicative of a negative female stereotype. What complicates the picture is that these qualities of empathy, moral struggle, expressing fear and doubt are positively coupled with the stereo-typically male heroic qualities of physical strength, decisiveness, prompt action, courage, and leading others out of danger. Male protagonists in games and young adult fiction are rarely drawn in such ways. For the sake of diversifying the leadership narrative, it would be better if both male and female protagonists were created that embodied these humanising characteristics along with at least some of the stereotypical heroic qualities. Courage rather than foolhardiness is desirable in a leader, as are a clear sense of right and wrong, empathy for others and a willingness to act on behalf of the common good rather than for individual gain. However, some progress is being made. Just as blurring gender roles in the novels helped to create a space for some of these couplings, the video game world appears to allow some fluidity in a playable character's formation. Gender stereotypes (including the depiction of women as nothing more than sex objects) and archetypal heroic narratives appear to be less popular with at least women gamers in this medium.

The rising interest in playing video/computer games among women aged eighteen years and older has surely had a positive impact on how women are portrayed in games. In addition, the huge success of the *Hunger Games* and *Divergent* books and movies can probably be attributed in some part to the excitement of seeing young women heroines. Narratives where young women successfully challenge adults and other authority figures, and succeed, capture the imagination of those who are trying to find their own identities. If they see leadership as taking initiative, dealing with fears, taking care of friends, having the determination and courage to overcome seemingly insurmountable obstacles and, at the same time, being ordinary women just like themselves, perhaps they will not feel the pressure to conform to a male version of leader. What matters is whether this attractive, 'badass' version of female leadership can withstand the further socialising young women go through as they ready themselves for the work place. The negative female stereotypes that limit women's leadership opportunities as Coleman (2002, 2011) outlined, have not been shattered with these new characters in fiction and games. But they have been called into question. We think the power of the books, movies and games lies in valuing women for using their intelligence, their capacity to reflect on their actions, and their humanity. None of these characters is a particularly 'good' person. Each character has flaws, tells lies, makes tactical mistakes – Tris pays with her life. Each makes enemies, and, although there are love interests in all the books, they are not romances.

We are hopeful that gender stereotypes and leadership have both been challenged by the ways these young women experience their worlds. There is still remarkably little ethnic or sexual diversity woven into the books and games. So the only small shifts we are seeing are those that emerge from imaginary, white, heterosexual women's experiences (although *Life is Strange* suggests a lesbian relationship and there are minor racially diverse characters sprinkled throughout the books and games). Perhaps the best outcome of all is that so many young women (and older women) are posting their views of the books, movies and games on the Internet. The debate about which is the more badass character Katniss or Tris is an excellent example. The many reviews of the new version of Lara Croft are another. We hope these conversations continue so that game developers and authors mix things up even more in the future. Eventually, gender and leadership stereotypes will lose their clout as young women and men explore even more nuanced narratives in the future.

References

Basu, B. (2013). 'What Faction Are You In? The Pleasure of Being Sorted in Veronica Roth's *Divergent*'. In B. Basu, K.R. Broad and C. Hintz (eds), *Contemporary Dystopian Fiction for Young Adults*, 19–33. New York: Routledge.

Broad, K.R. (2013). '"The Dandelion in the Spring": Utopia As Romance in Suzanne Collins's Hunger Games Trilogy'. In B. Basu, K.R. Broad and C. Hintz (eds), *Contemporary Dystopian Fiction for Young Adults*, 117–30. New York: Routledge.

Blackwell, W. (2012). 'Lara Croft, More Vulnerable But Stronger Than Ever'. <http://www.onlysp.com/lara-croft-more-vulnerable-but-stronger-than-ever/> accessed 14 June, 2015.

C., Sabrina (2014). 'Strong Heroines in Fiction: Katniss and Tris'. 17 July, <http://mvlteenvoice.com/2014/07/17/strong-heroines-in-fiction-katniss-and-tris/> accessed 4 April 2015.

Chambers, B. (2013). 'Lara Croft Is Dead. Long Live Lara Croft: Reflections on Tomb Raider'. <http://www.themarysue.com/tomb-raider-review/> accessed 5 May 2015.

Coleman, M. (2002). *Women as Headteachers: Striking the Balance*. Stoke on Trent: Trentham Books.

Coleman, M. (2011). *Women at the Top*. New York: Palgrave Macmillan.

Corriea, A.R. (2015). 'Not-So-Super Girl'. <http://www.gamespot.com/reviews/life-is-strange-episode-two-review/1900-6416079/> accessed 12 May 2015.

Couzelis, M.J. (2013). 'The Future Is Pale: Race in Contemporary Young Adult Dystopian Novels'. In B. Basu, K.R. Broad and C. Hintz (eds), *Contemporary Dystopian Fiction for Young Adults*, 131–44. New York: Routledge.

DeaVault, R.M. (2012). 'The Masks of Femininity: Perceptions of the Feminine in Hunger Games and Podkayne of Mars'. In M.F. Pharr and L.A. Clark (eds), *Of Bread, Blood and the Hunger Games*, 190–8. Jefferson, NC: McFarlane and Company.

Entertainment Software Association (2015). 'Industry Facts'. <http://www.theesa.com/about-esa/industry-facts/> accessed 12 May 2015.

Feminist Frequency (2015). <http://feministfrequency.com/> accessed 30 April 2015.

Fritz, S.S. (2014). 'Girl Power and Girl Activism in the Fiction of Suzanne Collins, Scott Westerfield, and Moira Young'. In S.K. Day, M.A. Green-Barteet and A.L. Montz (eds), *Female Rebellion in Young Adult Dystopian Literature*, 17–32. Burlington, VT: Ashgate.

Goodreads (2012). 'Divergent Question'. <http://www.goodreads.com/topic/show/860519-tris-or-katniss> accessed 30 April 2015.

Gilbert-Hickey, M. (2014). 'Gender Rolls: Bread and Resistance in the "Hunger Games" Trilogy'. In S.K. Day, M.A. Green-Barteet and A.L. Montz (eds), *Female Rebellion in Young Adult Dystopian Literature*, 95–106. Burlington, VT: Ashgate.

Green-Barteet, M.A. (2014). '"I'm Beginning to Know Who I Am": The Rebellious Subjectivities of Katniss Everdeen and Tris Prior'. In S.K. Day, M.A. Green-Barteet and A.L. Montz (eds), *Female Rebellion in Young Adult Dystopian Literature*, 33–50. Burlington, VT: Ashgate.

Hernandez, P. (2013). 'The New Tomb Raider Saved This Teenager's Life'. <http://kotaku.com/5990234/the-new-tomb-raider-saved-this-teenagers-life> accessed 14 June 2015.

Hogue, L. (2014). 'The Last of Us, Feminism and Misogyny'. 29 August, <http://lawrencehogue.net/wordpress/2014/08/29/the-last-of-us-feminism-and-misogyny/> accessed 5 May 2015.

Leithwood, K.A., and Riehl, C. (2003). 'What We Know About Successful School Leadership'. <http://www.leadersdesktop.sa.edu.au/leadership/files/links/school_leadership.pdf> accessed 1 May 2015.

Lenhart, A., Jones, S., and MacGill, A. (2008). 'Adults and Video Games'. Pew Research Center Report <http://www.pewinternet.org/2008/12/07/adults-and-video-games/> accessed 3 April 2015.

Lewit, M. (2012). 'Why Do Female Authors Dominate Young Adult Fiction?' <http://www.theatlantic.com/entertainment/archive/2012/08/why-do-female-authors-dominate-young-adult-fiction/260829/> accessed 12 June 2015.

Lo, M. (2012). 'YA Fiction and the Many Possibilities of Manhood'. <http://www.malindalo.com/2012/11/ya-fiction-and-the-many-possibilities-of-manhood/> accessed 12 June 2015.

Lord, E. (2015). 'Are you More Katniss or Tris?', 31 March <http://www.buzzfeed.com/emmamariemusic/are-you-more-katniss-or-tris-11sp6?responses#.hvrL2bPLN> accessed 30 April 2015.

Madigan, J. (2010). 'The Psychology of Immersion in Video Games'. <http://www.psychologyofgames.com/2010/07/the-psychology-of-immersion-in-video-games/> accessed 14 June 2015.

Moore, J.N. (2011). *John Marsden: Darkness, Shadow and Light*. Lanham, MD: Scarecrow Press.

McDonough, M. and Wagner, K.A. (2014). 'Rebellious Natures: The Role of Nature in Young Adult Dystopian Female Protagonists' Awakenings and Agency'. In S.K. Day, M.A. Green-Barteet and A.L. Montz (eds), *Female Rebellion in Young Adult Dystopian Literature*, 157–70. Burlington, VT: Ashgate.

National Endowment for the Arts (NEA) (2008). 'Reading on the Rise: A New Chapter in American Literacy'. <http://arts.gov/sites/default/files/ReadingonRise.pdf.> accessed 2 April 2015.

Olsson, S. (2006). '"We Don't Need Another Hero!" Organizational Storytelling as a Vehicle for Communicating a Female Archetype of Workplace Leadership'. In M. Barrett and M.J. Davidson (eds), *Gender and Communication at Work*, 196–210. Burlington, VT: Ashgate.

Pharr, M.F., and Clark, L.A. (2012). *Of Bread, Blood and The Hunger Games*. Jefferson, NC: McFarland & Company.

Pinchefsky, C. (2013). 'A Feminist Reviews Tomb Raider's Lara Croft'. <http://www.forbes.com/sites/carolpinchefsky/2013/03/12/a-feminist-reviews-tomb-raiders-lara-croft/> accessed 12 May 2015.

Pulliam, J. (2014). Real or Not Real – Katniss Everdeen Loves Peeta Melark: The Lingering Effects of Discipline in the "Hunger Games" Trilogy. In S.K. Day, M.A. Green-Barteet, and A.L. Montz (eds), *Female Rebellion in Young Adult Dystopian Literature*, 171–86. Burlington, VT: Ashgate.

Sarkeesian, A. (2013). 'Ms Male Character: Tropes v. Women'. 8 November, <http://feministfrequency.com/2013/11/18/ms-male-character-tropes-vs-women/> accessed 5 May 2015.

Sarkeesian, A. (2015). 'Tropes v. Women in Video Games'. 31 March, <https://www.kickstarter.com/projects/566429325/tropes-vs-women-in-video-games/> accessed 5 May 2015.

Shakeshaft, C., Brown, G., Irby, B., Grogan, M., and Ballenger, J. (2007). 'Increasing Gender Equity in Educational Leadership'. In S. Klein, B. Richardson, D.A. Grayson, L.H. Fox, C. Kramarae, D. Pollard and C.A. Dwyer (eds), *Handbook for Achieving Gender Equity through Education* (2nd edn), 103–30. Florence, KY: Lawrence Erlbaum Associates.

Starr, M. (2014). *The Risk of The Female Game Protagonist*, 6 August. <http://www.cnet.com/news/the-risk-of-the-female-protagonist/> accessed 12 May 2015.

Wetta, M. (2013). 'What We Talk About When We Talk About 'Strong' Heroines in Young Adult Fiction'. <http://www.yalsa.ala.org/thehub/2013/03/14/what-we-talk-about-when-we-talk-about-strong-heroines-in-young-adult-fiction/> accessed 12 June 2015.

PONTSO MOOROSI

Patriarchal Bargain for African Women in Leadership: Deal or No Deal?

Introduction

Marianne Coleman's work has consistently challenged gendered stereotypes that rendered women powerless in leadership positions in both education and the private sector. In challenging these stereotypes, Coleman's
attention has been focused on the role women continue to play in the
home despite their success in the boardroom and in leadership positions.
For Coleman, (and many others) this unequal distribution of roles and
responsibilities in the home, benefits men and works against the advancement and progression of women in leadership, thereby perpetuating the
gender inequality. In her latest book, *Women at the Top: Challenges, Choices
and Change*, Coleman (2011) presents a compelling analysis of women's
experiences of success against challenges they face in the domineering
masculine cultures of the workplace and difficult choices they have had
to make in the path towards change. This inspiring piece of work, breaks
boundaries by not only examining women's experiences of success in leadership, but by problematising the gendered intricacy between challenge,
choice and change, across the different sectors. In celebrating Coleman's
scholarship, this chapter will draw on findings from research that examined constructions of masculinities by corporate male and female leaders
in South Africa, with specific focus on women's experiences of navigating
a balance between family and work. The chapter will make a comparison between these African women's experiences and those examined in
Coleman's work. It will argue that in negotiating a balance between work

and home,[1] women end up striking a 'patriarchal bargain' that is both empowering and disempowering. By way of amplifying Coleman's work, the chapter will argue that challenges faced and choices made lead women to strike the patriarchal bargains in the home and take advantage of the corporate policies that are indeed supposed to benefit them and enable change. However in doing so, they perpetuate the stereotypes about the role of men and women at work and in the home.

This chapter is a contribution to a volume that honours the work of a great scholar, Marianne Coleman. Participating in such an important academic exercise is in and of itself an honour and distinguishing one's contribution from others was not an easy task. It may also seem unjust to merely focus on one piece of text out of the numerous available from Coleman's outstanding collection. Coleman is after all the greatest scholar of her time in the field of gender and leadership. I approach this chapter, however, from a comparative analysis perspective – comparing and contrasting women's experiences in the United Kingdom with some South African experiences of women managers. I build the chapter on the three themes of Coleman's book: challenges, choices and change. These are *challenges* that women face in pursing their leadership career and *choices* that they make along the way and how these challenges and choices influence *change* – change in the organisations and change in people's attitudes towards gender and work. As one of Coleman's latest contributions to the field, the book was a timely and much welcomed contribution to the field. In comparing and contrasting similarities and differences between women based in the UK with those based in South Africa, the intention is to highlight gendered challenges that are experienced by women in different contexts. These challenges, it is argued, force women to make difficult choices between family and work, and those who are married to accept some deals (or no deals) that appear to work for their families, but at the expense of their careers. It is not my intention to condemn or condone such strategies but

---

[1]   Work-home or work-family balance is usually referred to as work-life (e.g. Connell 2005b), but Coleman insists that work is an important part of women's life. I choose to use work-family in honour of Coleman.

the intention is to argue and problematise the extent to which they lead to change in combating the battle against gendered discrimination and gender inequality. Using the patriarchal bargain as a conceptual framework, I will analyse two cases of female managers who participated in the study of masculinities and compare their backgrounds and experiences to those of women in Coleman's book.

Following this introduction, the first part of this chapter serves to provide an overview of Coleman's book– appreciating the work and mapping the theoretical background on gender stereotypes in relation to leadership. the second part of the chapter will unpack the concept of the patriarchal bargain, which I use as a framework to analyse experiences of women in leadership in some of my own work. In this part I will also present a brief methodological note backgrounding the interviews from which I draw. The third part will compare South African women's experiences to UK women in Coleman's work using three key themes from Coleman's book: challenges, choices and change. Finally, the conclusion will highlight work that still requires attention in the field in continuing the legacy of Marianne Coleman for women in leadership.

Women at the Top

Women at the Top: Challenges, Choices and Change (hereafter, *Women at the Top*) serves as the highlight of Coleman's work. It is inspiring and varied – covering women's leadership across various sectors. In this book, Coleman foregrounds the problematic nature of the tradition that associated women with the supporting role to men while the role of leader has been associated with the male image. This has been largely due to the influence of gender role stereotyping and gender role socialisation on how women are perceived by society and how women perceive themselves and their capabilities in the work place. In this sense, it is perhaps not surprising that family responsibilities are still the main challenge to women's progression in leadership. Very early on in her writing in the 1990s, Coleman stated that the identification of women with supportive roles and of men with leadership roles is a stereotype that may be linked with processes of socialisation, which lead women to believe that the public domain is not suitable for them because they have been socialised into the private domain. Over decades this male and female dichotomy of roles has narrowed career choices available to women, pigeonholing women in jobs and roles within jobs that are unlikely to provide a route to promotion. In recent years we have also learnt that the public/private dichotomy is inadequate to explain the underrepresentation of women in leadership positions as more women got exposure into the world of work. However, although many countries have intervened politically and legally with strategies that guarantee equal access to all occupations and careers, Coleman and other researchers (e.g. Fuller, Cliffe and Moorosi 2013) note the subtle and more persistent gender discrimination that still exists, preventing women from reaching the very top in their chosen careers including those that they dominate. This discrimination is also deceptive, as even women sometimes fail to recognise or acknowledge its existence. For example, the study by Fuller et al (2013) asked women to narrate their experiences of discrimination, which they denied having, only to go on giving examples that demonstrate experiences of discrimination on the basis of gender. *Women at the Top*, shows how deeply ingrained stereotypes are in today's organisations, forming the foundation for the *challenges* women face in negotiating their way to the top of organisations. These stereotypes are manifest in the perceptions about and attitudes towards women at work that effectively block their career progression.

Using authentic voices of sixty high-flying women, Coleman (2011) skilfully problematises women's success with *choice* and change. By so doing, she illustrates that for most women to be successful, [sometimes difficult] choices have to be made. These choices have to be made because women still bear the brunt of domestic responsibilities. It is in making these choices that a patriarchal bargain has to be struck by some women, subjecting them to criticisms about their commitment [or lack of it] to work. In analysing women's commitment to employment, Bimrose (2008) identified three groups of women as: (i) those committed to their full-time employment (hence career); (ii) those giving priority to domestic life and (iii) those combining work and family.[2] Women in the first category are often the ones condemned for not having time for family as they are more interested in and focused on their career. These are the women who can spend long hours at work [with men] and adopt all the necessary skills to perform in a male dominated and masculine culture. In this vein, one would be inclined to think that the sixty highflying women at the top in Coleman's book fall in this category. However, *Women at the Top* presents a more thoughtful, complex and nuanced account than that, befitting of Coleman's standing. The majority of the highflying women are typical category (iii) who combine career and family. These women are wives and mothers who have or have had small children and not the typical executives with 'a wife at home' (Dunlap and Schmuck 1995: 44). The book is then filled with experiences of women and how they broke the glass ceiling as mothers and wives. What is pertinent to some of these accounts is the role that men as partners have had to play to support the women signifying the change in society and disrupting the masculine and feminine notion in domestic roles. However, Coleman highlights an important issue that more of this support is needed, as women are still playing the significant part of the domestic responsibility. This, convincingly remains Coleman's most compelling, useful and recurring message throughout the book.

Another message that is equally striking, is that of the changing world of work that makes it possible for women to arrange flexible working hours. Although the book is focused on interviews with sixty women, their constructions of gender and what happens in the workplace is not confined to their own experiences, but these are largely seen in the context of what is happening in broader society. This is what one would expect from an outstanding piece of work such as Coleman's. Her conceptualisation and portrayal of *change*, seen through the changing culture of work and the 'attitudes towards, and perceptions of the role of women' (147), represents modernity and the transforming world of work as seen through the experiences of the sixty successful women. However, the complexity of the challenges the women continue to experience brings to the fore the question of

---

2   These categories are similar to those drawn by Hakim's (2004) theory of preference.

and the extent to which this change is genuine. When we consider change in terms of the main challenges that the interviewed women experienced, i.e. gender stereotypes and family responsibilities, it is evident that real change is going to be painfully slow as it is not only organisational but also cultural.

But what does this tell us about the current situation of women in leadership and what questions does Coleman's work leave us with? In answering this it is perhaps important to consider that Coleman's work, at least in *Women at the Top*, focused on England with mostly white, first world women, whose experiences may be different from those of women in other parts of the world. After all, Coleman herself warned against essentialising women's experiences and as one of her interviewed participants articulately puts it; 'intelligent feminists have never argued that women as a [gender] are all equally victimised' (120). So, what can we take from this in pursuing or developing an understanding about what happens in the other parts of the world? The sections that follow, attempt to address this question.

The section below provides a brief theoretical underpinning and a methodological background to the discussion that is to follow. From there onwards, the intention is to bring other voices from another part of the world but also to highlight some other perspectives to the work that is similar to Coleman's. Through *Women at the Top*, Coleman has provided us with a useful tool that we need to take further in enriching our knowledge and possibly finding solutions to some of the long-standing problems of so few women at the top leadership of organisations. That, amongst others has been Coleman's quest and we cannot do that meaningfully unless we bring together knowledge from different parts of the world.

Gender and Leadership: Theoretical Underpinnings

Gender role stereotyping subjects women and men to certain roles and leaves women with certain perceptions about themselves and their capability to perform in leadership. It is considered a significant internal barrier that sometimes contributes to the confinement of women to the private space as opposed to the public. Although Coleman (2011) joins others in acknowledging that the division of gender roles along the public and private lines is no longer sufficient to explain the inequalities we see in the workplace today, her work illustrates a 'bedrock of stereotypes' (35) that underpins the way organisations continue to operate and discriminate against women. A shift in the way women perceive themselves has been observed, through women developing more confidence and actually going for these leadership positions. This shift[3] puts the spotlight on external barriers to women's progression that are mainly driven by perceptions about who can do what. I try to provide an alternative view, which forms the basis for the discussion that is to follow.

The Patriarchal Bargain

The patriarchal bargain was first introduced by Kandiyoti (1988) as a strategy used by women to deal with different forms of patriarchal norms. It refers to the choice that women make to accommodate and adapt gender roles that would otherwise put them at a disadvantage. According to Kandiyoti, patriarchal bargains may manifest in different forms according to class and ethnicity within a particular society and are subject to change and renegotiation depending on historical transformations or 'economic phases' (Moorosi 2015), and the areas of struggle they open up between genders (Kandiyoti 1988: 275). Arielli (2007: 20) suggests that the patriarchal bargain describes the 'constraints and the resources available for women to assume agency without disrupting the patriarchal system'. As such, one could argue that patriarchal bargains represent another type of world different from classic patriarchy[4] where women try to maximise their power

---

3   Previous literature focused on internal barriers that included women's low self-esteem and lack of confidence as barriers to progression, thereby blaming women for their underrepresentation.

4   Classic patriarchy means the system where girls are given away in marriage at a young age into households headed by their husbands' father where they become subordinate

by appearing subservient to patriarchy and conforming to the gendered societal norms on gender roles (Kandiyoti 1988).

I have found patriarchal bargain a useful concept in explaining the deals or strategies that women appear to make within families where men play the traditional economic provider role and women the supportive housewife (see Moorosi 2015). Whether the strategy is adopted to keep the peace at home or because it works for them as a coping mechanism, is arguable. It is significant that the patriarchal bargain appears to remove the victim label from women, but sees them more as strategists (or manipulators) who are in charge of their situations. The power and agency of women in this context is however, arguably overplayed, given the entrenchment of patriarchy and other forms of gendered oppression such as colonialism and apartheid [in the case of South Africa]. This would assume that women have the agency and power to negotiate their own terms within a patriarchal society – a debatable issue, I argue.

A Brief Note on Methodology

This chapter analyses two interviews held with women who were holding managerial positions, but yet not at the chief executive level at the time of the interview. These women were aged thirty-nine and forty-four, but the ages of the women in the sample ranged from thirty-five to fifty years of age. The study largely involved interviews with both men and women and focused on constructions of masculinity, gender and change. Most of the participants were in middle to senior management positions of decision-making; and were regarded as elite due to what they had achieved at the time of the interview. Fifteen women were interviewed altogether but for the purposes of this chapter (as already mentioned), only the stories of the two women are presented. The interviews were conducted using a life history approach which has credibility as a productive strategy for elite

---

not only to men, but even to other senior women and especially their mothers in law (Kandiyoti 1988: 278).

masculinity research (Connell 2005a; Messerschmidt 2000). The life-history interviews lasted between forty-five to seventy-five minutes and those of the two women were each more than an hour long. The interviews combined a range of topics from childhood, education, work and career, family, sexuality and conflict in the workplace. This range of topics max-imised rapport allowing the emergence of personal narratives. It is in these narratives that patterns are drawn that are comparable to Coleman's analysis.

The choice of the two women's stories is based on the relevance of the themes used for analysis (challenges, choice and change). They both work for large financial investment institutions and were both in asset management where every section is completely male dominated. Their stories both represent and illustrate the complexity of challenge, choice and change. Their circumstances are similar but they have made choices that have impacted differently on their career progression. The women's names have been changed to protect their identity, but the report and analyses made here are based on the actual interviews held with them in 2011. Below is a summary of the two women's profiles:

> Lulu was a forty-four year old woman, married with two children. She works in asset management in a large merchant bank. She has been with her current employer for the past eight years but her experience is largely in asset management as she has been with various companies over the years. Lulu studied a Bachelor of Commerce degree after working in the banking sector. Working for an asset management company that is male dominated meant that she would be expected to give a great amount of time to her work to be on par with her male colleagues. However, spending time with the children was important for her. Her husband earns a lot more than her and that put her in a comfortable position to negotiate and exploit the company's family friendly policies.
>
> Marina was a thirty-nine year old woman also married with two children. She works for a large financial multi-national institution and she is also based in a multi-manager asset management sector as a marketing specialist. Marina studied English and French and Media Studies for her postgraduate degree. She never expected to work in marketing, but she joined as a junior and worked her way up to a senior marketing consultant. Marina earns more than her husband, and that meant she could not afford to take any time out, as that would not only compromise her career, but her pay as well.

Although the intention is to compare these women's experiences, the two women chosen above are both black and are deliberately chosen to counter the white and first world experiences in *Women at the Top*.

Challenges, Choices and Change

Challenges

In *Women at the Top*, Coleman identifies three types of challenges that women face as they attempt to progress into leadership positions. These are: i) challenges experienced by women in finding their way in the masculine cultures of work; ii) challenges encountered by women through stereotypes that portray women as housewives and as nurturers and which portrays men as breadwinners at home and leaders in the work place; and iii) challenges that are experienced by women as a result of the impact of combining family and career.

With regard to stereotypes and the masculine cultures at work, the organisations in which the two women worked were predominantly male. For Marina, the biggest challenge for women was that women and gender issues were not even on the agenda. Most of the men (who are predominantly white) earn a lot of money and 'outsource' child responsibilities to their wives who are not working. So these men are not aware of issues that concern the women at work.

Asked whether there are different roles for men and women in the company Lulu confirms by saying:

> Without a doubt. And this is not just ... [current company] but the investment industry as a whole because that is where I have worked most of my career. The investment teams are male dominated, without a doubt – male and white dominated. And if you are a woman there is a huge struggle.

As she puts it:

> They guys there make huge monies [*sic*] and so their women and wives do not have to work, those who work, work because they want to. It is not a financial thing. I think because their wives are at home they cannot relate to the women needing time to look after children and stuff like that.

In terms of stereotypes, women and men were treated differently. There were no explicit roles for men or women, but it was largely [white] men in the top leadership positions.

Interestingly, Marina also raises the same issue about wives of the white males in leadership not working. Her response to the same question is:

> Not necessarily but you know for example the investment team for example they are all male and their wives don't work [...].

Lulu has been working in asset management almost all her career, and although she changed companies, asset management has always been dominated by white men.

Some of the women in Coleman's study faced challenges of not being taken seriously in the workplaces that were dominated my men. They found themselves isolated in the boardrooms and excluded from male networking sessions. Women in the South African study, were also not in the networks and although these networks are seen in terms of race, they clearly have even more dire implications for women. Bearing in mind that the majority of staff are male and white, Marina says:

> [...] three or four people studied together and they have known each other for a while and they socialise together. So that is something tangible, those are strong relationships, where we are new entrants, and they are hard to penetrate. Those systems are hard for us to fit in. We play according to their existing rules and that is going to take a while for black strong companies to emerge so we can also leave a legacy for our children.

The 'glass ceiling' is also real for these women. Marina left her previous organisation because of lack of upward mobility.

> When I left [previous company] I headed up a department of about eight people. You know I left because I realised I did not want to be there anymore. You know when you reach almost like a pinnacle in a company then you go like, 'what next?'

Marina also recalls being asked in an interview how she will balance work and family, commenting:

> I don't think they would have asked a man that question.

Lulu raises the age issue but more in terms of dealing with conflict. At forty-four she is the oldest woman on her team and although this is not mentioned in terms of discrimination or disadvantage, it is a factor she has to contend with at one level or another.

> And you know it is the age thing again, and it is the truth because in my team at forty-four I am the oldest and many of the girls are not even thirty yet. So they are young people and they look up to you and sometimes I feel the pressure to rise above issues and not come to their level.

This is raised in terms of dealing with conflict but it also has undertones of pressure brought by age in the sector. There is clearly discrimination on the basis of pay and because transformation has barely moved from issues of racial inequality, there is no sense of whether their success could be attributed to their gender. In terms of domestic responsibilities, they still carry the bulk of the work, but they manage because they have domestic helpers and Lulu made use of the company's flexible hours' policy.

Challenges that women face within the masculine cultures of work appear to be similar in London and Johannesburg. Having broken the mould of investment banking, these women are successful to some extent, but they are both in middle management –where they have been for more than eight years or so. Marina had been a middle manager before and left her previous company because she had reached the glass ceiling. Lulu on the other hand, is currently not able to progress further because of her childcare responsibilities.

How these women have become successful remains entirely down to their own drive and determination. Similar to women in Coleman's study, agency has been key. They have actively sought opportunities and never hesitated to go after what they wanted. Equally, they had the confidence to reject offers that did not suit their needs. Although Lulu's negotiations worked against her career progression, she had the confidence to negotiate terms of her contract to allow her to meet her family needs. Both women came from families with strong values where education was important and that carried them through. Lulu's parents were both working and Marina's parents were academics, so education was the order of the day. 'There was no question about that', Marina says.

Choices

In Coleman's study, subject choice is critical in leading women to certain careers and equally important, is choices that women make for family responsibilities. Lulu and Marina both made conscious subject choices, however these choices did not lead them to careers they initially wanted. Lulu wanted a career in banking after her first work experience, but Marina who landed in asset management marketing completely by default had her initial interest in journalism. As was the case with women in *Women at the Top*, subject choices were not always predictable but choices of jobs they made after that were conscious and driven by the desire to succeed and make it in the fields dominated by men.

Coleman has shown in her work that choosing to take a career break for family reasons significantly affects women's progression. In the developing countries' context where women have to work and make an equal [or even more] contribution economically, choice to take career break is not prevalent. However, Lulu made a choice to get a deskbound job and to work part-time so she would be able to collect her children from school and spend time with them after school. Marina on the other hand is a primary earner at home and makes no mention of career breaks or time out, but says she does what she has to do. She elaborates:

If I have to leave early and take my child to the doctor, I do that.

But unlike Lulu, she has not made any formal arrangement. In terms of broader career planning, there does not appear to have been much choice and planning, even though they are now happy with what they do. That also applies to choice about which subjects to study, which careers to follow and whether or not to get married.

Take Marina's case for example, she studied English and French as major subjects at university and subsequently undertook a postgraduate degree in media studies and communications with the intention of working in journalism. However, she ended up working in marketing in a male dominated world of finance and investment management.

The whole question of choice is rather problematic as it assumes agency. I argue that choice in the absence of agency is not genuine. Lulu and Marina both represent women who combine family and career with restricted choices either way [albeit to varying degrees]. Coleman highlights the choice not to have children that some women make so that they can follow a career or sometimes a choice they make to continue to work and be homemakers despite their success in leadership positions. However, in a patriarchal society women's choices may be limited as their capacity to bargain only goes so far. Choice to have children or not does not appear to be the kind of choice that these women make, but these are life experiences that occur and experiences around which they have to adjust their lives. The depth of patriarchy also makes domestic responsibilities inescapable for women. These experiences suggest the limited choice these women have in claiming freedom from domestic responsibilities. However, choice for these women is not simplistic. It is influenced by their life experiences some of which are pre-determined for them such as experiences of apartheid that rendered black people (both men and women) powerless. The extent to which they can escape that reality and claim their freedom of choice is debatable, to the extent one would argue that by choosing to get married, they inevitably succumbed to oppressive patriarchal norms.

Change

There are three types of change identified in *Women at the Top*: change affecting women at work, change in attitude to families and children and change in work practices. In terms of change affecting women at work, Marina's story provides a perfect illustration of the South African context. Here change is seen as a two-fold transformational process that is linked to broader societal change: Transforming the ownership of business from the predominant white minorities to black majorities and getting women to the top exercising key leadership roles in private organisations. Marina's story reflects complexities of the interaction between race and gender. However, the most significant issue she mentions centres around the lack of attention to gender issues because the country is still grappling with racial issues, as she says below:

> I also think just looking at where I worked, I think there is also the racial issue in terms of power-play, work pressure politics, and you know in terms of male to male. I don't think they are at the level of looking at women to men issues. [...] They are not even talking about gender issues because the issue is still racial.

Marina's story leaves us with a significant understanding of the complexity of South African issues, a complexity that puts gender issues in corporate South Africa further down the ladder. From her perspective one can deduce that things are not about to change soon for women. She further says:

> I think that for some of the men because for them child rearing and everything has been outsourced to their wives who do not work, they don't understand the challenges facing working women.

In terms of change in attitude to families and children, Marina's is what in patriarchal terms could be referred to as a typical 'no deal' story. She is the primary earner in the home, but still also bears greater responsibility for domestic responsibilities. As a modern woman she thinks the arrival of children sometimes changes things for women. Her husband was a typical progressive who did his share of household duties, however that attitude changed when their two children were born.

> I think after children you know things change. Before we had kids, roles were more balanced and after kids there is a shift and now there is like 60/40. And you know this is the same guy that I never used to tell to do anything but now I have become like a nagging wife you haven't done this you haven't done that.

Lulu's story partly resonates with first world women's experiences who technically 'step off the career ladder' to take care of family, losing out to their male counterparts (Coleman 2011: 148). Of significance in Lulu's story is also the patriarchal bargain that she makes with her husband as she says that she allows her husband to take care of her:

> [...] I don't earn as much as my husband earns and I let him take care of me and I am not going to compete about the roles.

This suggests that Lulu's husband is a traditional man who sees his role primarily as a provider and has no share in the domestic roles. She is concerned about the messages this is sending to her two boys, since the roles in the home appear more traditional than progressive. Lulu's example is an interesting one that suggests on the one hand, a slow pace of change for women and gender roles that are unconsciously being passed on to young boys.

On the other hand, Lulu provides a classical example of *change in the work practice* through flexible hours and work practices. In this case she is able to negotiate her terms as part of her contract and although she negotiates for a desk-bound part-time type of arrangement to allow her to pick up her children from school, which impacts negatively on her upward mobility career-wise, we do see through her, a progressive work environment. This is however complex as it suggests that the terms she negotiates come with a price, namely, lower pay, hence the patriarchal bargain with her husband.

Discussion: The Three Cs

Gender studies in leadership have shone the spotlight on gender-based inequality in the home and the workplace. The intricacy between challenges, choices and change is evident in the South African women's experiences as it was in Coleman's study. The role of women in family is often at the centre of debates around women's capability to perform in high profile jobs. This is based on the 'suspicion' usually cast upon women aspiring for leadership and the stereotypical belief that women cannot lead, which has often led to discrimination purely on the basis of gender. This has led to the systemic and unrelenting underrepresentation of women in important positions that bear decision making powers, which the presentation above suggests may persist for some time. Without losing sight of the significant gains made in recent years, that saw more women achieve leadership of key decision-making positions in politics, the corporate world and elsewhere, it is evident that a lot more work needs to be done to address the challenges that women still face in attaining top positions in their chosen careers.

Having said that, this chapter, echoing Coleman's scholarship, indicates that some progress has been made with drive and determination as key ingredients to success.

The aspect of choice seems rather complex in the South African context. Lulu's apparent comfort in her situation indicates the 'strategic nature of women's choices' (Kandiyoti 1988: 283), which could also find support in Hakim's (2004) theory of preference. She is not, however, an outright 'home-centred' woman as she still works but her choice leans more towards family. This choice is enabled by her economic circumstances, and it is a choice that Marina could not afford to make because of her different set of circumstances, which render a 'no deal' situation for her. But perhaps more significantly, Lulu's choice shows the power of patriarchy and the extent to which women are forced to succumb to the patriarchal norms despite their levels of education and their freedom of choice. Lulu is an accomplished woman in her own right who knows she is resourceful, capable and competent. However, she chooses to take care of family at the expense of her own career. Her choice is genuine in that she chooses to be part of her children's life instead of relying on domestic help. But it appears that only she (and not her husband) could make that choice and on that level the genuineness of the choice is questionable. Lulu is empowered by the ability to make such a choice, but it comes at the expense of her career and is thus disempowering. This reflects complexity of choice and change and that change can only happen if it is allowed to happen, and sometimes this becomes just a matter of choice. As Kandiyoti, concluded, 'patriarchal bargains do not merely inform women's rational choices but also shape the more unconscious aspects of their gendered subjectivity, since they permeate the context of their early socialisation' (285).

The South African experiences also bring another issue to the table, an issue missing from *Women at the Top*: the intersection of gender and race. The racial issues are still so prominent that they are receiving more attention at least at the level of recognition. And what keeps them alive is the visibility of black men in the corporate boardrooms albeit not in top leadership positions. The same cannot be said about their black sisters, as they are still invisible. The latter's invisibility is even more problematic as it does not bring the gender issue to the table. The [white] men who still make the decisions on issues that deserve attention have their wives at home taking care of the family while they make money, and perhaps for these men the home is still where women belong. In this context it is difficult to ignore the impact of the intersection of colonialism, patriarchy and apartheid on the lives of black women [and men]. Arndt (2002: 32) labelled these 'oppressive mechanisms' of women and the people of Africa. These mechanisms present a challenge for black women to be accepted in predominantly white and male institutions that were created during colonial times and institutionalised by the unequal laws of apartheid that favoured the white minority. On the surface, South African women may appear to be on par with their sisters in the developed world in terms of access to opportunities, freedom of choice and agency. However, these oppressive mechanisms, through their deeply embedded and subtle power, underplay women's agency and limit their freedom of choice thereby impeding change.

Conclusion: What's Still To Be Done

I conclude by bringing to the fore the work that still needs to be done building on Coleman's legacy. This is done in the strong conviction that a hallmark of great scholarship is to open up avenues of work to be pursued for generations to come. The patriarchal bargain enables choice and strategies that empower women to strike deals that work for them. However, the more they bargain the more things on the gendered stereotypes front remain the same. Women strike deals that keep them as players in the domestic sphere, and are empowered to negotiate working arrangements that are flexible, but that flexibility keeps them further down the career ladder. Connell (2005b) notes that family friendly policies exist to support women's domestic responsibilities. Thus, the extent to which the patriarchal bargain and the flexible family friendly policies that are supposed to enable change, empower and benefit women, is the extent to which they appear to perpetuate the stereotypes about the role of men and women at work and in the home. There is a need to look elsewhere, perhaps the answer is more in the determination and drive that individual women seem to possess. And perhaps Lulu's and Marina's cases and some of the women in Coleman's (2011) research show us that a gain in the workplace should not necessarily mean a loss in the home.

References

Arndt, S. (2002) 'Perspectives on African Feminism: Defining and Classifying African-Feminist Literatures'. *Agenda* 17 (54), 31–44.

Arielli, D. (2007). 'The Task of Being Content: Expatriate Wives in Beijing, Emotional Work and Patriarchal Bargain'. *Journal of International Women's Studies* 8 (4), 18–31.

Bimrose, J. (2008). 'Guidance with Women'. In J.A. Athanasou and R. Van Esbroeck (eds), *International Handbook of Career Guidance*, 375–404. Dordrecht: Springer.

Connell, R.W. (2005a). *Masculinities* (2nd edn). Cambridge: Polity.

Connell, R.W. (2005b). 'A Really Good Husband: Work/Life Balance, Gender Equity and Social Change'. *Australian Journal of Social Issues* 40 (3), 369–83.

Coleman, M. (2011). *Women at the Top: Challenges, Choices and Change*. London: Palgrave Macmillan.

Dunlap, D., and Schmuck, P. (eds) (1995). *Leading Women in Education*. Camberwell, Victoria: Australian Council for Education Research.

Fuller, K., Cliffe, J., and Moorosi, P. (2015). 'Women's leadership preparation within the Senior Leadership Team', *Planning and Changing* (forthcoming).

Hakim, C. (2004). *Key Issues in Women's Work: Female Diversity and the Polarisation of Women's Employment: Changing Lives and New Challenges*, Cheltenham: Edward Elgar.

Kandiyoti, D. (1988). 'Bargaining with Patriarchy'. *Gender and Society* 2 (3), 274–90.

Messerschmidt, J.W. (2000). *Nine Lives: Adolescent Masculinities, the Body, and Violence*. Boulder, CO: Westview Press.

Moorosi, P. (2015). 'Breadwinners and Homemakers: How Constructions of Masculinities Affect Women's Progression in Leadership'. In E.C. Reilly and Q.J. Bauer (eds), *Women Leading Education Across the Continents: Overcoming Leadership Barriers*. Lanham, MD: Rowman and Littlefield.

HELEN SOBEHART

Weaving the Fabric of Legacy: An Epilogue

How we marvel at tapestries, carpets, clothing and other woven goods that were made by artists many, many years ago. Ancient work affects us today, even though the artists did not consider how their work might intersect with others in the future.

Though we do not know who crafted the first weave of tapestry or cloth, by medieval times it was a male domain. Interestingly, a modern-day female novelist, Tracy Chevalier, imagined the plausible tension between genders in that era as she fictionalised comments by the wife of major character, Georges de la Chapelle, a medieval master weaver:

> Warp threads are thicker than the weft, and made of a coarser wool as well. I think of them as like wives. Their work is not obvious – all you can see are the ridges they make under the colorful weft threads. But if they weren't there, there would be no tapestry. Georges would unravel without me. (Chevalier 2004: 113)

Perhaps that tension is why I have been intrigued for years with a small loom that sits proudly on the credenza in my office. It was a gift from a Turkish colleague who is one of the members of the network, Women Leading Education across Continents (WLE). This group, founded in 2007, pursues the goal of conducting research and sharing practice about the issue of gender in educational leadership. As the founding chair, in cooperation with the University Council for Educational Administration (UCEA) and the American Association of School Administrators (AASA), I had the privilege to invite thirty-five leaders to a meeting in Rome. They were all passionate about the issue of underrepresentation of women and minorities in the highest levels of educational leadership. They came from around the globe, each writing a scholarly paper about the issue in their respective countries. We spent four days together, not only sharing research from authentic contexts and identifying further work, but also getting to know each other. One of the many wonderful colleagues I met during that time was Marianne Coleman. She contributed an important chapter to the first of several books fostered by WLE, *Women Leading Education Across the Continents: Sharing the Spirit, Fanning the Flame* (Sobehart 2009).

It was evident, even then, that Marianne and her work had impacted each of us in a variety of ways. Getting to know her as a person underscored her stature as the inspiration and backbone of work in this field. She was, and remains, a true role model – in her life and in her work. Her interaction with members of the group made us better scholars, better practitioners and better people. She helped us intertwine knowledge, skill, and courageous spirit.

So as I gaze at the loom, I think of Marianne. For those of you not familiar with weaving, there are two main components – the warp and the weft. As noted in the earlier quote, the warp consists of the cords held taut by the bars of the loom. They must be strong and straight in order to carry the weight and beauty of the threads, the weft that will intertwine across them. Warp cords are also beautiful in their texture and strength. In my loom, there is a partially woven tapestry. The weft threads across the warp are of lovely colour and pattern. Reds, blues, greys and yellow move according to a Turkish motif that is striking and intentional in its design. As the colours move up the tapestry, they begin to surround a weave of all white thread in the shape of a block. Inside the block, woven in striking black, is my name.

The motif continues for a distance above the white block. Then it ends, revealing the strong cords of the warp that support it. At the top of the loom there are more skeins of yarn, the colours of the motif. There is also a tool with which to continue the tapestry. Since I am not knowledgeable about weaving in the literal sense, I dare not try to extend the tapestry. However, the image of the unfinished tapestry with the warp awaiting skilled hands to continue the design makes me envision Marianne and her legacy.

Marianne's work has given us strong threads of warp on which to intertwine our own research, thoughts and action. I describe below the threads of warp which Marianne has gifted to us. Giving colour to those cords are concepts taken from a few of her many works. The cords, the themes, are those that I see at this time. Certainly, there are others. Nevertheless, they provide backbone for the arguments, ideas and findings that are the weft woven by authors in this collection. Allow me to illuminate Marianne's tapestry as I envision it in my mind's eye.

The Warp: Cords of Marianne's Work

Leadership, Diversity and Intersectionality

Marianne was a pioneer in identifying this particular thread of the tapestry. The survey she conducted with headteachers in England and Wales at the beginning of the twenty-first century has been replicated many times and in many countries. In a chapter on leadership and learning she contends that the values most relevant to diversity are moral leadership, servant leadership and authentic leadership (Robertson and Timperly 2011: 174). She also emphasises how important it is to recognise the complexity in the many faces and types of diversity. She gives as examples not only common categories of race, gender, religion or ethnic background, but also cultural contrasts such as perceptions of power, distance between employees and employer, individualism versus collectivism, uncertainty avoidance, masculinity and femininity, as well as long-term and short-term orientation (177). In that same work, she identifies ways in which leadership can impact diversity in a positive way, including policies, targets and monitoring that respect and support a diverse atmosphere of thought, structure and personnel (178). Using Marianne's empirical evidence to illuminate leadership, diversity and intersectionality gave legitimacy to further study.

Life Story Narrative

Perhaps Marianne's greatest contribution to this weave is her own life. In their book *Shaping Social Justice Leadership*, Linda Lyman, Jane Strachan

and Angeliki Lazaridou use critical evocative feminist portraiture to analyze
the stories of over twenty women who were original members of WLE,
Marianne among them. Each woman wrote her own story, but the book's
skilled authors intertwined their experiences with themes related to social
justice. Here are highlights of Marianne's story.

Marianne's life began at the end of World War II in Leeds, an industrial
city in England. She lived in a multigenerational family. Ongoing family
illness and an extended illness of her own spurred her interest in reading.
Nevertheless, growing up in a poor economic environment caused her to
say that by the age of five she 'had quite a sophisticated understanding of
the class system' (Lyman, Strachan and Lazaridou 2012: 91). Though the
system initially placed her in the bottom stream class, her family's finances
improved after primary school. That, and the fact that her mother constantly prodded the school to recognise Marianne's talent, allowed her to
move into the top level.

As a teenager Marianne became somewhat rebellious and political,
joining the youth branch of the Campaign for Nuclear Disarmament and
supporting the anti-apartheid movement in South Africa. She notes, 'during
this, I began to develop critical awareness and a realization that people
might be influenced by their circumstances so that society was responsible in part for the problems that beset individuals' (92). She became an
exchange student in the USA and reported that to be a 'culture shock'
as she experienced being a 'foreigner' herself. So, international work and
travel became an interest (92).

Marianne returned to attend the London School of Economics to
study sociology. In her last year there she became involved in and aware
of the student unrest that affected universities in several countries in the
latter half of the 1960s. She noted, however, that race and class were seen
at this time as far more important than gender inequality. Even though she
now had an excellent education, she still felt 'rootless, unsure, and lacking
in confidence' (93). She became a secretary briefly and then a mid-level
university administrator. She married towards the end of the 1960s but,
since maternity leave did not exist, she had to quit her job when she became
pregnant, with no promise of a job in the future. Interestingly, she found
no comfort in the feminist movement at the time. It made her feel that it

was impossible to be a successful wife, mother and worker. Laws changed by the time she had her second child and she was 'the first person at my school to successfully return after maternity leave' (94). She worked for several years as a secondary teacher in economics and politics, and then in a county advisory teacher role that required her to develop educational reports. She notes that 'this made me realize that what I would really like to do was research and writing' (94).

Through a chance meeting with a professor, Tony Bush, she became a research associate at the University of Leicester. Completing her master's degree, she eventually became a senior lecturer at the university. With full support of family she engaged in research and teaching in countries across three continents. This led to a doctoral dissertation regarding the issue of women in educational leadership followed by a substantial body of influential research and writing. Her work continues even today as she joyfully embraces status as a grandmother, emeritus reader and consultant.

Marianne lived the experience faced by many women with families and children as they encounter challenges in pursuit of successful and fulfilling lives. So the strong backdrop of Marianne's own story supports not only the braid of life story narrative on the loom, but also many themes captured in this book.

Ways of Knowing

In her 2002 book *Women as Headteachers: Striking the Balance*, Marianne described two approaches that she used to gain knowledge about the status of women leaders in the UK. The first approach was the previously mentioned survey sent to female headteachers in England and Wales. However, she also conducted in-depth interviews with some of these women. Using this knowledge, she summarised each section of the book with 'learning points for aspiring women' and 'learning points for headteachers'. For aspiring women she offered such wisdom as, 'Aim for a spread of experience and stay wary of pastoral pigeonholing' and 'Look for, and take the small but significant career opportunities, e.g. a visible role as a short-term project leader'. She advised current headteachers to 'Offer mentoring widely'

(34). In this way, she not only underscored the ongoing importance of research, but also recognised that data informed findings can be distilled as kernels of wisdom, especially for practitioners in the field – another way for them 'to know'.

Marianne also extolled the contribution of qualitative research as another way of knowing, citing that of Hall (1996) and Schick-Case (1994). Marianne noted that such studies 'bring depth of observation and long scrutiny' (Coleman 2002). She emphasised that by noting in the Schick-Case work, 'studies of male and female communication show consistent differences in male and female speech which must surely affect the ways they manage and are perceived to manage' (118). She also underscored the importance of ongoing and thorough literature review as a source of knowledge even as she returned to interviewing in her recent book, *Women at the Top: Challenges, Choices and Change* (2011). There she synthesised learning from interviews of sixty top female leaders in their fields. The findings in that book contribute heavily to the next length in Marianne's warp of tapestry, mentoring.

Mentoring, Networking and Role Modelling

The interviews that Marianne conducted with the sixty successful women provided evidence that women need not, and should not, be alone in their journey to and through leadership. She culls the wisdom of these women into admonitions for success, such as: 'Join networks, both mixed and all women, ensuring that both your affective and instrumental needs are met; Establish one or more good mentoring relationships; Take note of female role models; Make use of coaching for specific short-term purposes; Be aware that you are acting as a role model to younger women' (172).

The mentoring theme dates to some of Marianne's earliest work. One example appears in her chapter on Managing for Equal Opportunities in the book, *The Principles and Practice of Educational Management* (Bush and Bell 2002). She avers that her survey of female headteachers supported the need for mentors, even though half of the respondents said that they had been mentored by men (143). Marianne also warns about the 'subtleties that may be involved in the management of a specific case' (143). Systemic efforts to support women can sometimes cause misunderstanding or resentment among male employees. This example leads to the next powerful ligature of Marianne's warp – systems change to improve equality of opportunity must first be based on deeply held values. Those values become actions. Actions turn into systems that support the growth of human and social capital. If actions are not based on the sincere value of respect for all aspects of humanity, the system may go awry.

Turning Values into Systemic Action

In her previously cited chapter (Bush and Bell 2002), Marianne outlines elements of a system that operationalises the core value of respect for diversity. She notes that such systems must not only touch upon mentoring in the provision of role models but also on: 'appraisal and training for appraisal; managing curriculum and equal opportunities; inclusion; personal and social education; gender issues and achievements; and the educational environment' (143–6). She cites recommendations of researcher L. Burton: 'ensure that equal opportunity is on the agenda, talked about and discussed; have a woman in a senior role who is providing a role model; provide career opportunities which draw on nonconventional sources or provide differently constructed openings; monitor and use the results of the monitoring exercise to make changes; ensure that interview panels are representative; peruse all institutional documentation from an equal opportunities perspective looking at language, metaphors, images; create close links with the community and listen to what they're saying about the institutional obstacles that are experienced.' (Burton 1993: 287, as cited in Bush and Bell 2002: 147).

Marianne urges caution about systems that are not based on deeply held values of respect and appreciation for diversity. She provides several examples of situations where actions may appear to be congruent with positive systemic change, but do not display integrity in daily reality. 'One woman, appointed as deputy, recalled being met by 'expectations that I would be pastoral care – look after girls/flowers/coffee/tampon machines' (142).

Another is the experience of a newly appointed headteacher, 'On my third day of headship I had to cope with a very irate member of staff who took great pains to inform me that I had only got my job because I was an Asian female' (142). The values of human dignity and respect not only need to be openly discussed among existing staff but be part of the employee interview process since congruent values strengthen the system.

Imagery

Though Marianne only occasionally refers to the concept of imagery, her life and the entire body of her work illuminate that concept. The strength of her research, as outlined in the themes cited above, represent the strong ropes held taut on the loom, confidently supporting the cross weave of the tapestry. The strength of her life, despite socioeconomic challenges, illness, gender discrimination, and many challenges of managing work/life balance also represents the cord of imagery. Interestingly, early feminist Hildegard of Bingen in the 13th century relied greatly on imagery as she saw visions throughout her remarkable life. She always visioned wisdom as a woman. In her book *Scivias* ('Ways of Knowing'), she captured the essence of so many women's life stories. Here is a paraphrase of a key vision – The woman was in the flame but not consumed by it. Rather it flowed from her. That vision became the logo of WLE. Marianne's life is certainly an example of that image. So I see imagery as one of the most powerful threads that Marianne has given us – and the one upon which I have built this epilogue.

The Weft: Crossweaves of Many Artists

So the strong warp that Marianne Coleman created provides support for the weft of many researchers, including those who contributed to this book of celebration. Tony Bush anticipated this in his Foreword as he applauded the quality of authors who contributed to this book. He also touched on life story narrative, describing how Marianne kept her composure while interviewing a male principal in China who made a gender-biased remark.

Kay Fuller, for example, weaved her thread through cords of life story narrative, mentoring and ways of knowing as she elucidated the story of headteacher Rita. Rita did not tell her own story. Instead, those whom she affected described her life beautifully through tales of mentoring and support that she provided. So learning about the life of another through the eyes of those whom she has positively affected, is indeed a different way of knowing a life story narrative.

Joan Smith decries organisational systems gone awry due to the lack of a values base of respect for diversity. Ironically, Joan asserts that the role of motherhood, commonly seen as a positive model, has become an overly idealised, socially constructed norm. It impacts life and career decisions of aspiring female leaders. It also contributes to a lack of systematic, organised support for women teachers with children, even as the extended family concept declines. So Joan's research on career decisions and experiences of women teachers intertwines with Marianne's threads of role modelling and values-based systems.

Marianne's warp lines of leadership, diversity and intersectionality, as well as ways of knowing, support *Victoria Showunmi*'s weft that notes the inadequacy of leadership perspectives as they continue to be dominated by a mostly male and Western world view. She provides an additional way of knowing by reflecting upon and evaluating the western model of leadership, making comparisons and suggesting there be space in the weave for alternative models of leadership to emerge.

Jacky Lumby's contribution rests heavily on the thread named leadership, diversity and intersectionality. She argues against researchers who purport to convey findings from subjects in another culture without taking context into account. She even cites the fact that Marianne's survey has been translated and used in a variety of countries. She notes that some of those efforts did not make a thorough attempt to assure that the research and findings were explicated in the language and conceptions of the given culture. She grapples with the reality that all researchers, in a sense, speak for the subjects of their studies. Specifically as it applies to gender equity, Jacky illuminates the path by which those interested in the topic may be true to their research methodology while also being true to the authentic voices of the women they represent.

Marianne's cords of diversity, systems and ways of knowing fully support the work of *Mary Cunneen* and *Judith Harford*. As they explore the continuing question of why educational leadership remains such a male-dominated field, they use the image of space that is between the many variables in a system, such as cultural, societal, organisational and personal. They pursue a life history perspective of twelve women principals working in post-primary schools in the Republic of Ireland. Their findings illuminate answers to the question about male domination in the field but also light a path towards change. They find that women who occupy, or aspire to occupy, leadership positions do so because they want to impact a system that will promote more equality of opportunity.

The role of imagery is the name of the thread that *Tanya Fitzgerald* weaves across Marianne's warp. Tanya underscores the powerful impact of the ongoing image of leadership as masculine. She asserts that this concept, consciously or unconsciously, often results in women being seen as transgressors in a field that conventional wisdom sees as rightly male. She is understandably concerned about how this image may shape public consciousness, and draws on Marianne's work to identify ways by which that image might be destabilised.

Ways of knowing is an element seen in *Jill Sperandio* and *Jennifer Polinchock*'s study, as they use a convergent mixed methods design. They draw from a state-wide survey in Pennsylvania, USA, regarding career pathways of female superintendent aspirants. In addition to a random sample survey of those women, they pursued three case studies. Among their several findings are the importance of mentorships and professional networks to promote women's attainment of district leadership positions. So Marianne's emphasis on role modelling and networking indeed spurred the work and findings of Jill and Jennifer's study.

Margaret Grogan and *Klara Wahlster* clearly build on the cord of imagery as they also provide a new way of knowing. They studied the current conception of women as leaders in contemporary young adult and adult fiction. As they find that the male ideal as leader dominates, even in fiction, they credit Coleman's ongoing work that draws attention to gender stereotypes that impact our thinking. Margaret and Klara's work gives further credibility to imagery as a tool in the understanding of and inspiration for leadership.

An authentic weft of African context is woven by *Pontso Moorosi*. Building on Marianne's conceptual supports of diversity and leadership, Pontso's research examines feminine and masculine aspects of corporate managers in South Africa. The theme of systems provides additional insight to the finding that women often strike a less than grand bargain as they balance work and life on the corporate ladder. She coins the term 'patriarchal bargain' to describe the arrangements made by men, women and their roles that perpetuate a dichotomy of femininity and masculinity. All too often, she asserts, enabling policies in the corporate world that appear to benefit women actually perpetuate stereotypes about the role of men and women in the home.

The work of *Izhar Oplatka* provides yet another thread across the cord labelled ways of knowing. He asserts that historical analysis offers a new approach by charting topical research contributions over time. Specifically, Oplatka reviews the literature in educational management during the last four decades. Within that, he pays special attention to scholarship that regards behaviours of men and women engaged in educational management. He suggests that such a systematic review provides for meta-epistemological reflection of a relatively new area of study. In this case, it enables others to view the development of the concept of 'gender' as it has grown in the field of educational management, thus contributing to both theoretical and applied knowledge.

The Tapestry of Legacy

So we see how Marianne Coleman constructed the strong warp of her tapestry regarding women and educational leadership. We also see how that work has supported many threads woven by the authors of powerful chapters in this book. It exemplifies the quote that wife of fictional medieval weaver Georges described at the beginning of this epilogue. Marianne's warp 'was not always obvious, allowing us to sometimes see only the ridges under the colourful weft threads. Nevertheless, if they weren't there, there would be no tapestry.'

This epilogue envisions Marianne's tapestry. Weft threads woven by the various authors in this book create a motif, just as the Turkish tapestry does on my loom. Somehow, however, I imagine the design woven by the authors of this collection as more flowing than in my tapestry, just as the motifs of women's lives flow beautifully among the various opportunities and demands of their complex yet fulfilling existence. Similarly, I see the colours of Marianne's tapestry not as the reds and blues and greys in mine, but rather shades of purple and green – shades central to the feminist view – with swaths of yellow, black, pink, etc. The colours speak the beauty of diversity.

However, I see two aspects of my tapestry that should remain on Marianne's. There should still be a pure white centre that proudly weaves the name of Marianne Coleman. It should not be a block, however. Rather, it should be a circle, the shape of the world that Marianne has so strongly affected. Or perhaps the centre should be just a star since Marianne's work shines the light of truth into the shadows of discrimination.

The other important aspects of my tapestry that must continue on Marianne's are the strong fibres of warp still clearly visible as unfinished. Those strong threads have not yet been touched by the next weaver, but they will be. There are spools of purple and green and other yarn, waiting to be used. The skilful weavers of knowledge, such as the contributors to this book, will take that strong thread of material and continue to weave, still supported by Marianne's background warp. The pattern will become lovelier as each artist's hand threads new learning through the enduring strings that Coleman's work still holds taut.

The tapestry of your work, Marianne, will grow over many more years – so many that you and we may never see the completed work. That does not matter, our friend. The tapestry described in the fictional work at the beginning of this chapter, created by the fictional character Georges, you may suppose was a figment of imagination. But it is not. It hangs today in the Musée National du Moyen Âge in Paris. It is called *The Lady and the*

Unicorn. Though the artist that created it is not known, people nevertheless stand in awe of its beauty day after day. And so will scholars of the future stand in awe of the tapestry you have fostered as a legacy, Marianne. We began that tapestry for you in this book, building on the warp you created. If your warp wasn't there, there would be no tapestry. However, we have intentionally left your tapestry unfinished, though we boldly wove in your name so that generations to come will know the master weaver who gave us the background on which to intertwine our colourful weft of learning.

So here, Marianne, is our gift to you. It is a strong, flowing but unfinished tapestry. It is your legacy. You support both the finished and the unfinished part. We thank you for this gift that we now give back to you, embellished with our learning and our love. May you celebrate, have peace and share joy for many, many years to come. May you gaze on this tapestry and smile.

References

Burton, L. (1993). 'Management, "Race" and Gender: An Unlikely Alliance?'. *British Education Research Journal* 19 (3), 275–90.

Bush, T., and Bell, L. (2002). *The Principles and Practice of Educational Management*. Thousand Oaks, CA: SAGE.

Chevalier, T. (2004). *The Lady and the Unicorn*. New York: Dutton.

Coleman, M. (2002). *Women as Headteachers: Striking the Balance*. Stoke on Trent: Trentham Books.

Coleman, M. (2011). *Women at the Top: Challenges, Choices and Change*. New York: Palgrave Macmillan.

Hildegard of Bingen (1990). *Scivias*. Trans. C. Hart and J. Bishop. New York: Paulist Press.

Lyman, L., Strachan, J., and Lazaridou, A. (2012). *Shaping Social Justice Leadership: Insights of Women Educators Worldwide*. Lanham, MD: Rowman and Littlefield.

Robertson, J., and Timperley, H. (2011). *Leadership and Learning*. London: SAGE.

Sobehart, H. (2009). *Women Leading Education Across the Continents: Sharing the Spirit, Fanning the Flame*. Lanham, MD: Rowman and Littlefield.

Notes on Contributors

TONY BUSH is Professor of Educational Leadership at the University of Nottingham (UK and Malaysia) and Visiting Professor of Education at the University of the Witwatersrand, Johannesburg. He is a vice president and Council member of the British Educational Leadership, Management and Administration Society (BELMAS) and was given the Society's Distinguished Service Award in 2008. He has edited the BELMAS international journal, *Educational Management, Administration and Leadership (EMAL)*, since 2002. Tony has published extensively on many aspects of school leadership and management, including the influential *Theories of Educational Leadership and Management*, which is now in its fourth edition and has been translated into several languages. He has directed many research projects for the former National College for School Leadership, and for many other clients in the UK and several other countries. Tony has been researching in South Africa for twenty years. He was director for the evaluation of the national ACE: School Leadership pilot programme for current and aspiring principals, from 2007-2011, funded by the Zenex Foundation. He has been a consultant, external examiner, invited keynote speaker or research director in more than twenty countries on all six continents. He is also a fellow of the Commonwealth Council for Educational Administration and Management (FCCEAM).

MARY CUNNEEN is a doctoral candidate in the School of Education at University College Dublin, focusing on the area of gender and leadership. She was a post-primary teacher for over twenty years and now works in the area of teacher education.

TANYA FITZGERALD is Professor of Educational Leadership, Management and History at La Trobe University (Australia) and Head of School, Humanities and Social Sciences. She is the author of numerous books and articles that examine historical and contemporary perspectives on gender, leadership and higher education. Recent publications include *Women Leaders in Higher Education: Shattering the Myths* (2013), *Women Educators, Leaders and Activists: Educational Lives and Networks 1900–1960* (co-edited with Elizabeth Smyth, 2014) and *Advancing Knowledge in Higher Education: Universities in Turbulent Times* (2014). Tanya is co-editor of the *Journal of Educational Administration and History* and Vice President of the Australian and New Zealand History of Education Society.

KAY FULLER is Associate Professor of Educational Leadership and course leader of the MA in Educational Leadership and Management at the School of Education, University of Nottingham. She is a member of the Centre for Research in Educational Leadership and Management (CRELM). Kay has published internationally in the area of gender and educational leadership. Her recent publications include *Gender, Identity and Educational Leadership* (2013). She is an elected member of the British Educational Leadership Management and Administration Society (BELMAS) Council and Co-Convenor of the BELMAS Gender and Leadership Research Interest Group. She is also an invited member of the worldwide network Women Leading Education.

MARGARET GROGAN is Dean and Professor in the College of Educational Studies, Chapman University, California. Originally from Australia, she received a Bachelor of Arts degree in Ancient History and Japanese Language from the University of Queensland. She taught high school in Australia, and was a teacher and an administrator at the International School of the Sacred Heart, Tokyo where she lived for seventeen years. After graduating from Washington State University with a PhD in Educational Administration, she taught educational leadership and policy at the University of Virginia and at the University of Missouri-Columbia. Among the various leadership positions she has held at her institutions and professional organisations, she served as Dean of the School of Educational Studies from 2008–2012, Chair of the Department of Educational Leadership and Policy Analysis at the University of Missouri-Columbia, 2002–2008, and she was President of the University Council for Educational Administration in 2003/4. A frequent keynote speaker, she has also published many articles and chapters and has authored, co-authored or edited six books including *The Jossey-Bass Reader on Educational Leadership* (2013). Her current research focuses on women in leadership, gender and education, the moral and ethical dimensions of leadership, and leadership for social justice.

JUDITH HARFORD is Senior Lecturer and Director of the Professional Master of Education (PME) at the School of Education, University College Dublin. She has published internationally in the areas of history of women's education, teacher education and education policy. She is Co-ordinator of the Teacher Education Policy in Europe Network and a Convenor of the Teacher Education Research Network of the European Educational Research Association (EERA). She is a Fellow of the Royal Historical Society (London) and an International Clinical Practice Fellow of the American Association of Teacher Educators.

JACKY LUMBY is Professor of Education at the University of Southampton. Her main interests are in educational leadership and management and particularly issues of equality and power. She is concerned to explore how leaders can be supported to lead people, systems and processes which offer success to all learners and staff in the context of living a life they value. Her work encompasses a range of perspectives, including critical theory and comparative and international perspectives. She is interested in challenging the appropriateness of Western-derived concepts, theories and suggested practice in different cultures and in an increasingly diverse UK culture. She has researched the practice of education leaders in South Africa, China, Hong Kong and the UK and has published widely in the UK and internationally.

PONTSO MOOROSI is an associate professor of educational leadership at North-West University, South Africa. She obtained her PhD from the University of KwaZulu-Natal and pursued post-doctoral research at McGill University, Canada. She has also worked at the University of Warwick and the University of Bedfordshire in the UK. Her research interests centre on gender and leadership, with a specific focus on leadership preparation and development. She has been involved in several research projects in different contexts including an international project on constructions of masculinities and femininities in corporate leadership. Currently, she is leading on a school leadership development project in four Southern African countries.

IZHAR OPLATKA is Professor of Educational Administration and Leadership at the School of Education, Tel Aviv University, Israel. He is Head of the Department of Educational Policy and Administration. Professor Oplatka's research focuses on the lives and careers of school teachers and principals, educational marketing, emotions and educational administration, and the foundations of educational administration as a field of study. His most recent books include *The Legacy of Educational Administration: A Historical Analysis of an Academic Field* (2010); *The Essentials of Educational Administration* (2015, in Hebrew); *Organizational Citizenship Behavior in Schools* (2015, with Anit Somech). Professor Oplatka's publications have also appeared in a wide range of international journals.

JENNIFER POLINCHOCK is currently Assistant Superintendent at Centennial School District, Bucks County, Pennsylvania, USA, having worked as Director of Teaching and Learning in the district for many years. She received her doctorate from Lehigh University.

VICTORIA SHOWUNMI received her doctorate from the University of Sheffield and is a lecturer at the Institute of Education, University of London. Her interests include diversity-related perceptions in leadership, Black girls' experience in education, and coaching and mentoring. She is an associate editor for the journal *Equality, Diversity and Inclusion* and a reviewer for the American Education Research Association: Black Education, Multicultural and Teacher Education Special Interest Groups. In addition to this, she is a committee member for the British Educational Research Association and was the Co-Programme Chair for the Black Education Special Interest Group in AERA between 2012 and 2015.

JOAN SMITH is Lecturer in Education at the University of Leicester, where she has responsibility for the leadership of the Doctorate of Education (EdD) programme. She has substantial experience of initial teacher education and postgraduate researcher development. Prior to moving into Higher Education she was a secondary school teacher and leader for almost twenty years, working in large urban schools in the English Midlands. Her research interests include teachers' career experiences, gender, leadership development and Higher Education pedagogy.

HELEN SOBEHART is Associate Academic Vice-President for Graduate Education at Point Park University in Pittsburgh, Pennsylvania. During her career of over forty years she has held positions as full professor and university president at Cardinal Stritch University in Milwaukee, associate academic vice-president, doctoral program faculty and director at Duquesne University, CEO of a non-profit organisation, school district superintendent, special education director and teacher. Both professionally and personally, she has been an advocate for the needs of underrepresented groups, including special needs students, minorities and women in the highest levels of leadership. Dr Sobehart has been recognised with numerous awards for her work, including the national Dr Effie Jones Humanitarian Award from the American Association of School Administrators (AASA) and the Legacy Foundation Education Award. She was recognised by the Pennsylvania State Legislature for her 'immeasurable contributions' to the education of special needs students. With AASA and the University Council for Educational Administration (UCEA), she founded Women Leading Education Across Continents, an international group of scholars and practitioners dedicated to impacting social justice issues related to the underrepresentation of women in educational leadership worldwide. The group's work represents all continents except Antarctica. She edited a 2009 book of the same name in addition to numerous other publications and international presentations in such countries as Germany, Sweden, Switzerland, Italy and Canada, as well as Oxford University in the UK.

JILL SPERANDIO is Associate Professor in the College of Education at Lehigh University, Pennsylvania, USA, teaching graduate courses in the educational leadership program. Her research has focused on gender issues in educational administration and leadership worldwide, and international education at the school and university level. Most recently she has researched and published on women in school leadership in Ghana, Bangladesh and the USA, and she is currently researching career paths of women teachers and school leaders in Indonesia.

KLARA WAHLSTER was born in Japan to multinational parents. She received most of her education in the USA and most recently received her Bachelor's degree in Film and Television and East Asian Studies from New York University. She works full-time as paramedic for the City of New York but spends her time involved in gaming, and writing about gaming. She has had her writing published by gaming blog Gamervescent (under Klara Boz) and she works on her own blog, Natural 20. When she isn't running table-top role playing game sessions for locals, she also helps design games with her friends (submitted to Come Out & Play festival for 2015).

Index

with full-time paid work 16, 249–50,
  252–3
images of 106
and patriarchy 262
precedence over workplace role
  43, 165
as primary female role 105, 151–2,
  158–9
shared 42–5, 49, 109, 110–11, 253
work-family balance 250, 252–3,
  266–7
  and degrees of
    commitment 252–3

Eagly, A.H., and Carli, L.L. 150, 163
Eagly, A.H. et al. 22–3
Educational Administration Quarterly
  (*EAQ*) 12, 14, 18, 25
educational management
  1960s and 1970s 13–16
  1980s 16–20
  1990s 20–5
  2000s 25–30
  barriers to women 10–11, 23,
    28–9, 150
  challenging research questions 30
  and educational attainment 24
  feminisation of administration
    15–16
  gender bias in journals 18–19
  gender concepts and styles of
    management 18
  global expansion of research 31
  internationalisation of research 29
  journals 12, 14, 18–19, 21
  male-female comparisons 17–18,
    27–8, 29
  race/ethnicity 26, 28
  research and Western values 39–40
  'sex' variable in studies 15, 17, 19,
    20–1, 24, 28

styles of leadership 22–3, 30
women's aspirations 29
*Educational Management, Administration
  and Leadership* (*EMAL*) viii, 12,
  14, 18, 25
elementary principals aspiring to district
  superintendency 177–203
  accessing positions in school and
    district leadership
  networking skills 193–4
  findings 198–203
    career decisions 201–2
    career development 200
    district-level positions 199–200
    implications for professional
      practices 202–3
    mentors and endorsement 201
  methods 179–81
    interview transcripts 180
    merging of quantitative and
      qualitative data 180
  participants 179
    case study profiles 182–3
    open-ended survey
      respondents 183–4
  research design 178–9
  research site 178
  results regarding career planning 181
  themes
    accessing positions in school
      and district leadership
      189–98
    career decisions 189–90
    communication and interper-
      sonal skills 192
    developing professional
      preparation 190–3
    external factors 194–5
    networking skills 193–4
    personal identities 195–6
    reflections on gender 196–8